CLASSIC FLASH 3

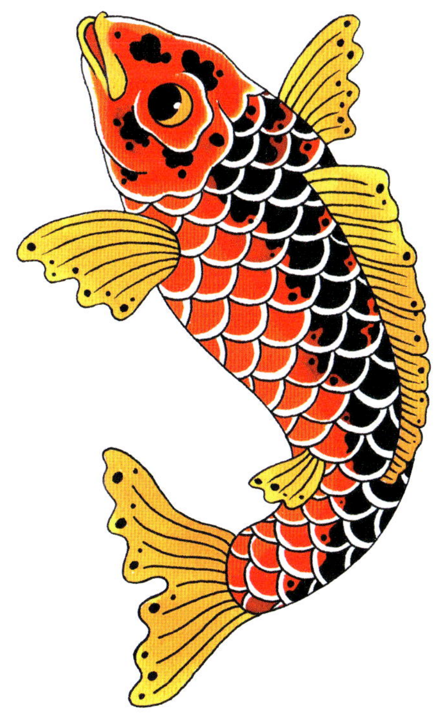

JAPANESE STYLE

Jeromey "Tilt" McCulloch | Justin "Lowercase j" Sellers

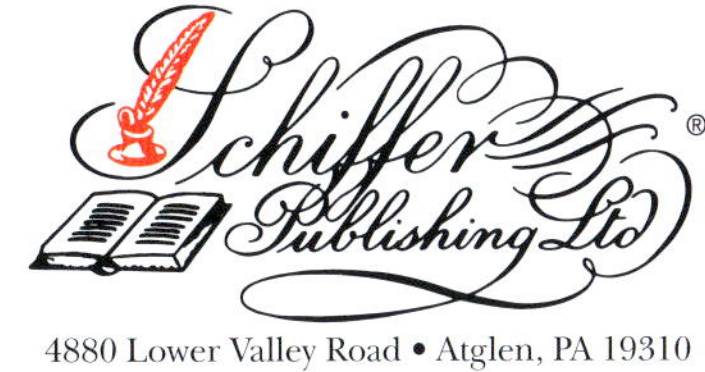

4880 Lower Valley Road • Atglen, PA 19310

OTHER SCHIFFER BOOKS BY THE AUTHOR

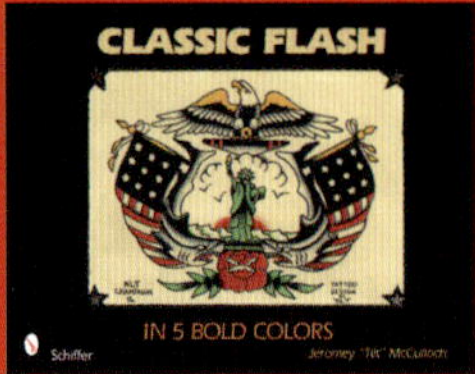

Classic Flash: In 5 Bold Colors
ISBN 978-0-7643-3165-7

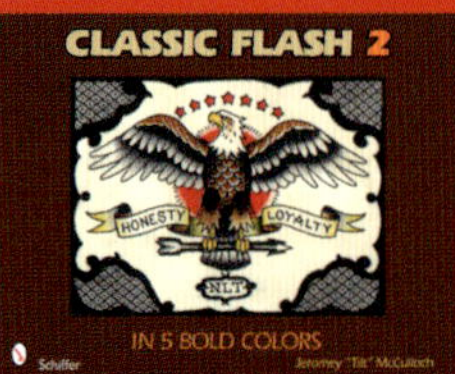

Classic Flash 2: In 5 Bold Colors
ISBN 978-0-7643-3867-0

OTHER SCHIFFER BOOKS ON RELATED SUBJECTS

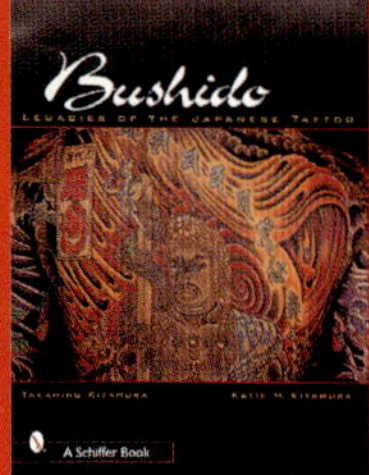

Bushido: Legacies of the Japanese Tattoo
Takahiro Kitamura & Katie M. Kitamura
ISBN 978-0-7643-1201-4

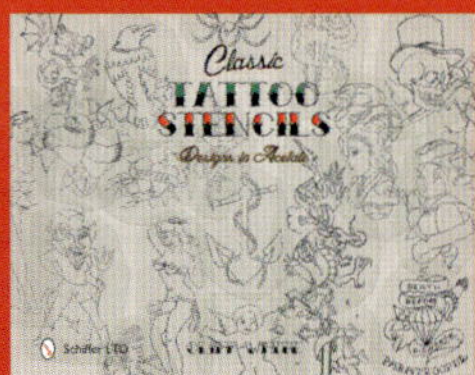

Classic Tattoo Stencils: Designs in Acetate, Cliff White
ISBN 978-0-7643-4999-7

Library of Congress Control Number: 2016933167

Published by Schiffer Publishing, Ltd.
4880 Lower Valley Road
Atglen, PA 19310
Phone: (610) 593-1777; Fax: (610) 593-2002
E-mail: Info@schifferbooks.com

Designed by Matt Goodman
Cover design by Justin Watkinson

Type set in Helvetica

ISBN: 978-0-7643-5100-6

Printed in China

FOREWORD

As I sat and watched my brother, Lowercase j, research and dive into his Japanesque paintings, I was quite pleased to see the humor he was born with pour out into his work. We spent many days painting together, and he was always making me laugh. When I saw the half-painted sheets coming in from his collaborator Tilt, I was amazed at this project the two decided to undertake. The paintings the two of them made together—one artist starting, the other finishing—were many things, but most importantly they were beautiful and completely tattooable. I saw the two of them feeding off each other's designs and the result is this awesome compilation. I am lucky to have experienced the process "behind the scenes." Good people, good art, great style.

—TimmyTatts, May 2015

ACKNOWLEDGMENTS

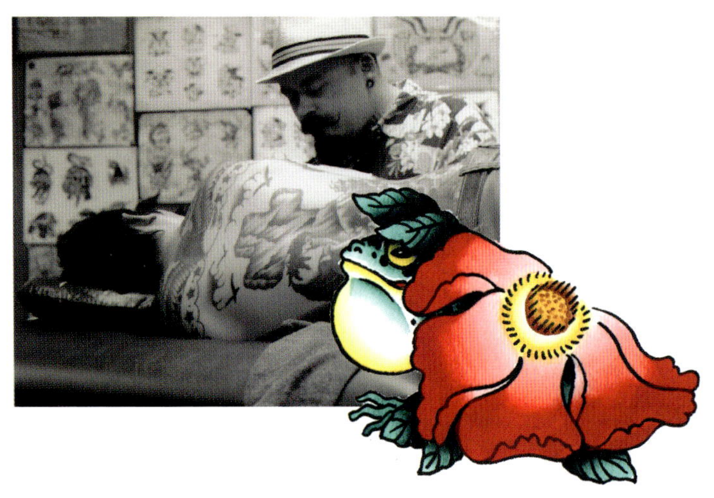

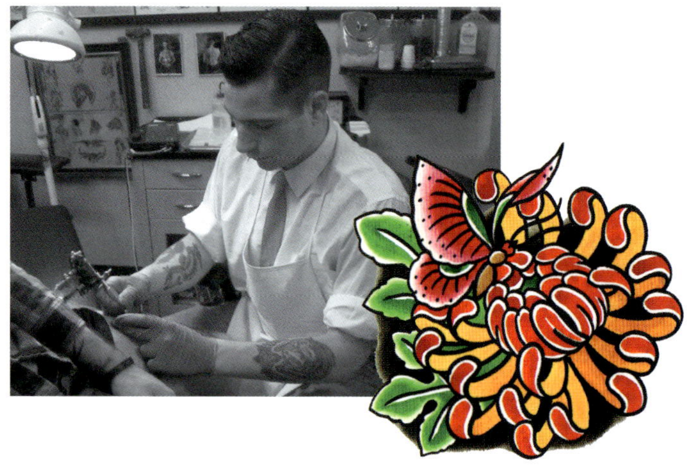

TILT

Thank you to my family—Bobbi, Auggie, and Zeke. And to the guys in OATTAN, the Brunsons, Lunchbox, Joel, Jim, Hata, Wizzo, Dr. Albarran, Mike, Al, McCrocklin, TimmyTatts, Cliff Raven, HoriHide, Don Nolan, Bruce, Mo, and countless other artists who have tried their hand at the Japanese tattoo. Also, special thanks to Lowercase j. His ever-playful designs inspire me to keep it fun and simple.

Tilt
NewLife Tattoos
404 E Green St.
Champaign, IL 61820
217-367-5320

LOWERCASE J

I'd like to thank my brother TimmyTatts for getting me into this, and all the others who helped me out along the way. Also, everyone in OATTAN, my girlfriend, Katie, and everyone who gets tattoos from me. I want to thank all of the amazing artists I referenced for this book, everyone who keeps traditional tattooing alive, and, of course, Tilt, for influencing me greatly and making this book with me.

Lowercase j
Tattoo Mark's
127 E. Beaver Ave
State College, PA 16801
814-237-6940

LOWERCASE J

Coming up in the field of tattooing, two styles stuck with me—traditional American/European and Japanese. I never really thought of them as styles, though, just simply what tattoos are. It's what my brother TimmyTatts always had around and tattooed. It was a case of monkey see, monkey do.

When Tilt and I started this project, I hadn't yet made a real attempt at painting Japanese motifs. I was excited to do it, though, because I loved the way he approached it. His work was bold and clean, with plenty of black. I could tell he had a great admiration for Japanese tattooing. It was fun to make some individual silhouetted designs rather than painting them into intricate background sheets.

While combing through the great prints and paintings for inspiration, I was amazed by the imagination and creativity in the Japanese folklore. Its whimsical nature really appealed to me. The style is characterized by a heavy black background with a colorful foreground; this contrast makes the subject matter stand out. The images are usually based on mythological beasts and traditional folklore. In the following tattoos, I hope you enjoy my take on the Japanese style. I still have a lot to learn, but I have learned a lot. Thanks to Tilt for doing this project with me, and to everyone who picks up this book.

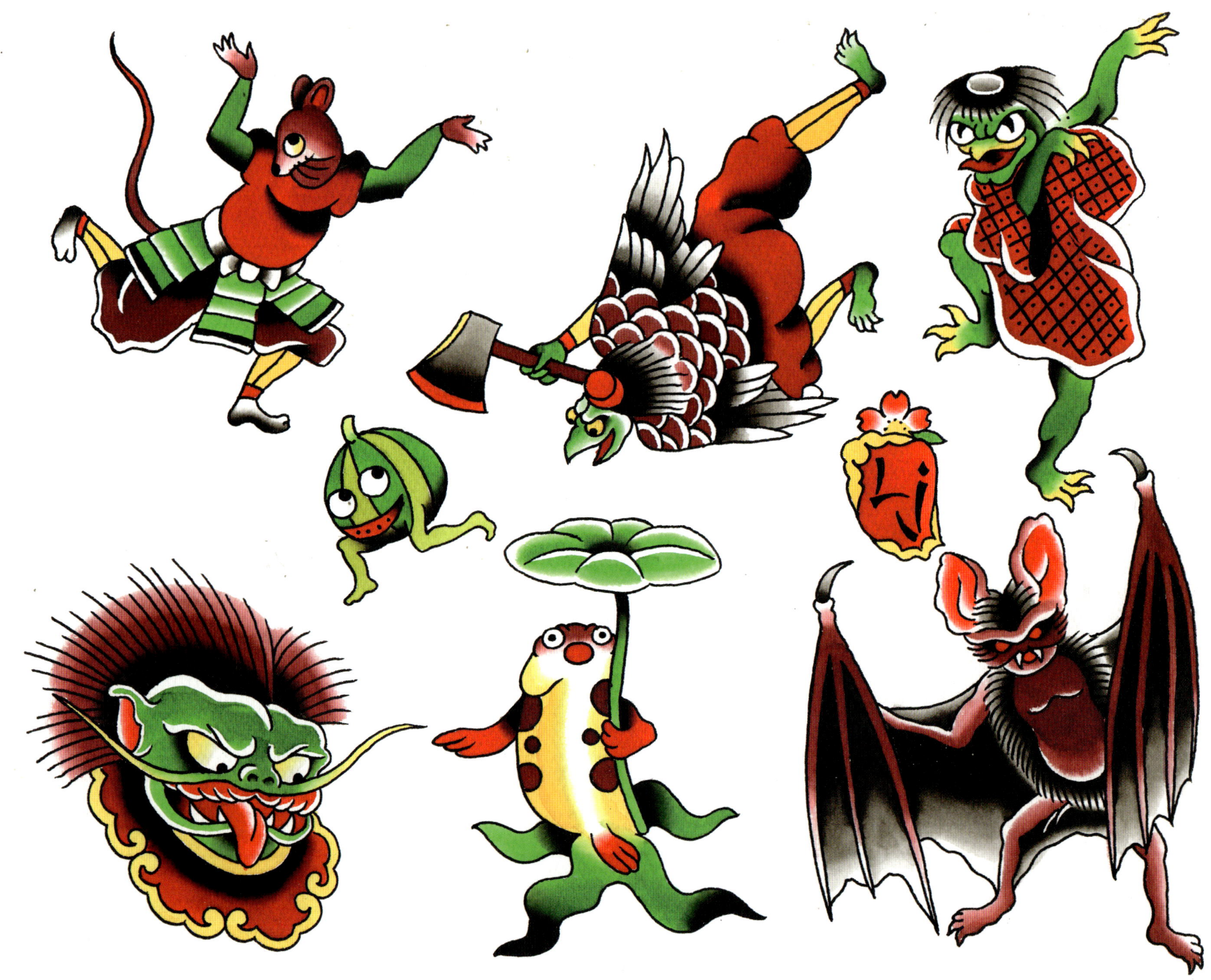

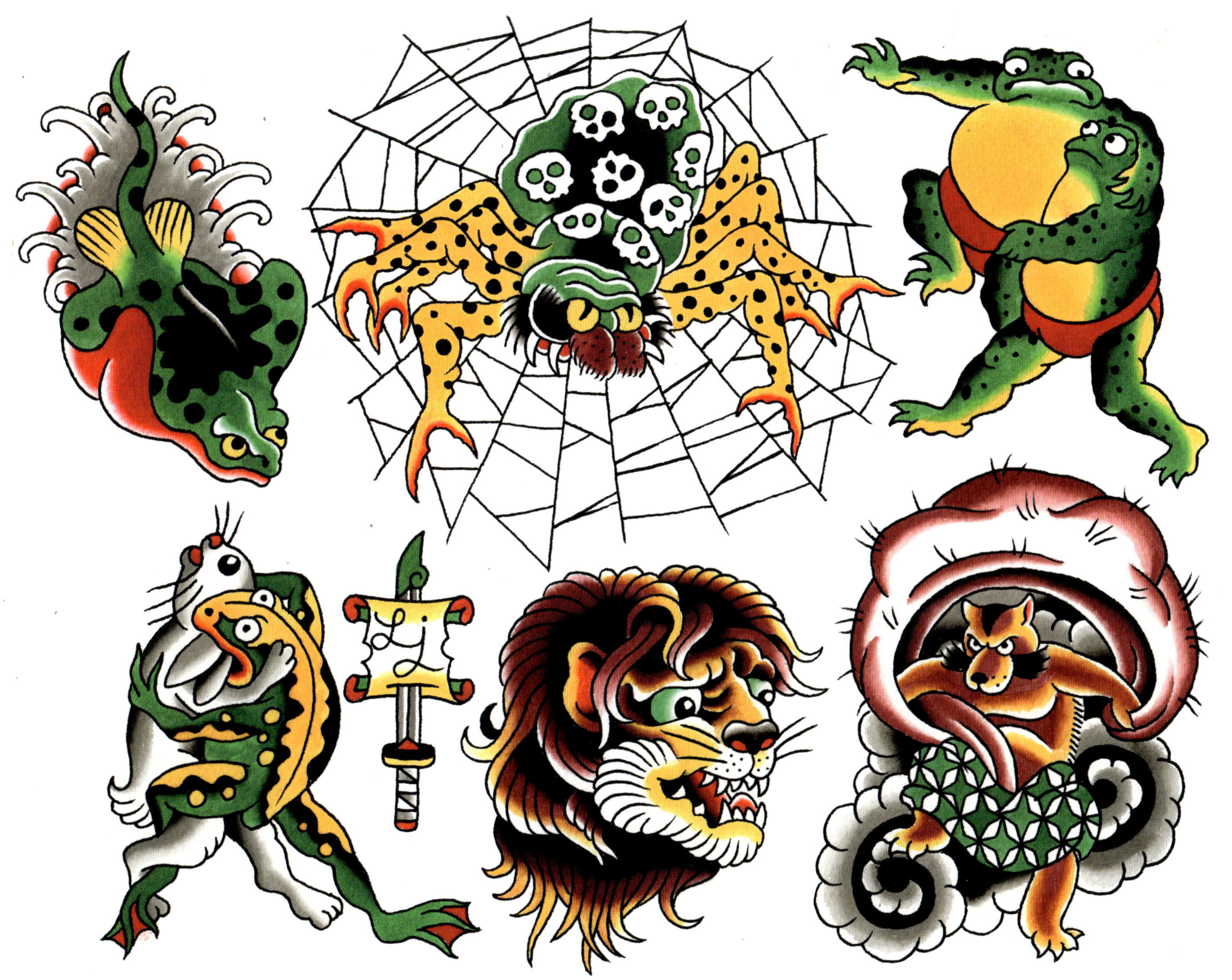

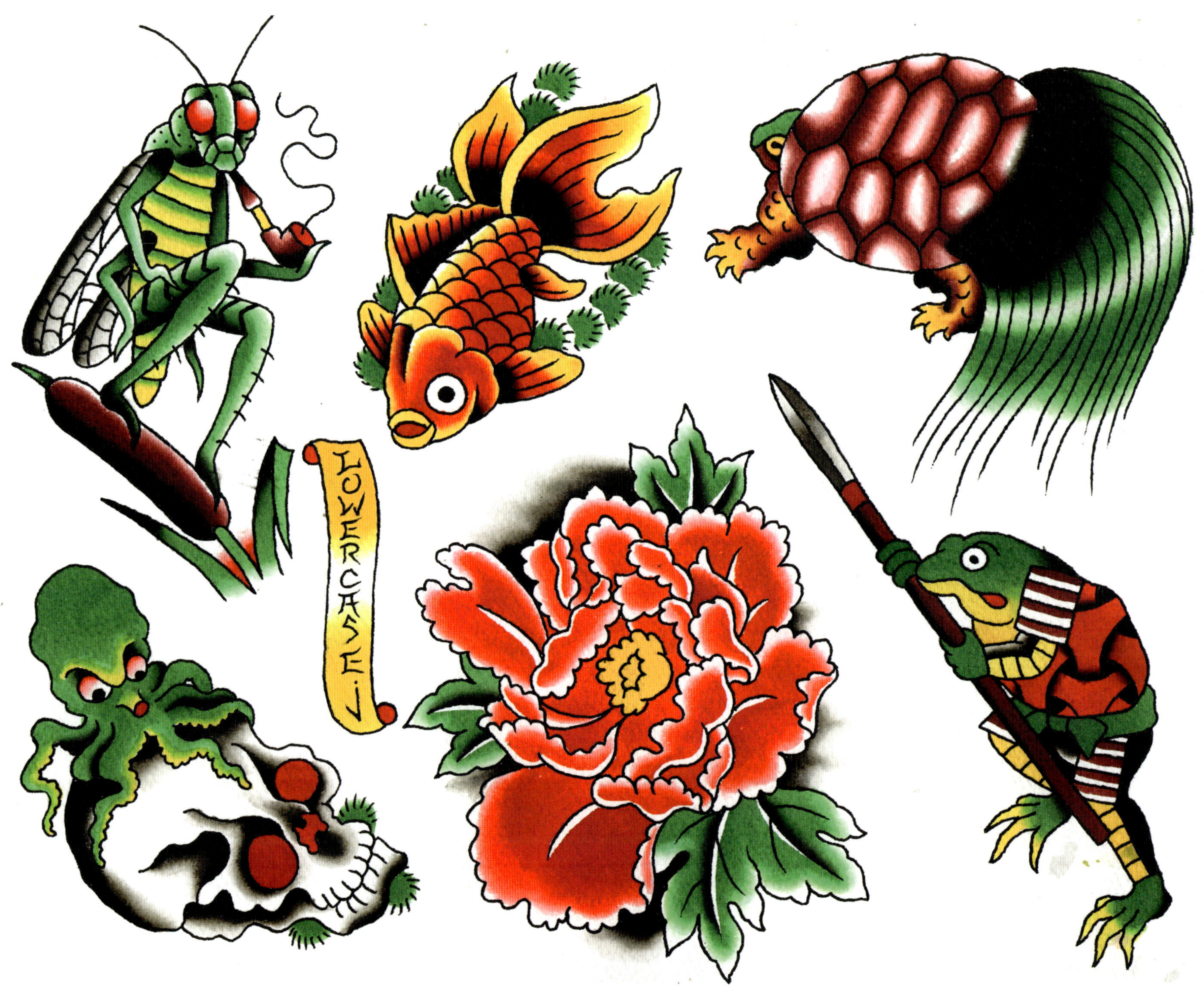
LOWERCASE J

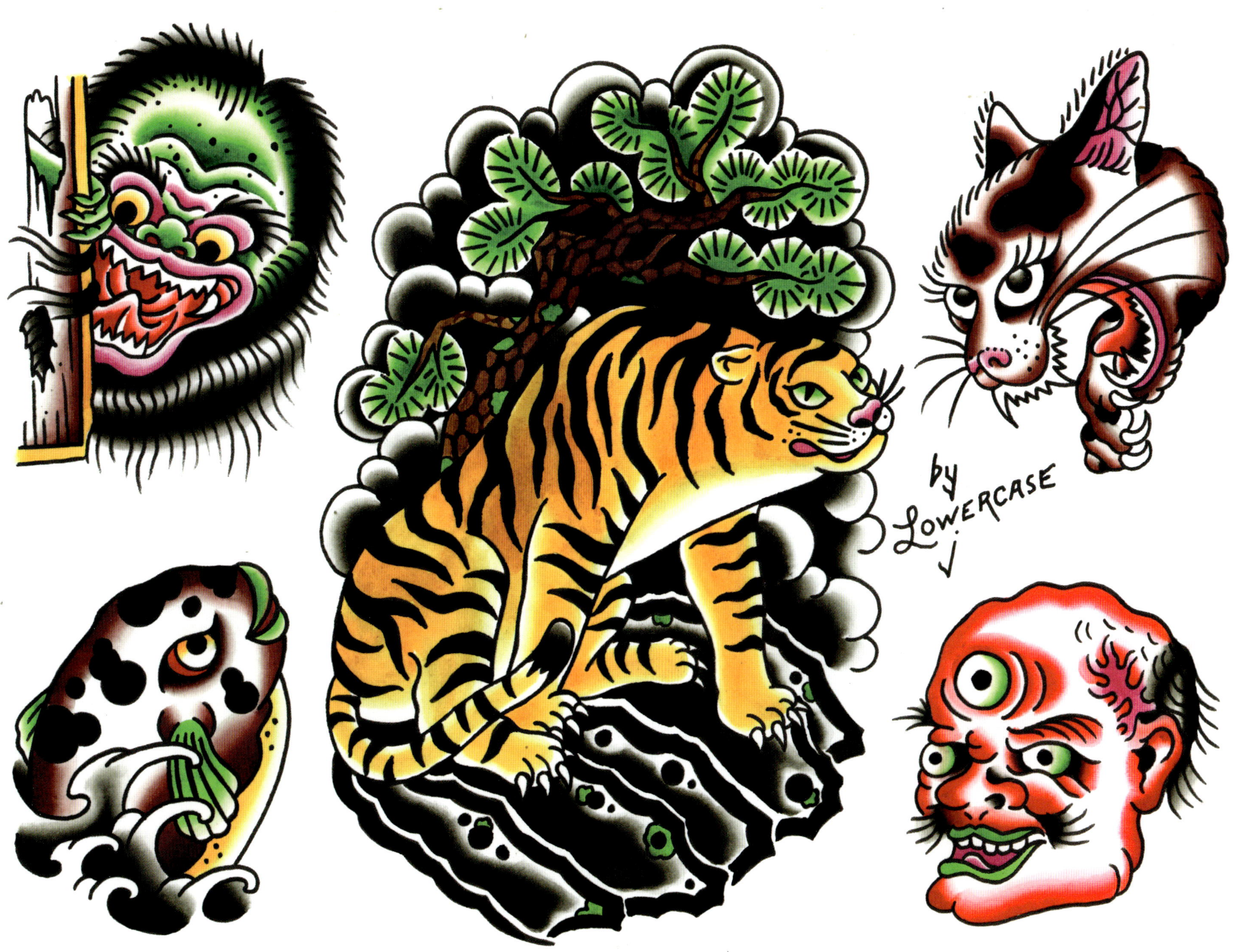
by
LOWERCASE
j

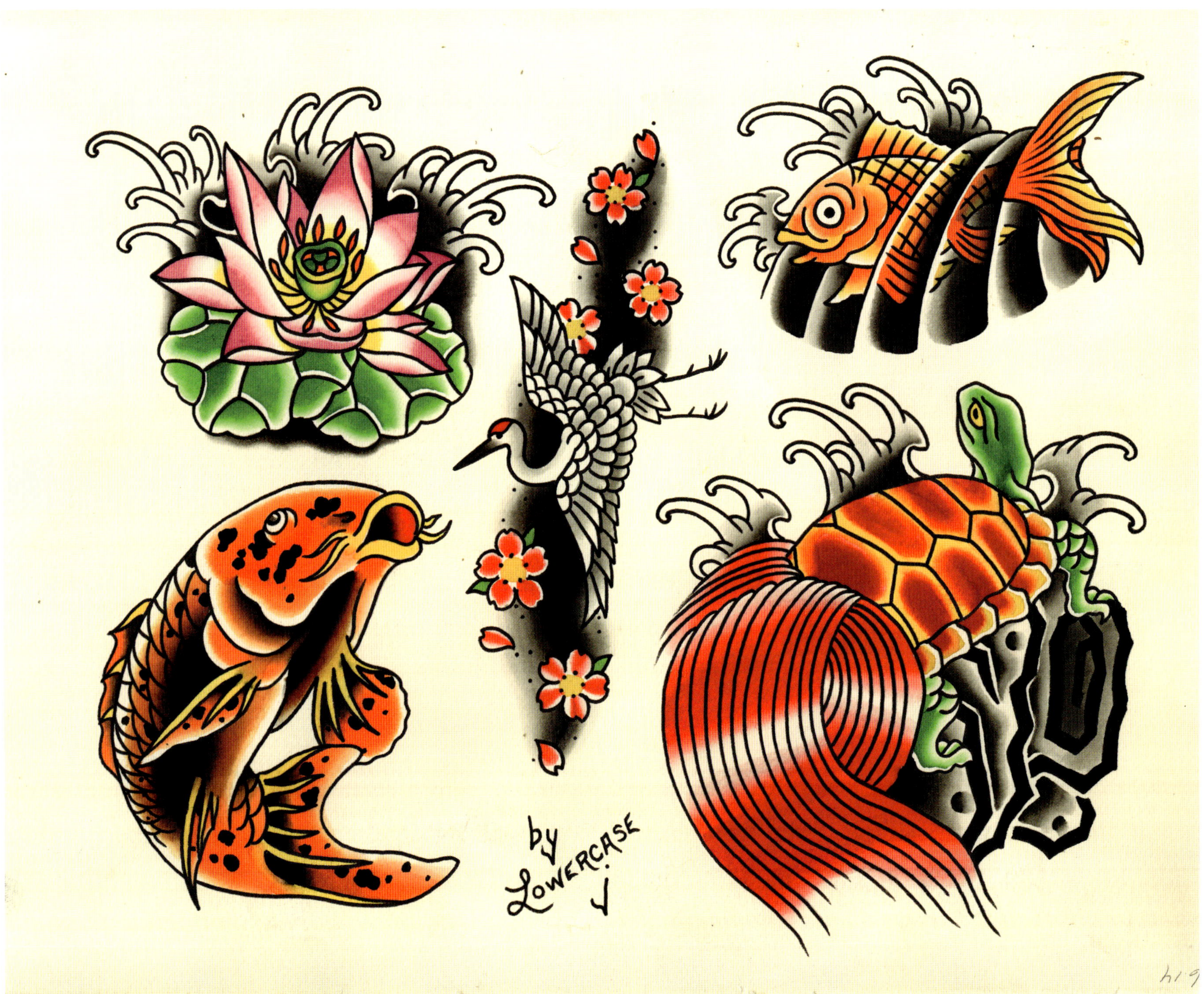
by
LOWERCASE

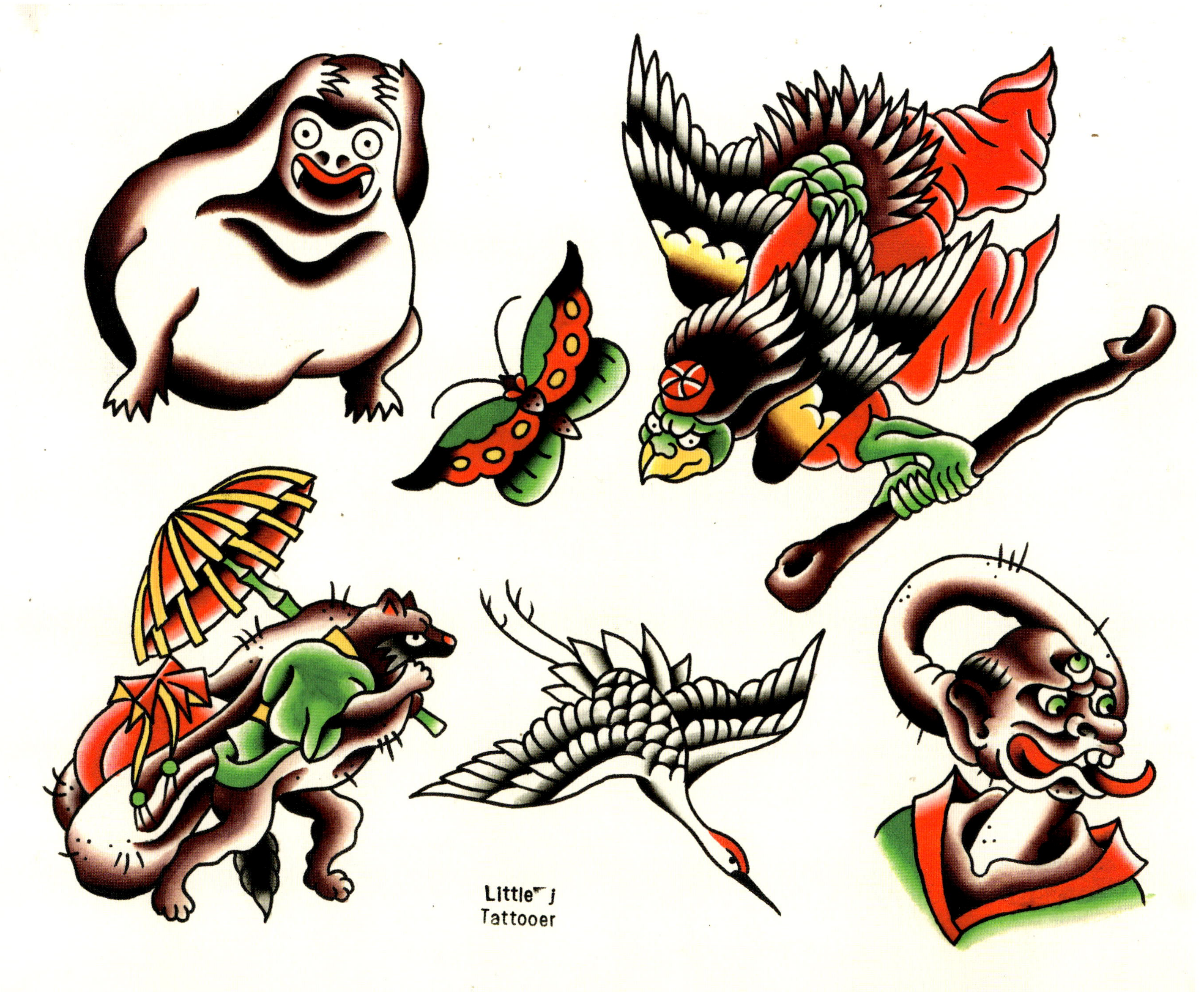
Little j
Tattooer

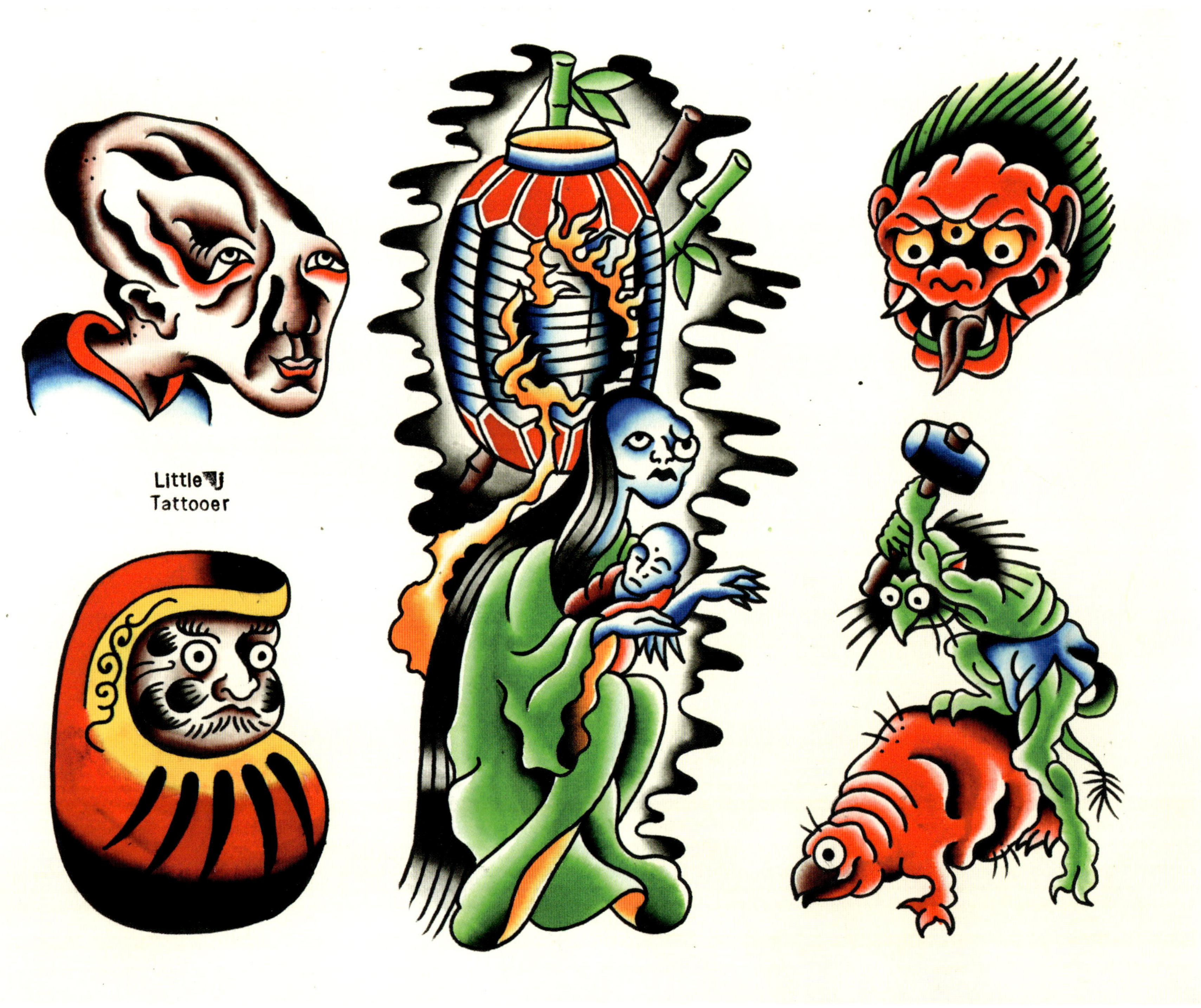
Little J
Tattooer

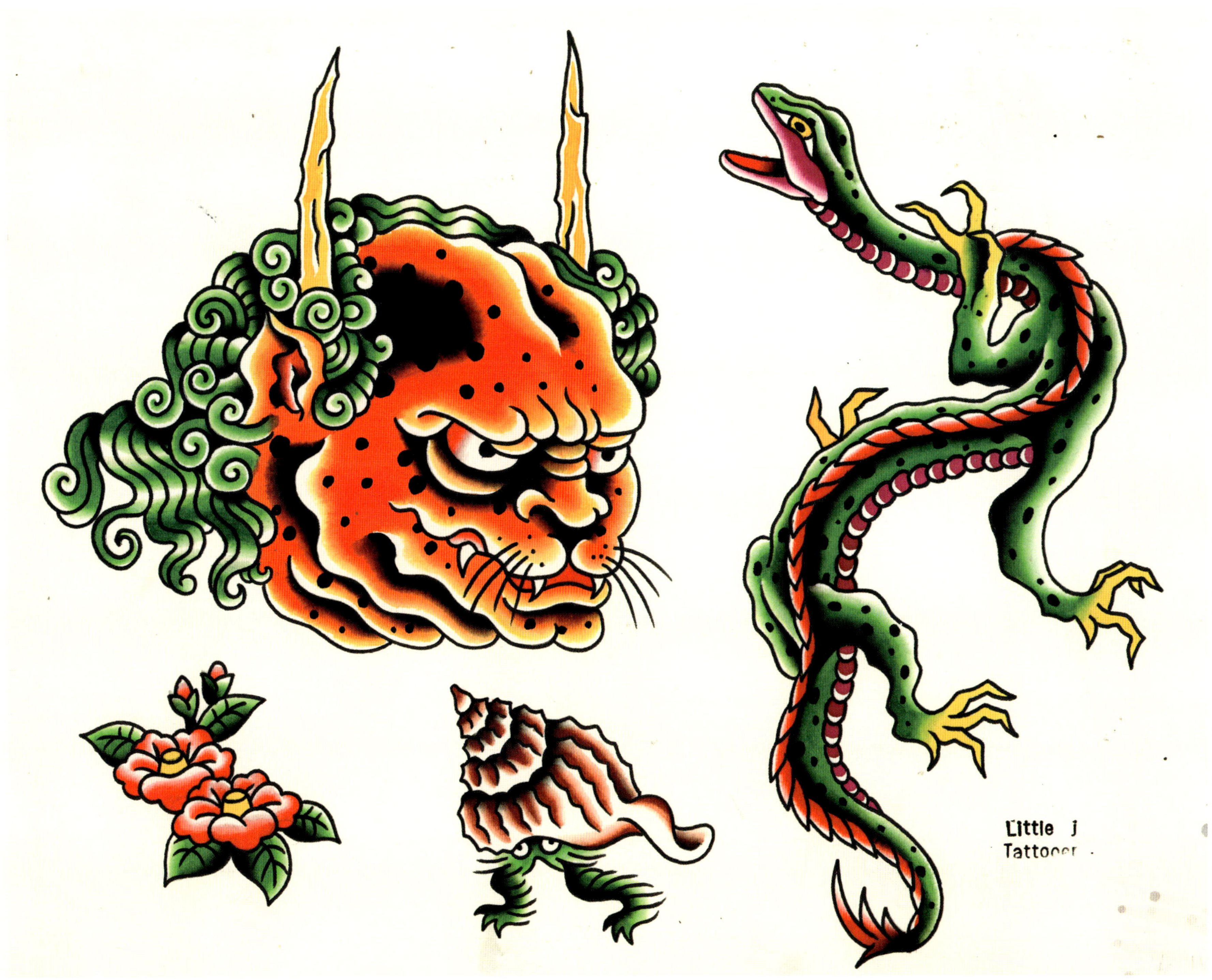
Little j
Tattooer

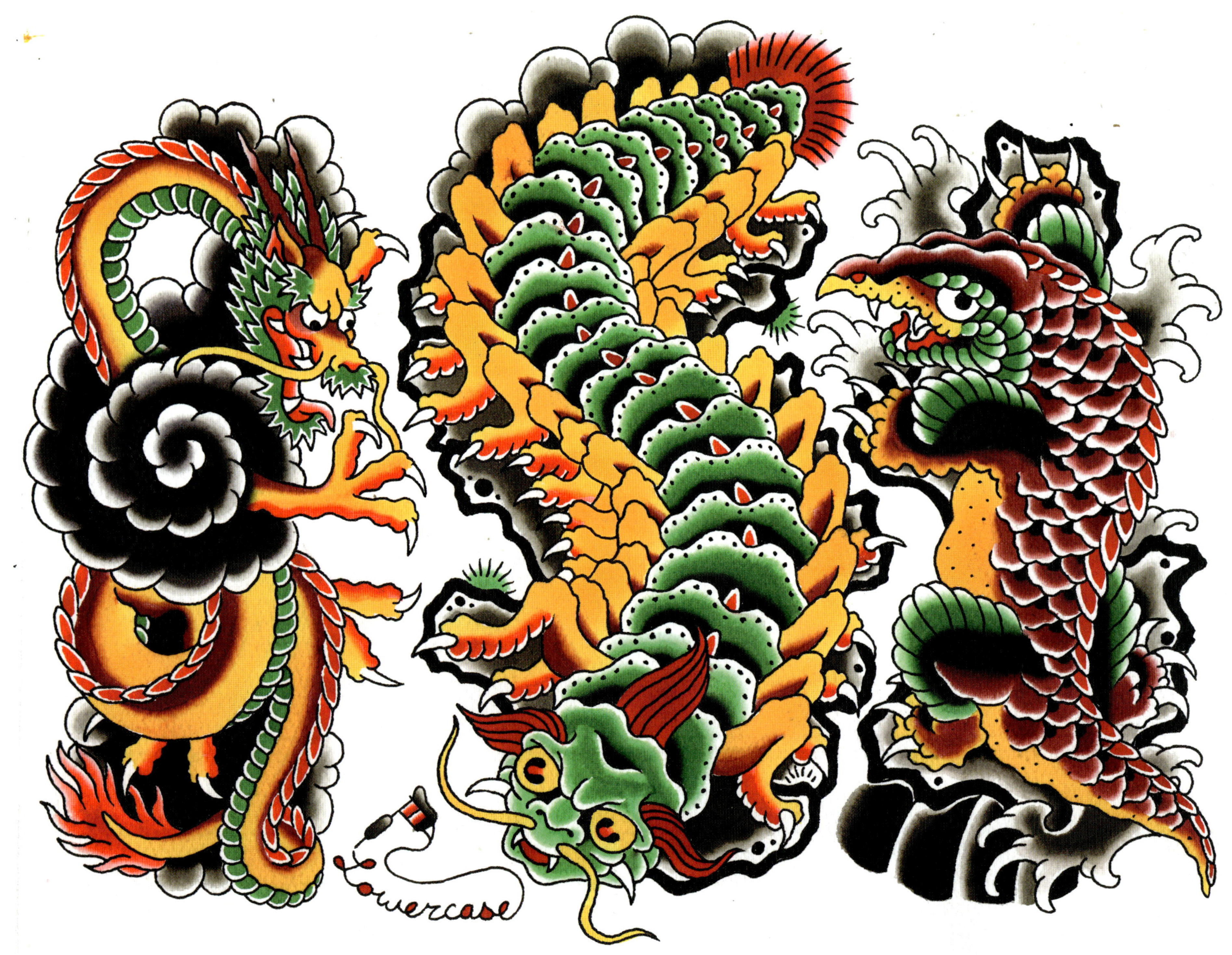
Lowercase

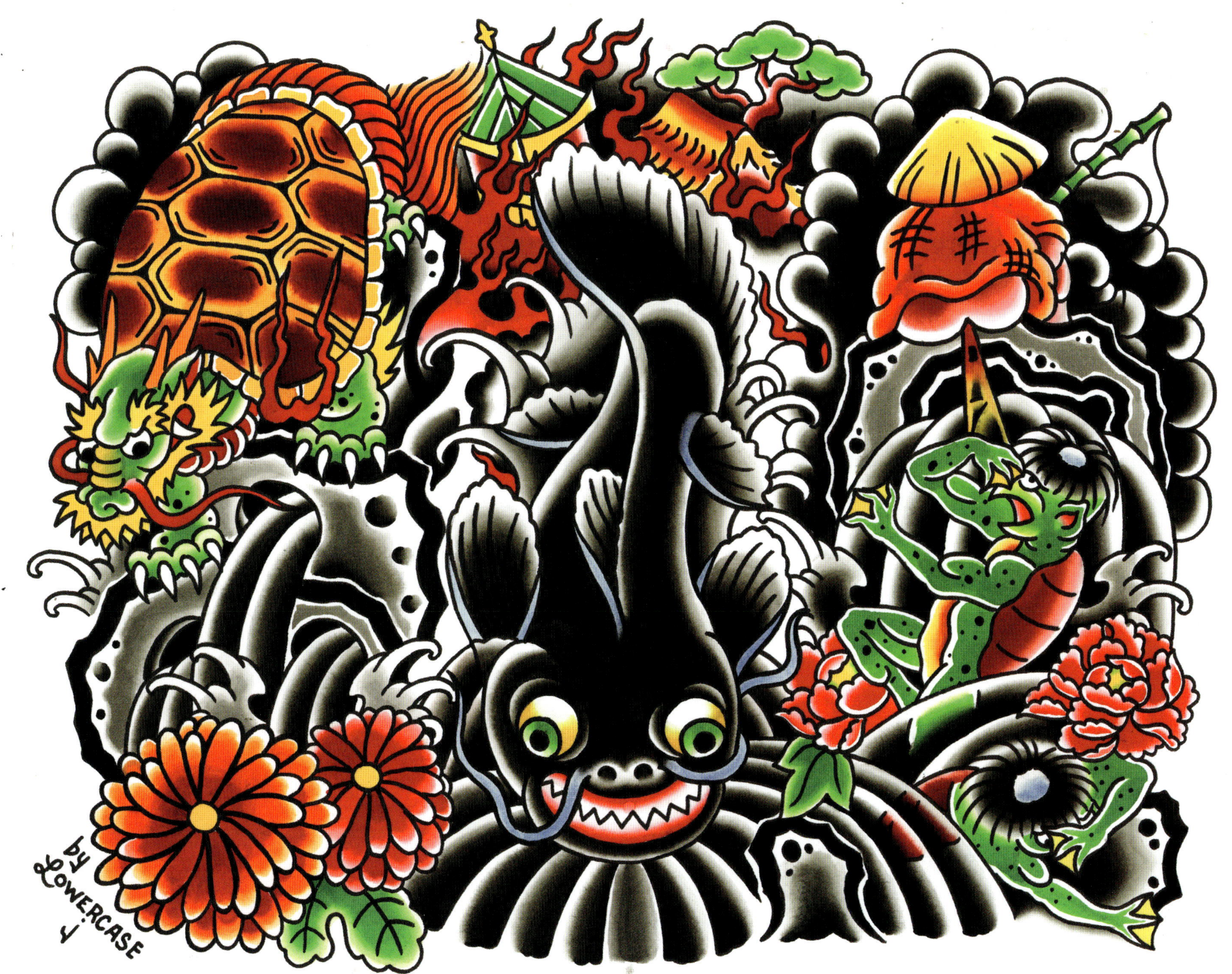
by
Lowercase
j

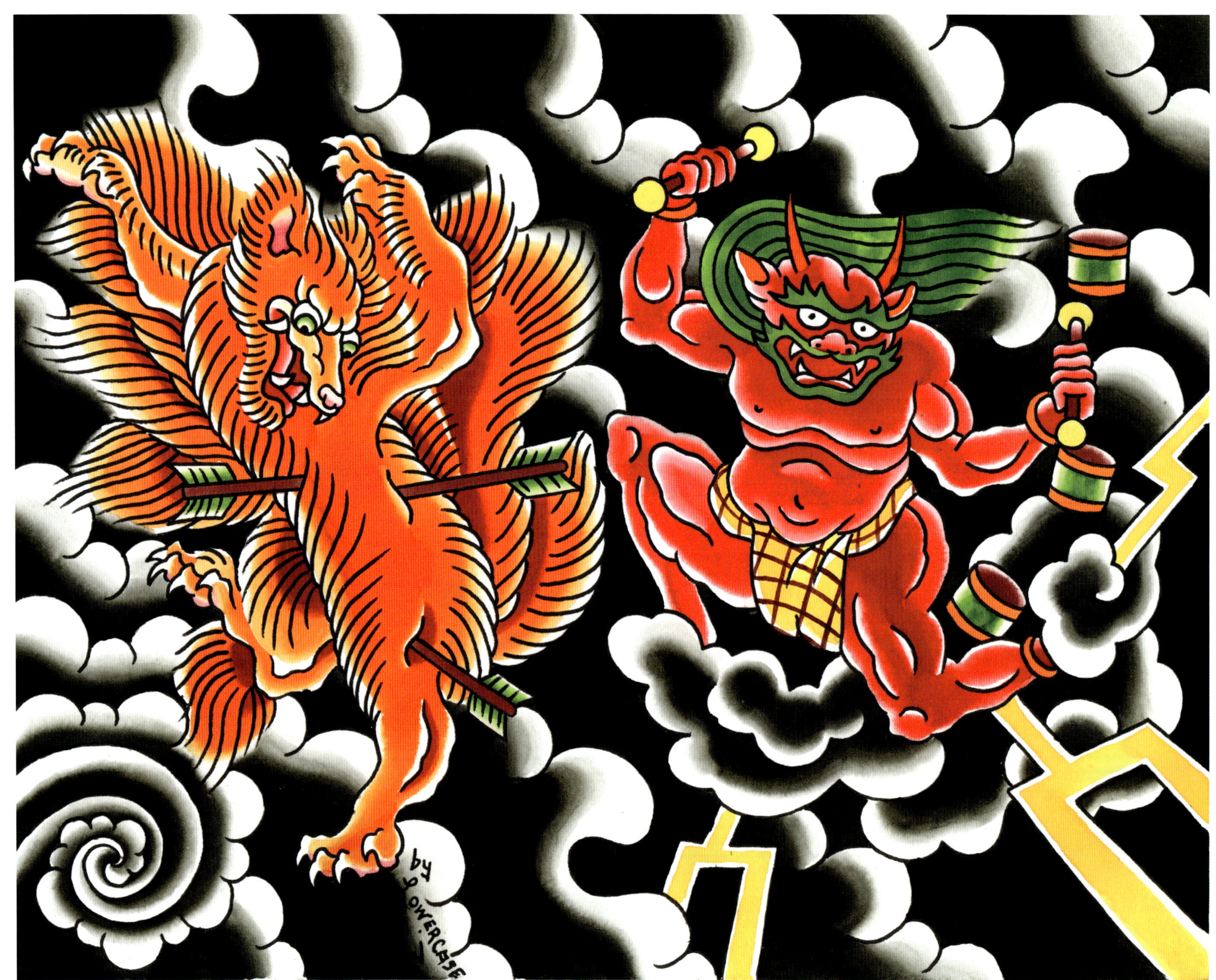
by LOWERCASE

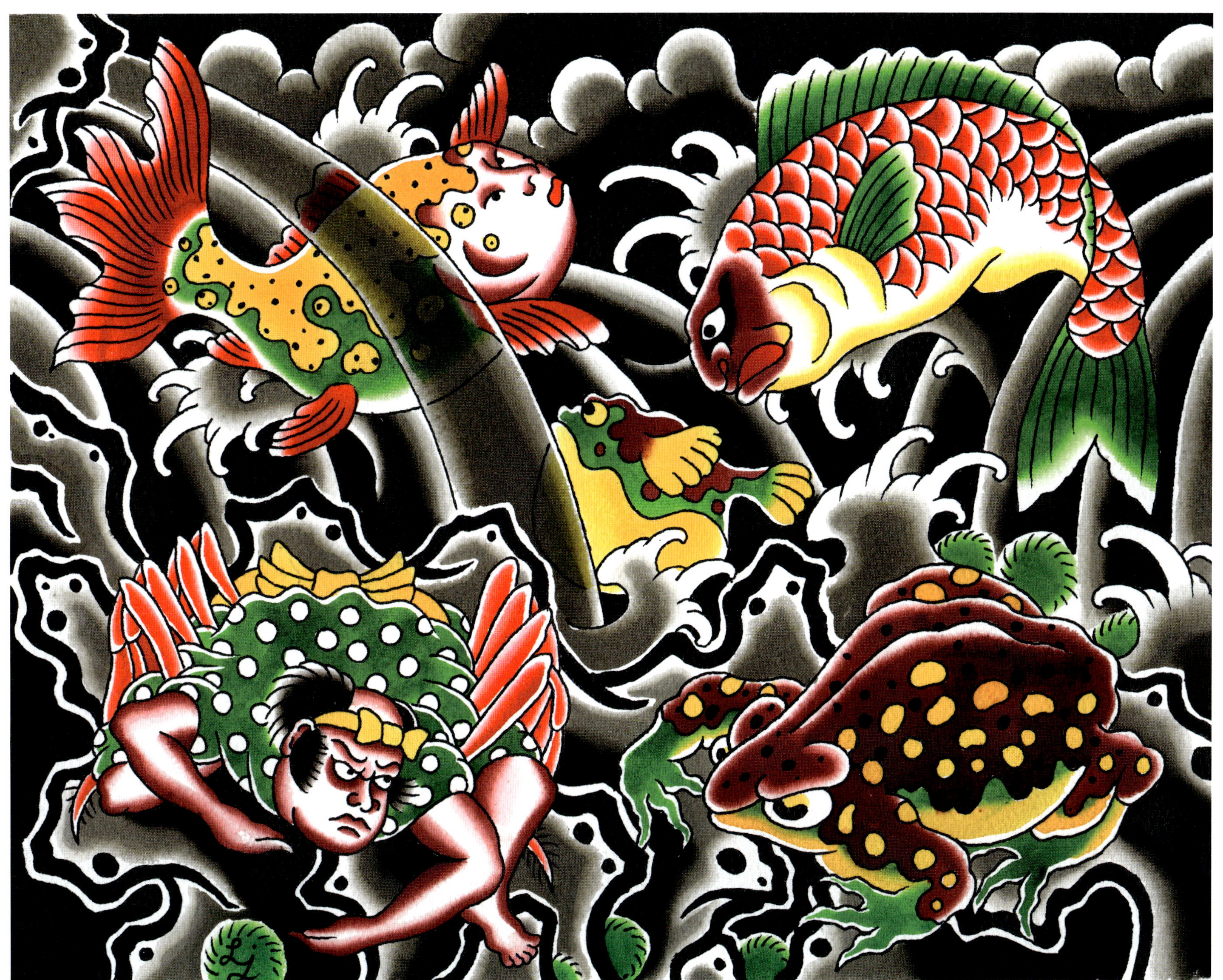

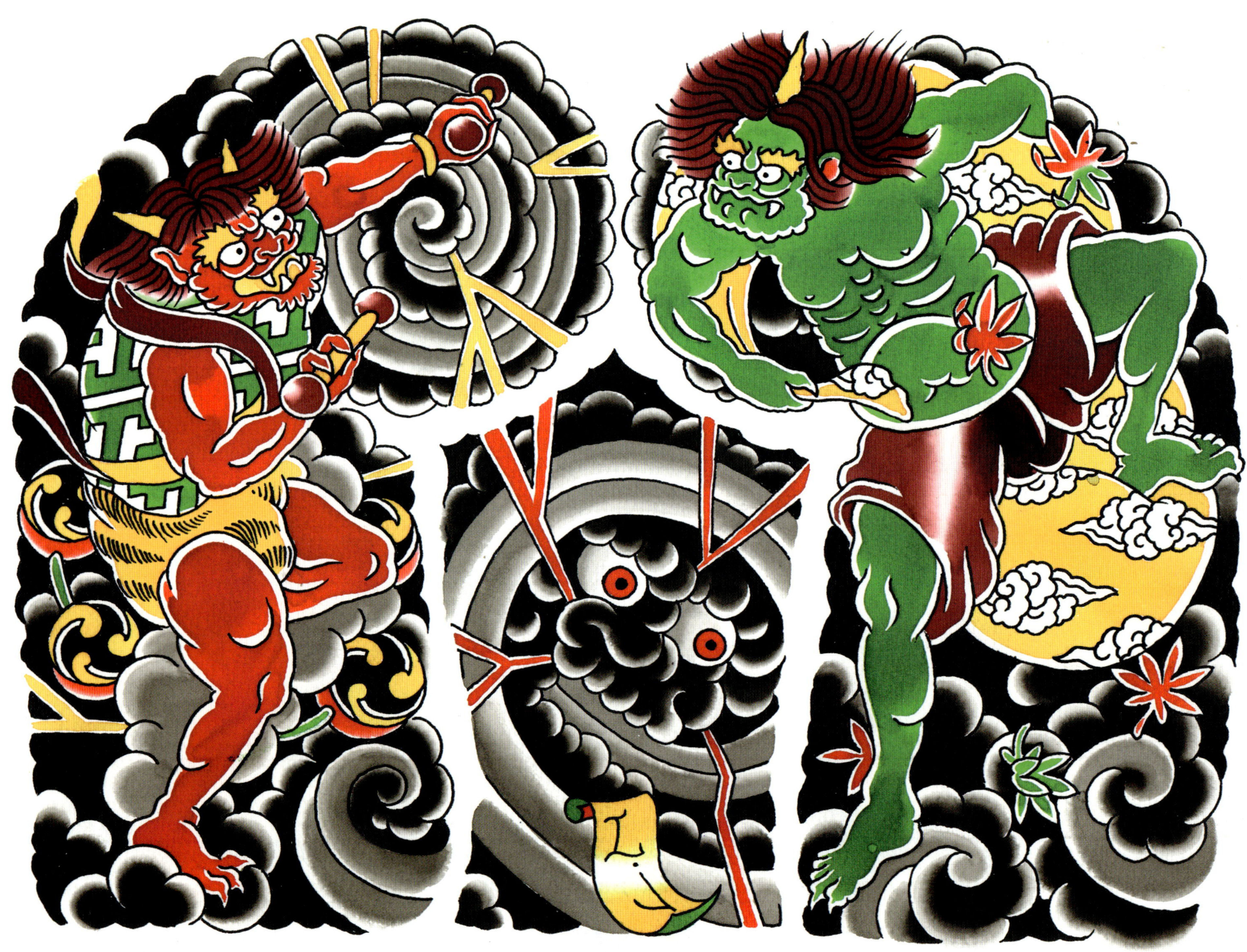

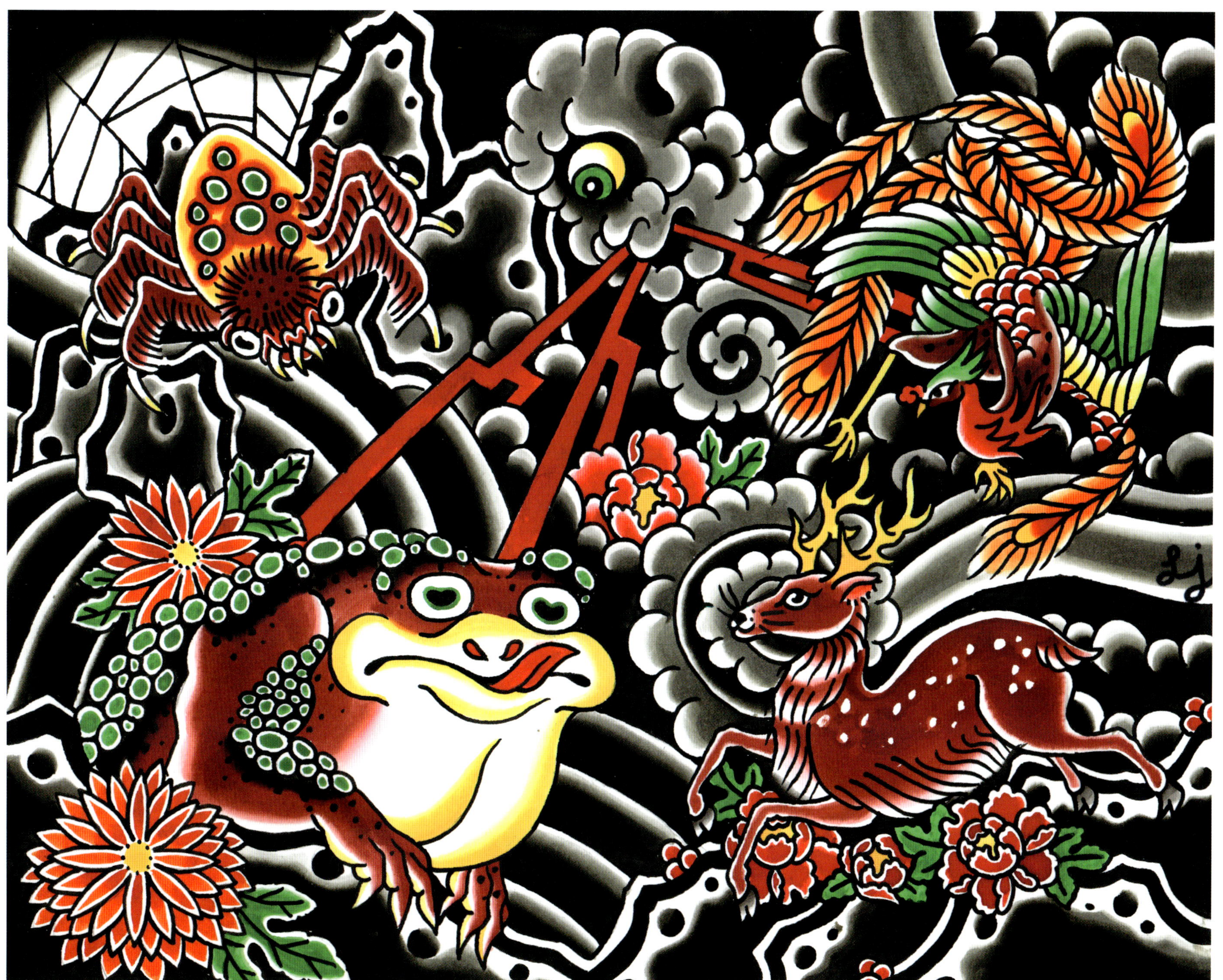
Lj

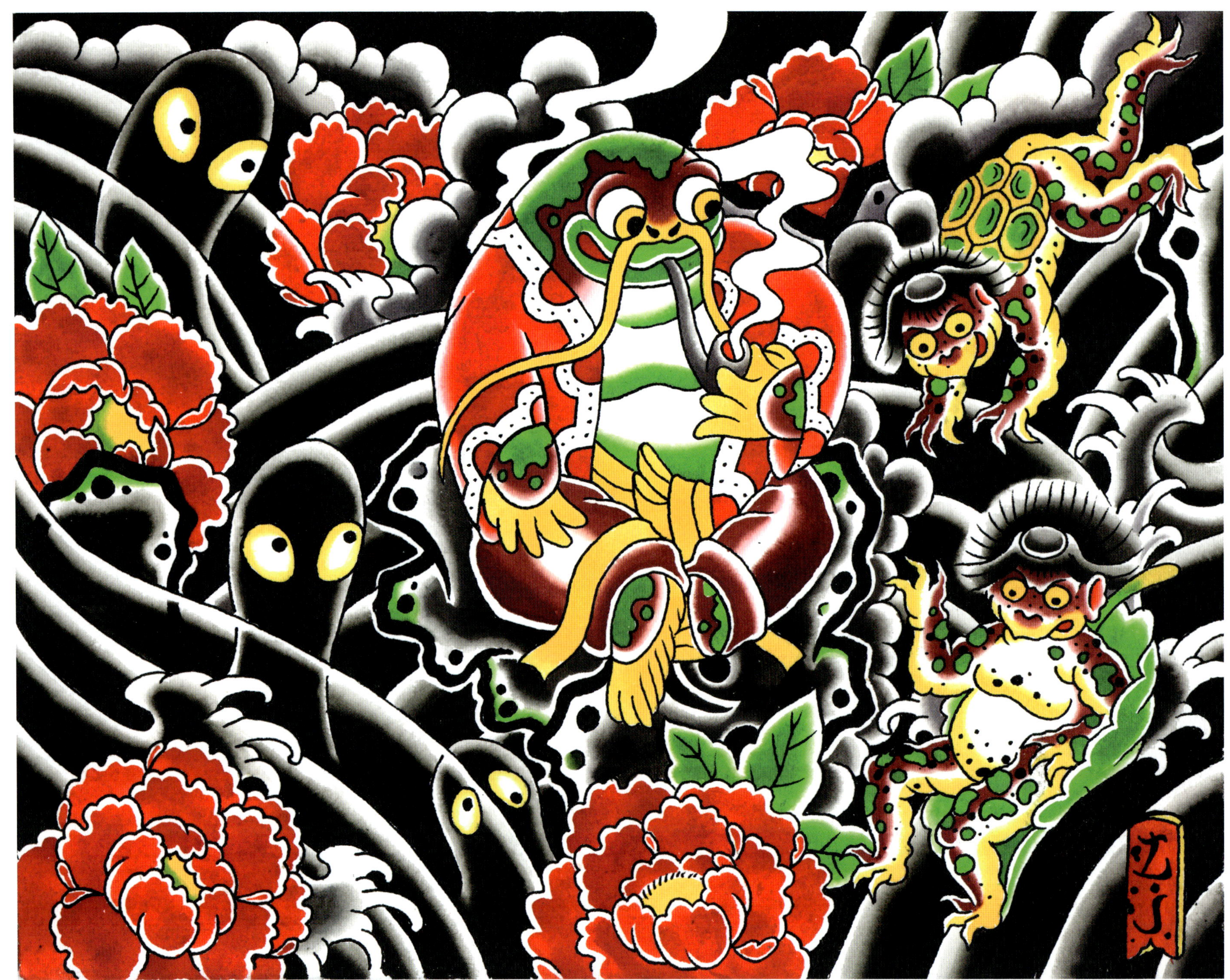

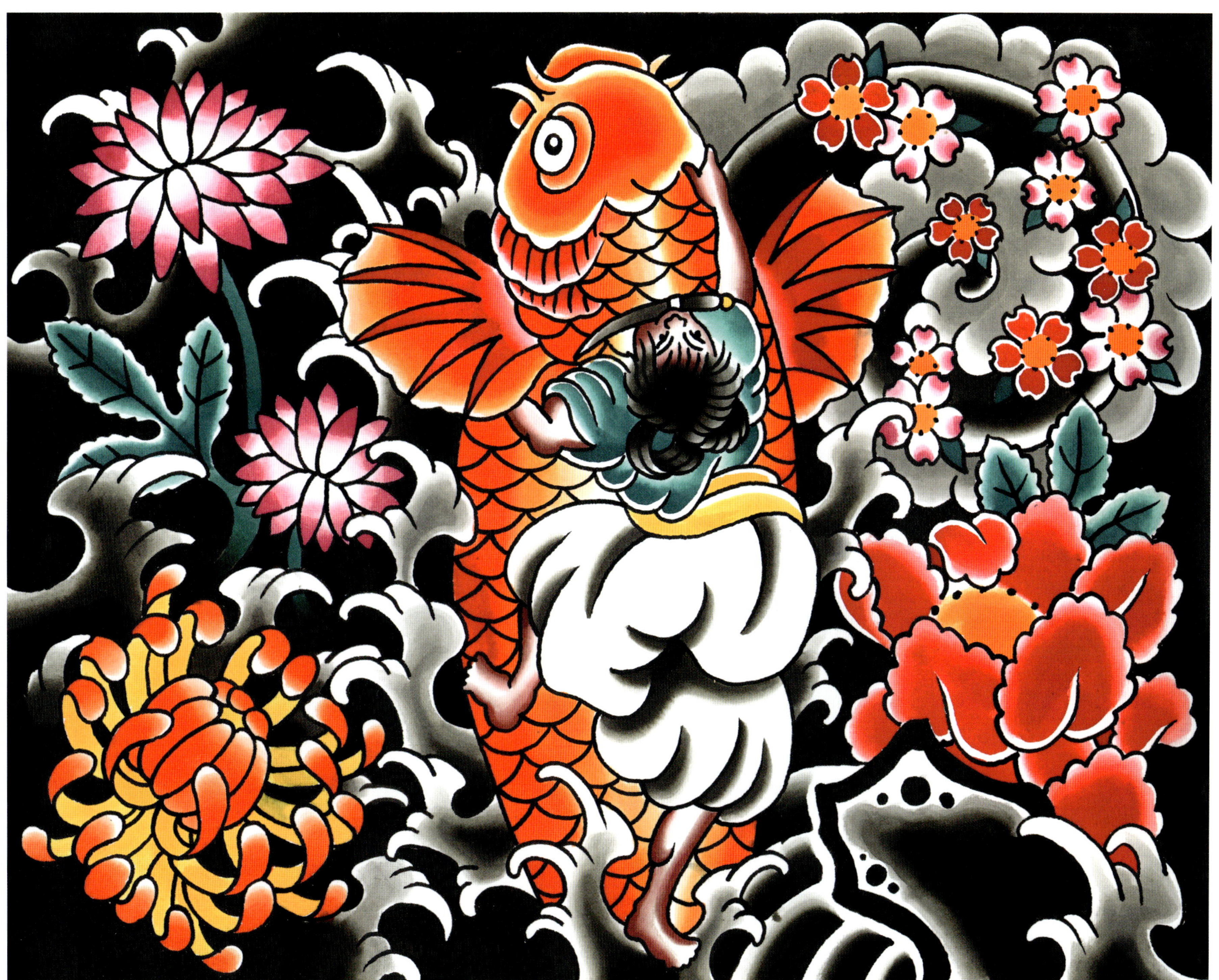

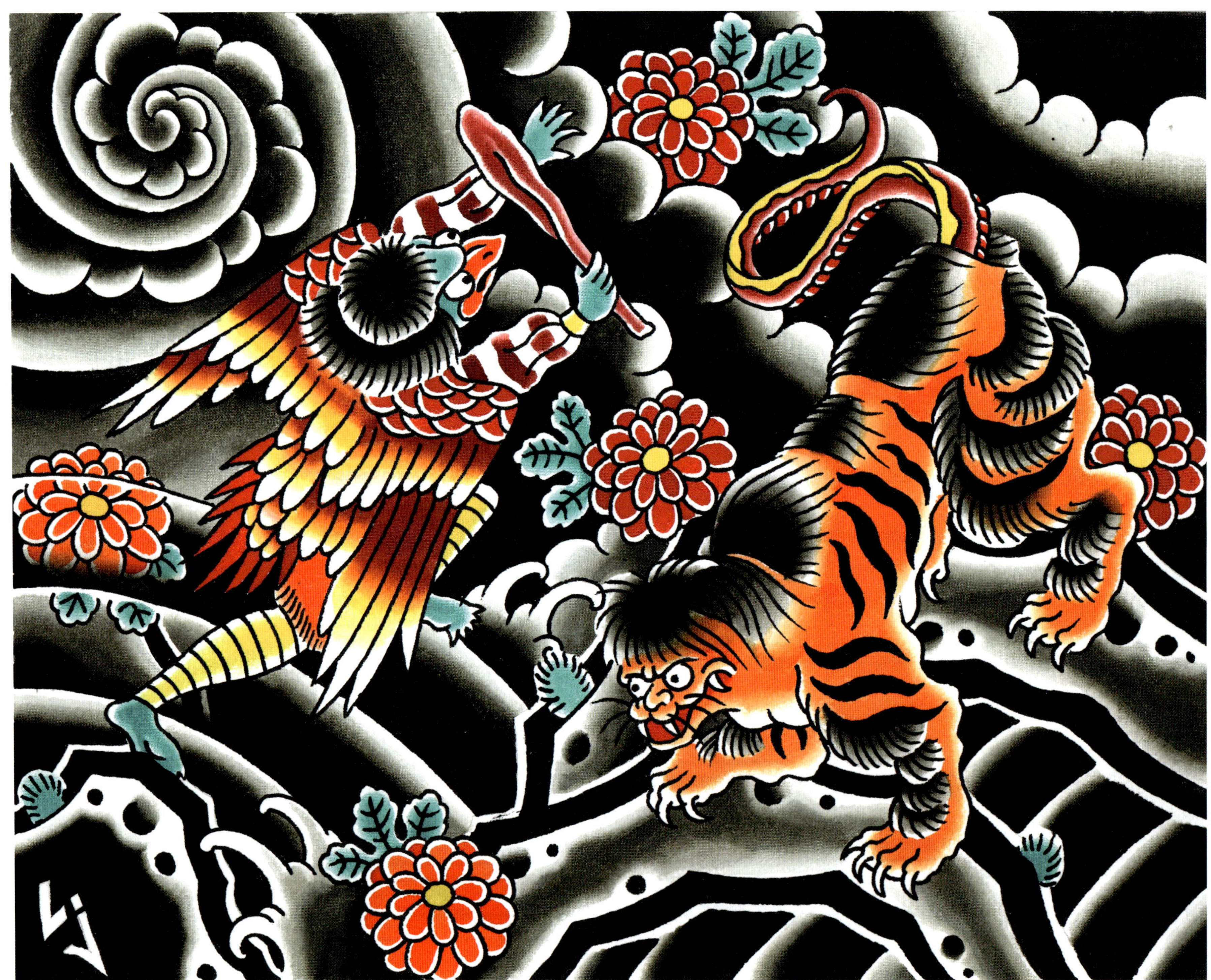

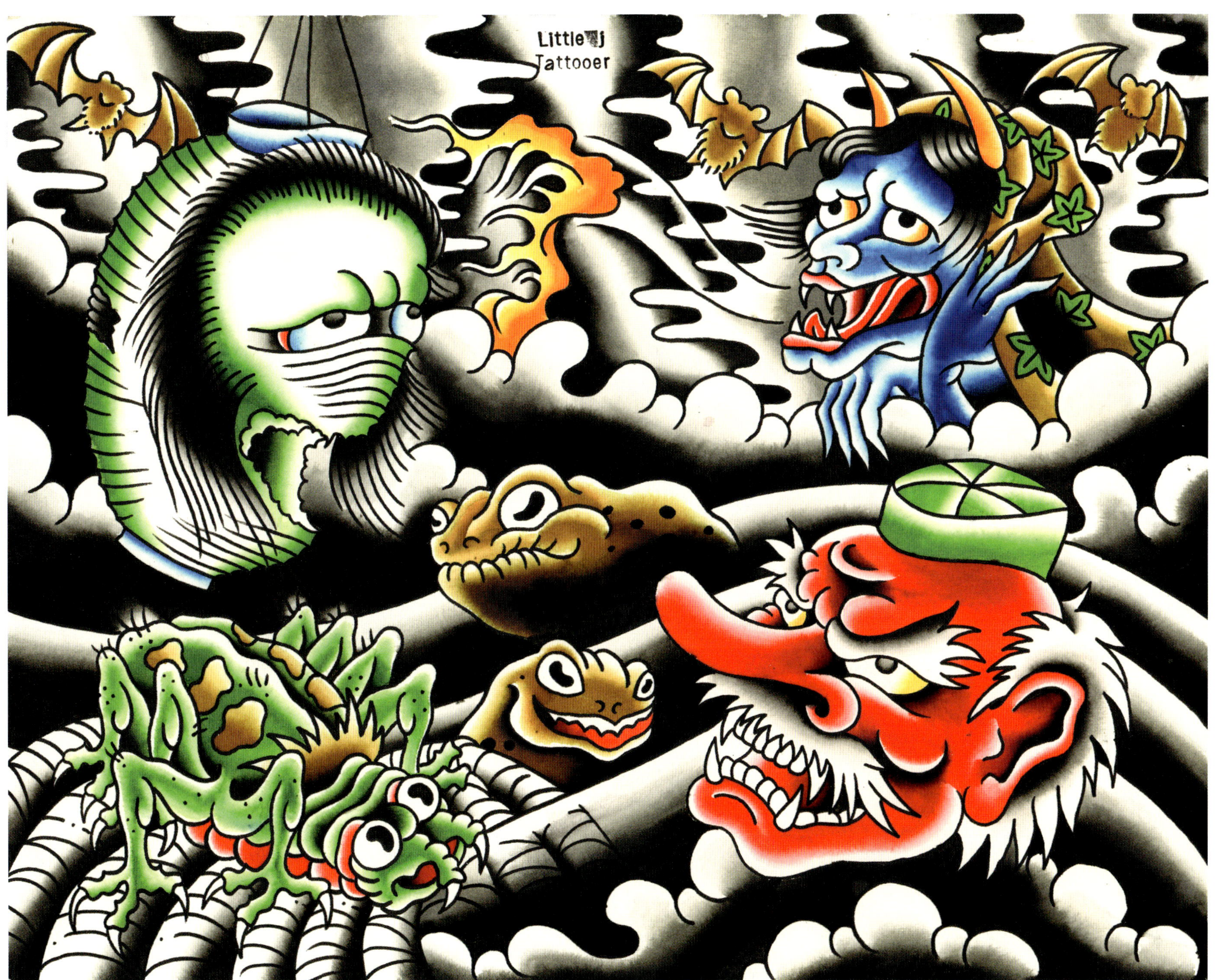
Little j
Tattooer

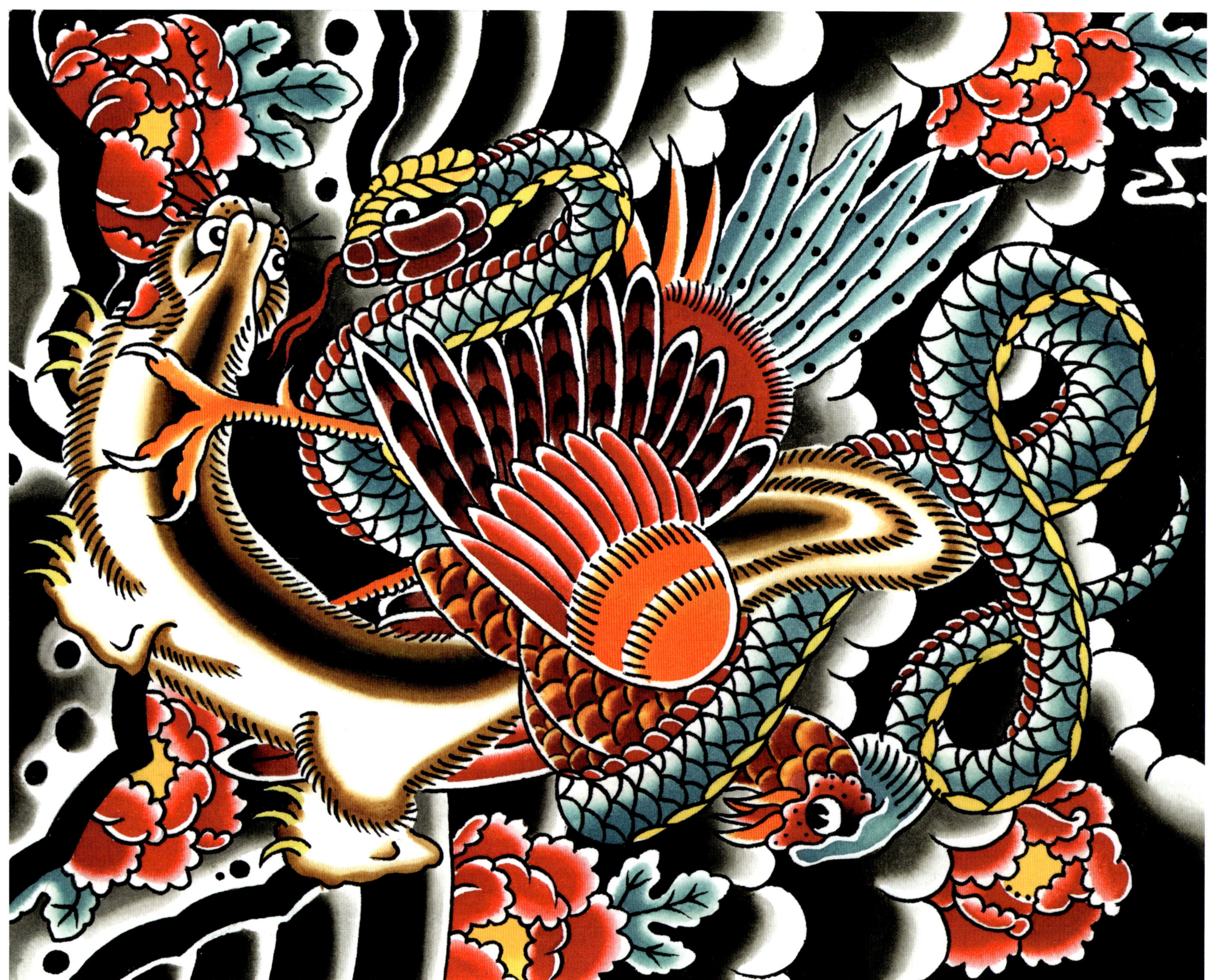

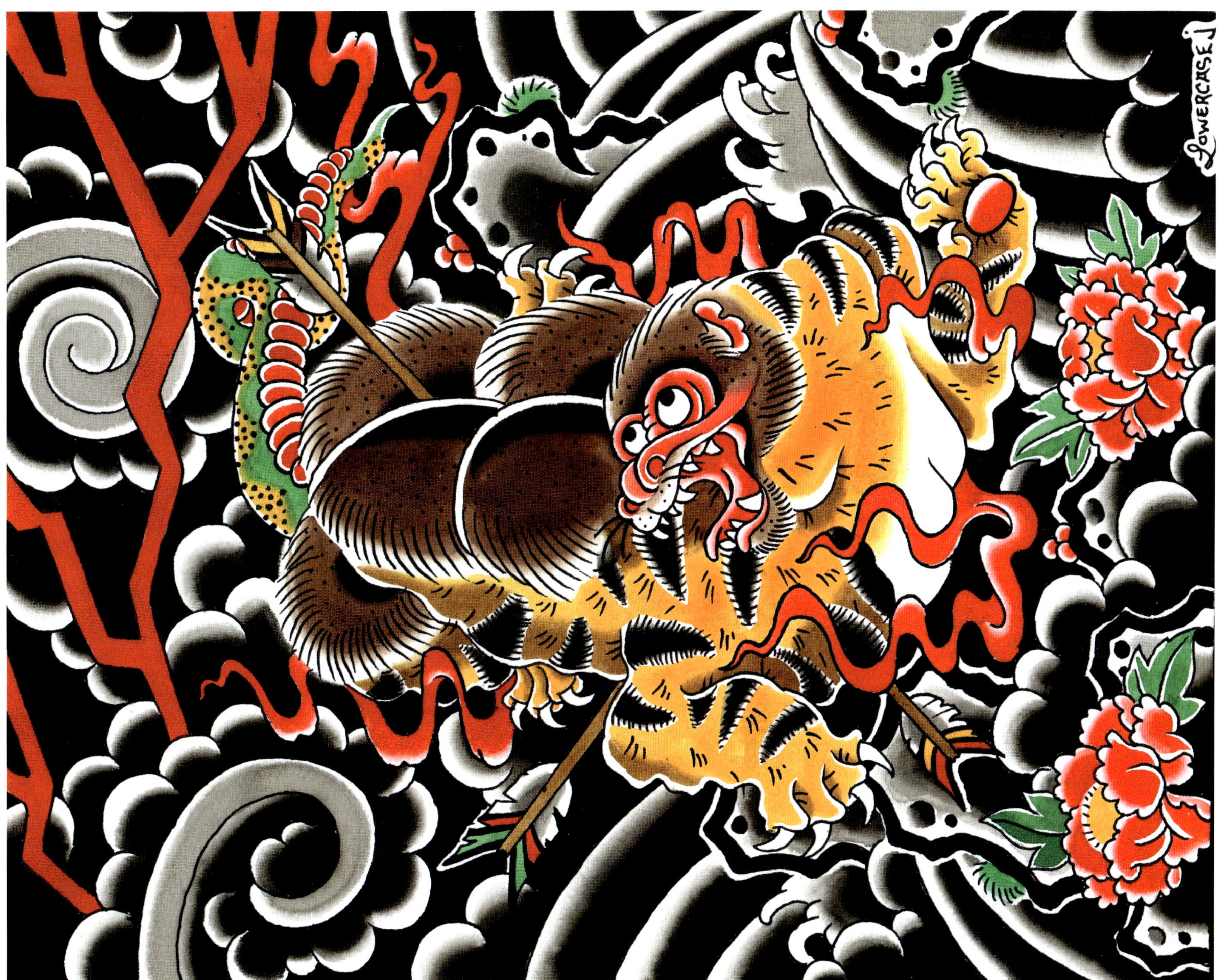
Lowercase j

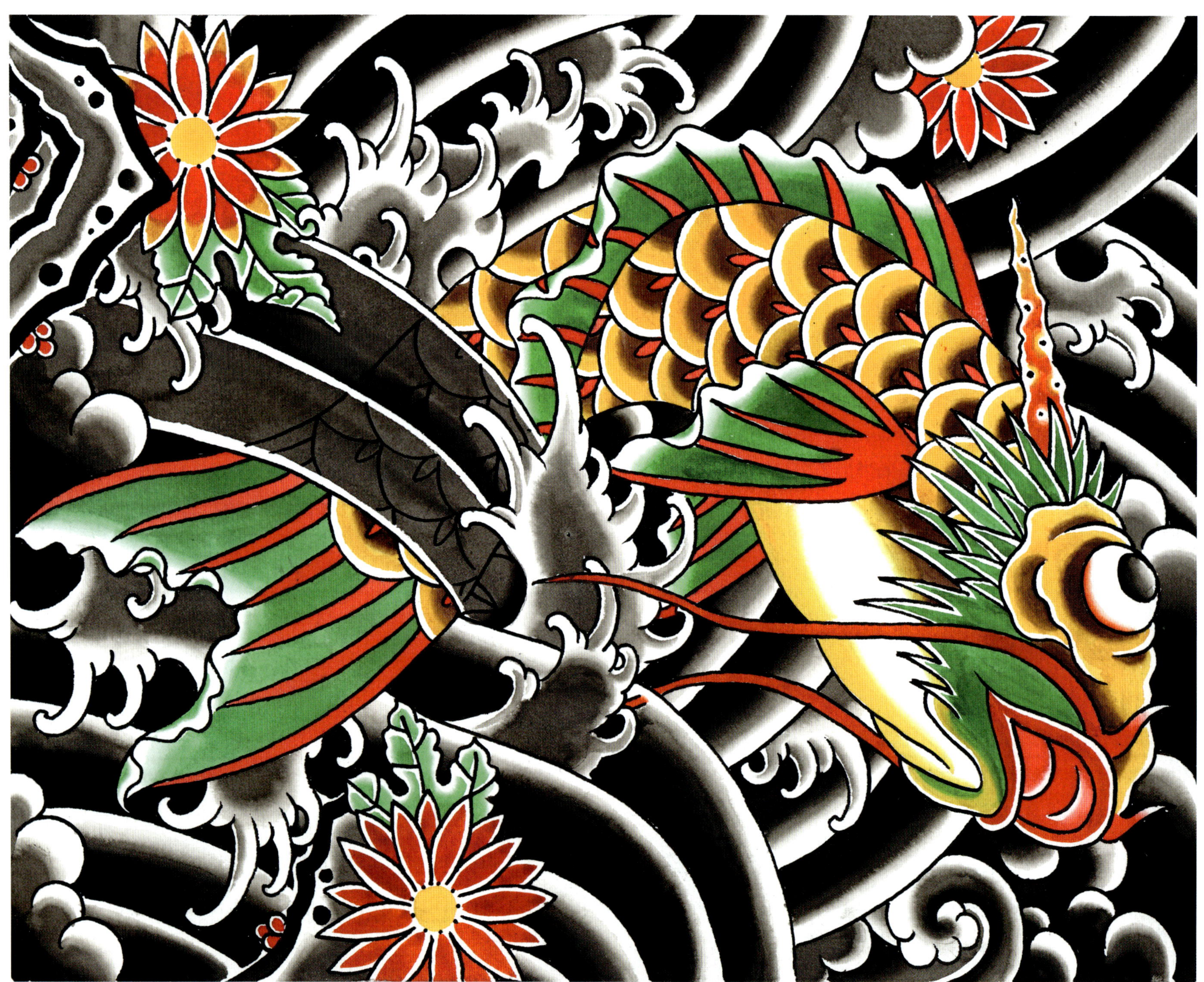

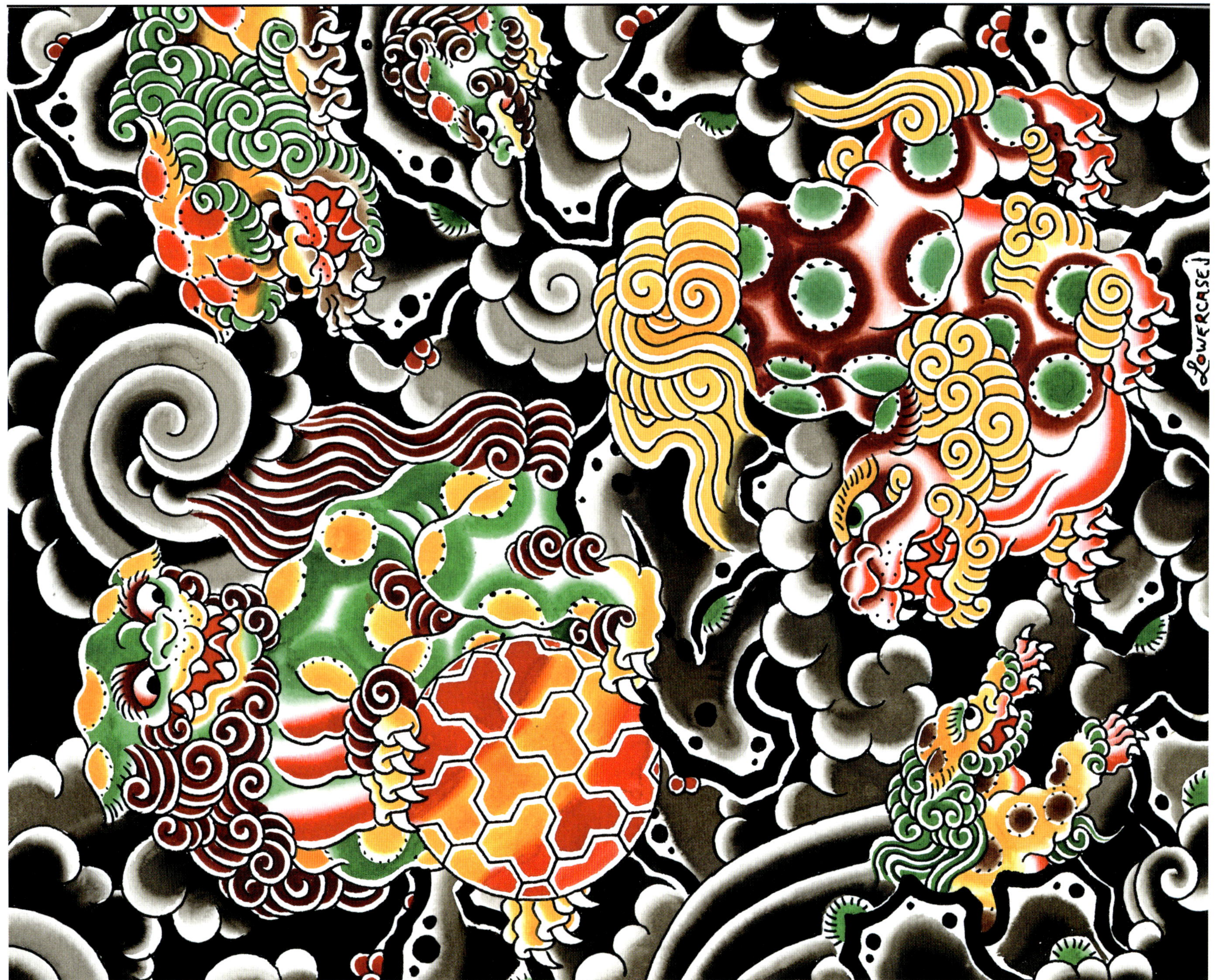
LOWERCASE J

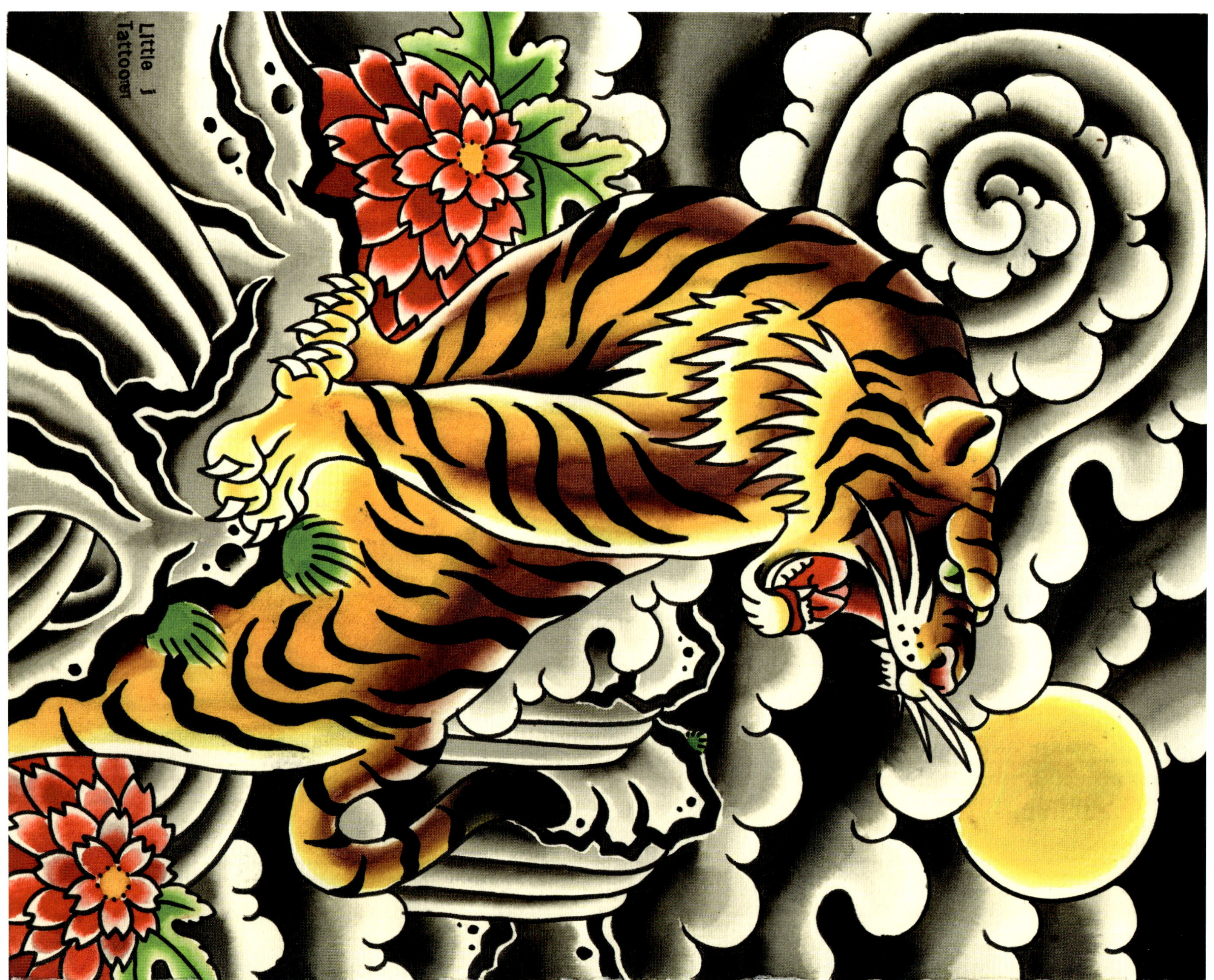
Little J
Tattooer

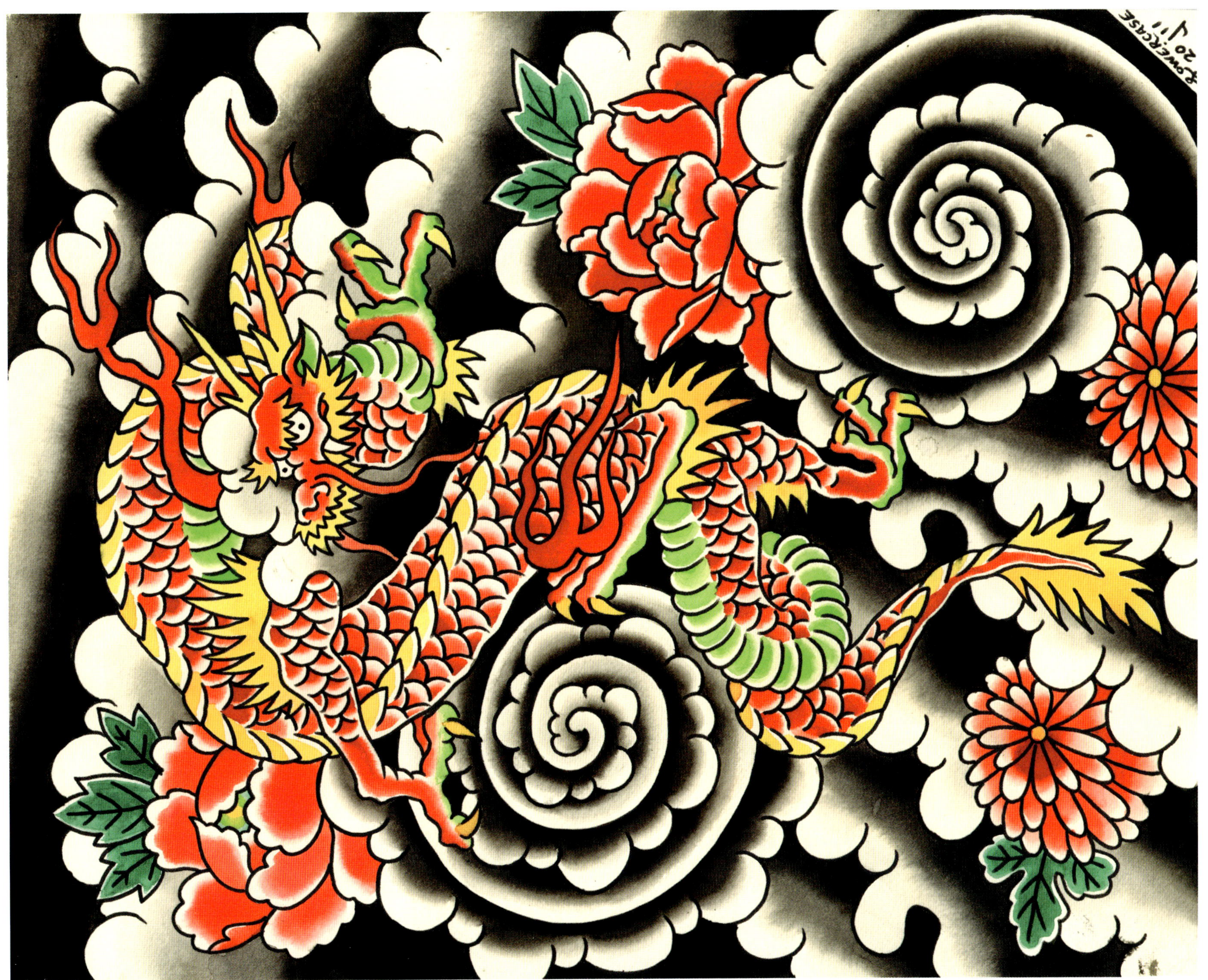

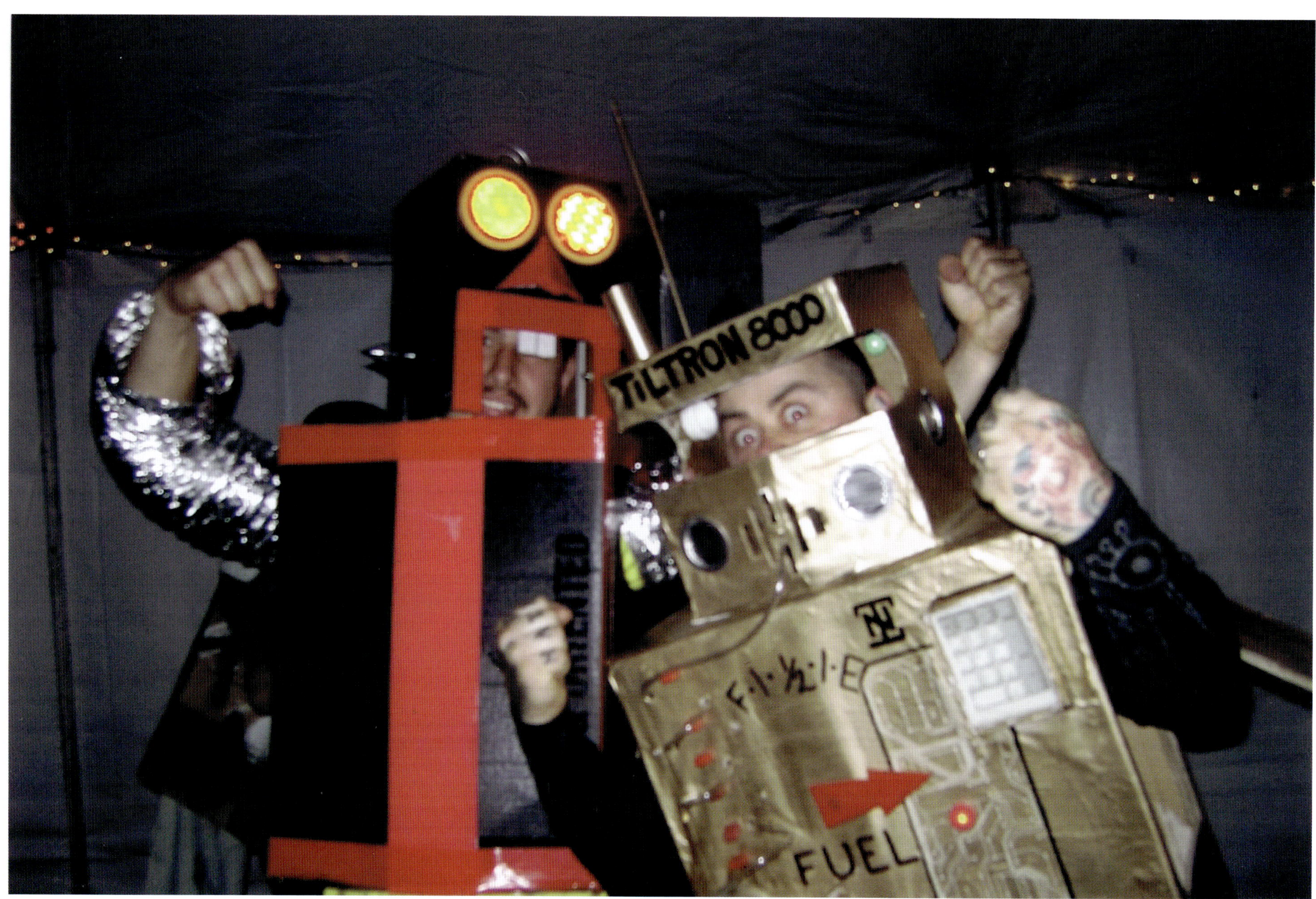
TiLTRON 8000
FUEL

COLLABORATING

Between publication of the first and third volumes of *Classic Flash*, I feel like I have done hundreds of designs with other artists. I get excited about working with pages that another person has started. Energy builds as you open the package and get the first glimpse of what you have to work with. In some cases, the ideas jump off the page as if they have always been there. Other pages take more thought and effort. When a couple of pages came in the mail at a time, I would first tackle the one that seemed the most exciting. However, when I reflected on the completed projects, I realized that the pages I put off working on were some of the best I made. That's probably because the "less exciting" layouts were the ones for which I spent more time studying the other person's work, which resulted in greater continuity and understanding.

In tackling any project of this scale, you really get to know your collaborator's style and design sense. It took Lowercase j and I a couple of years to complete the drawings shown here. He would send half of a painted page and I would add the other half, or vice versa, and we would surprise each other with the finished painting. We have been to each other's shops and like a lot of the same stuff, and I knew what he was thinking by the way he started a page.

Lowercase j has taught me to embrace the fun side of design. As I reflect on this long collaboration, my biggest lesson is that there are many lessons to be learned, and it's more fun to explore those lessons with a buddy.

—Tilt

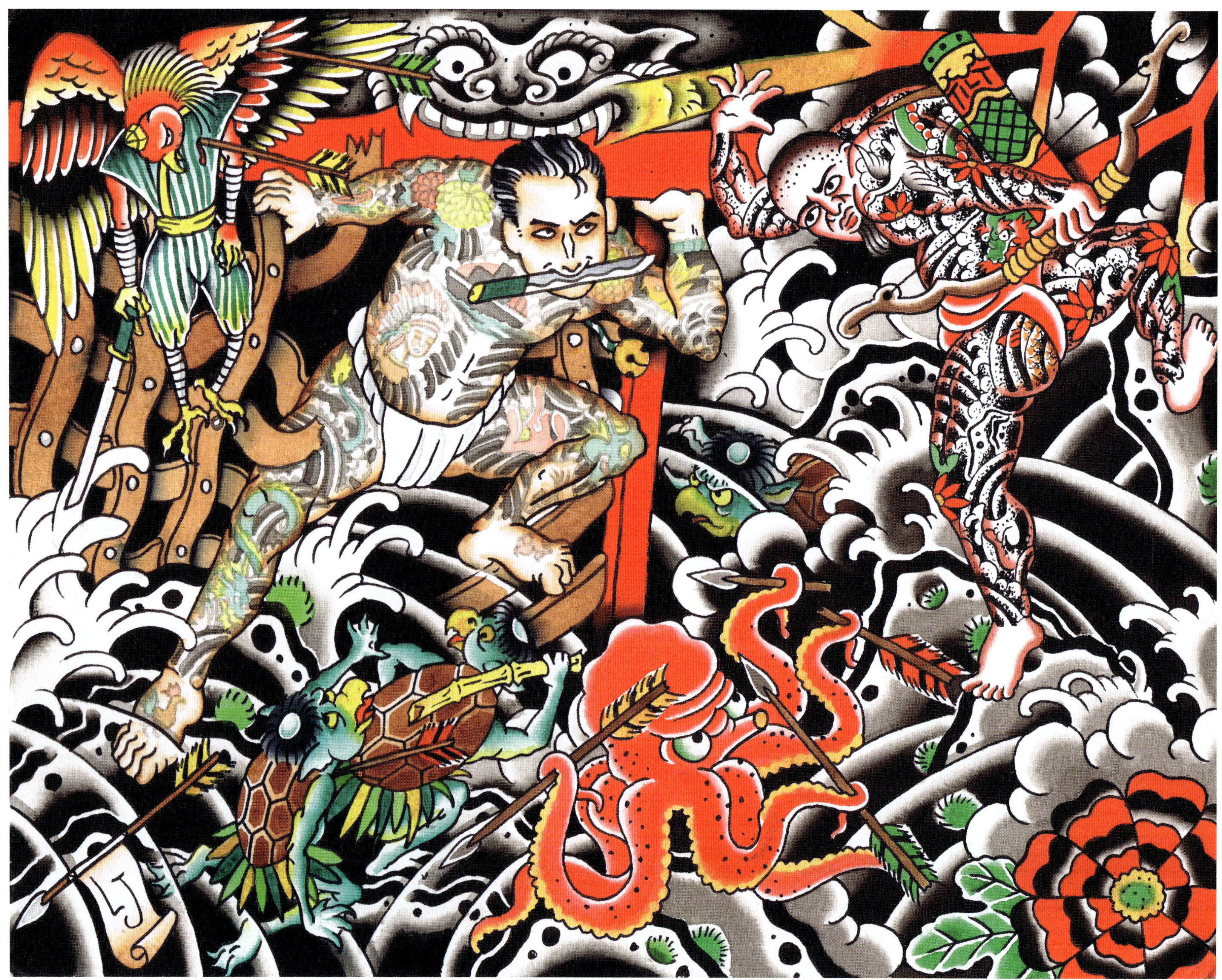

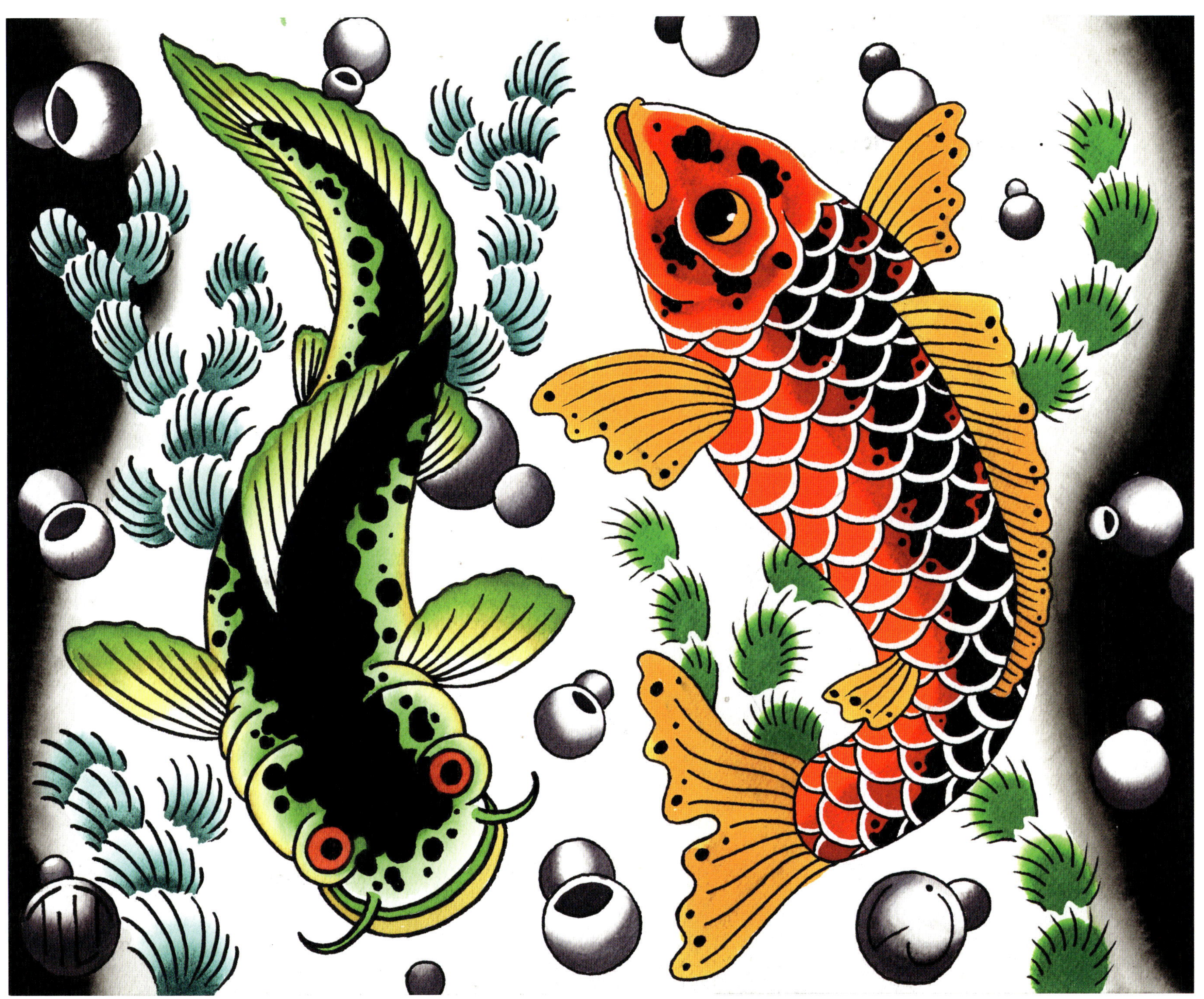

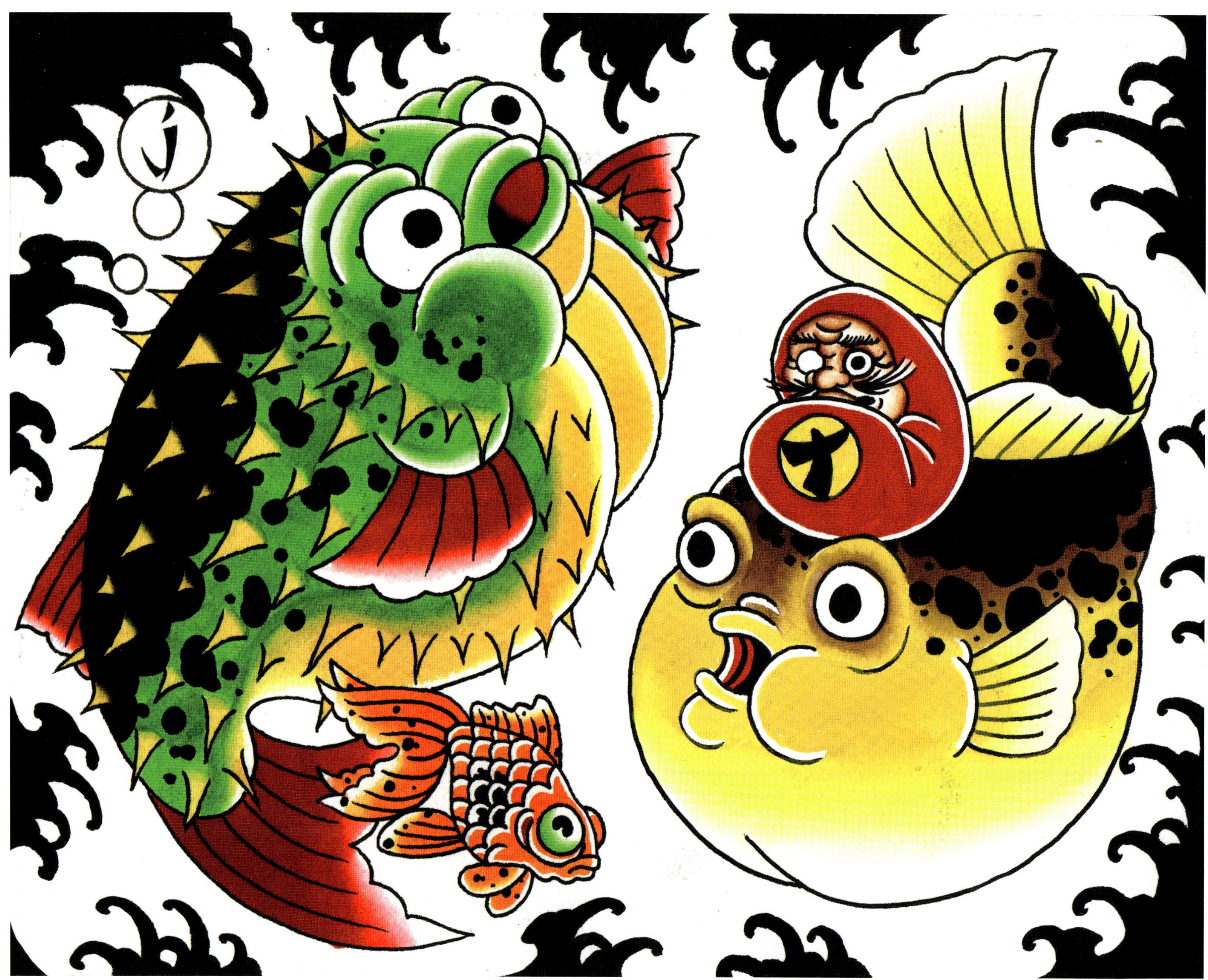

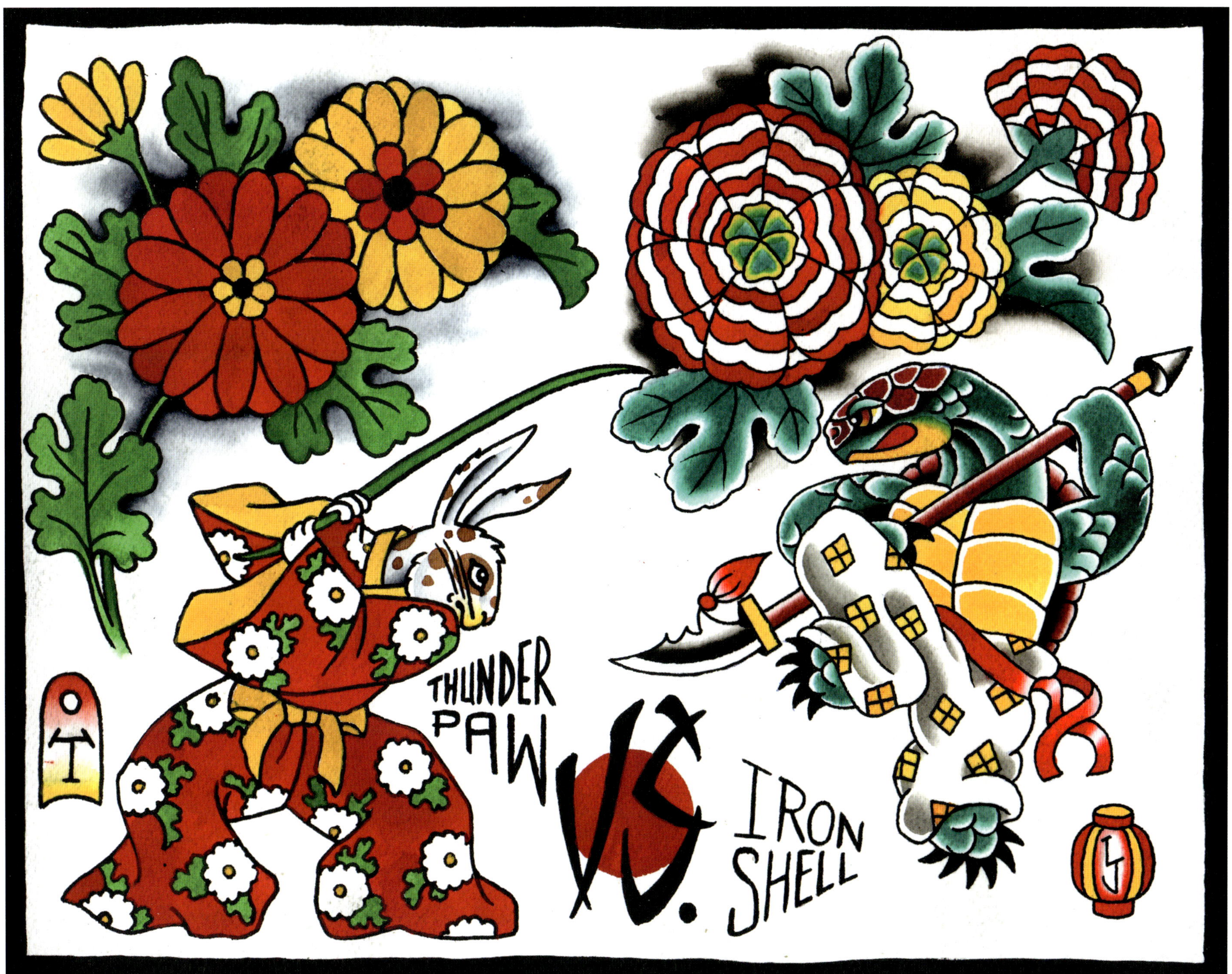
THUNDER
PAW
VS.
IRON
SHELL

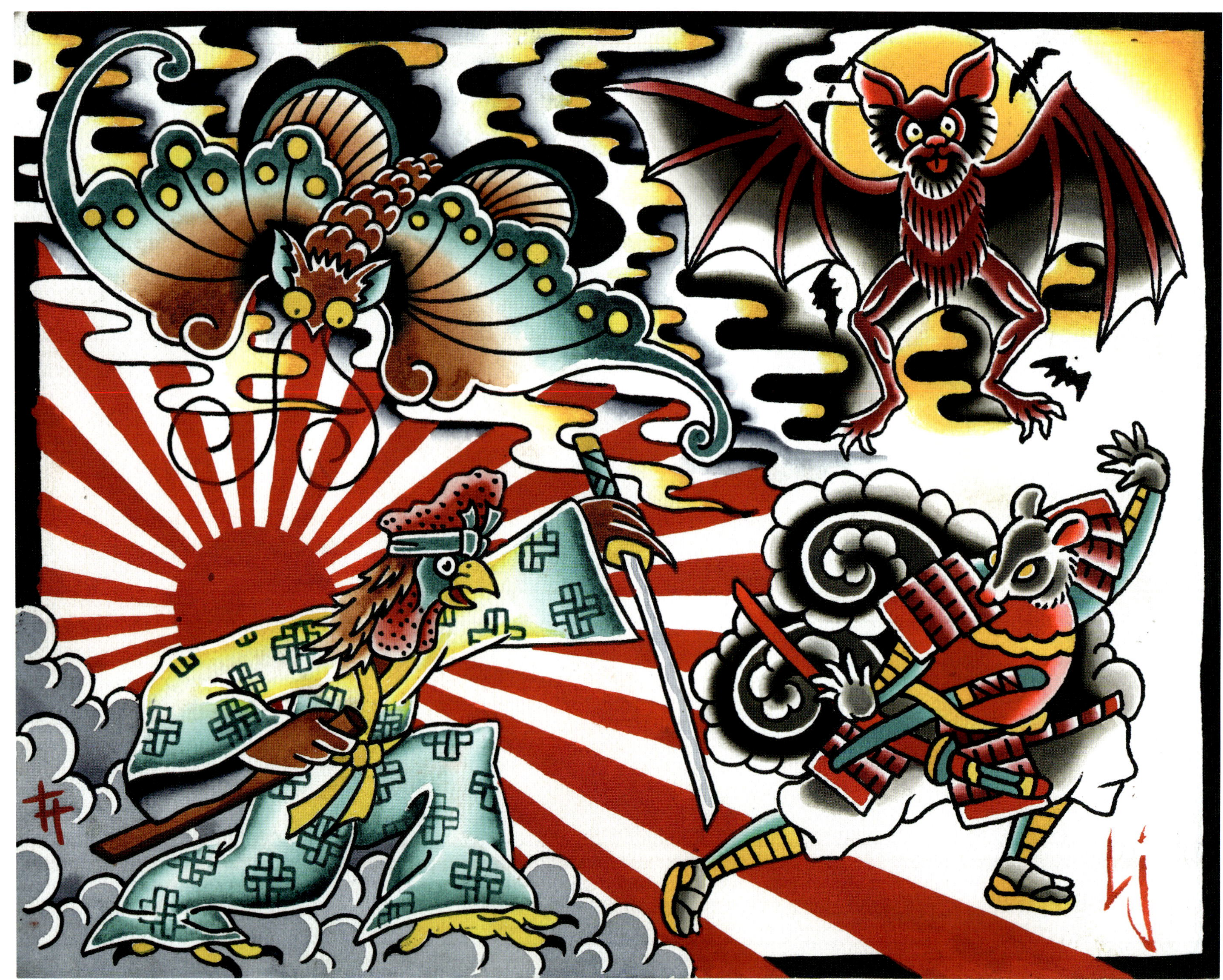

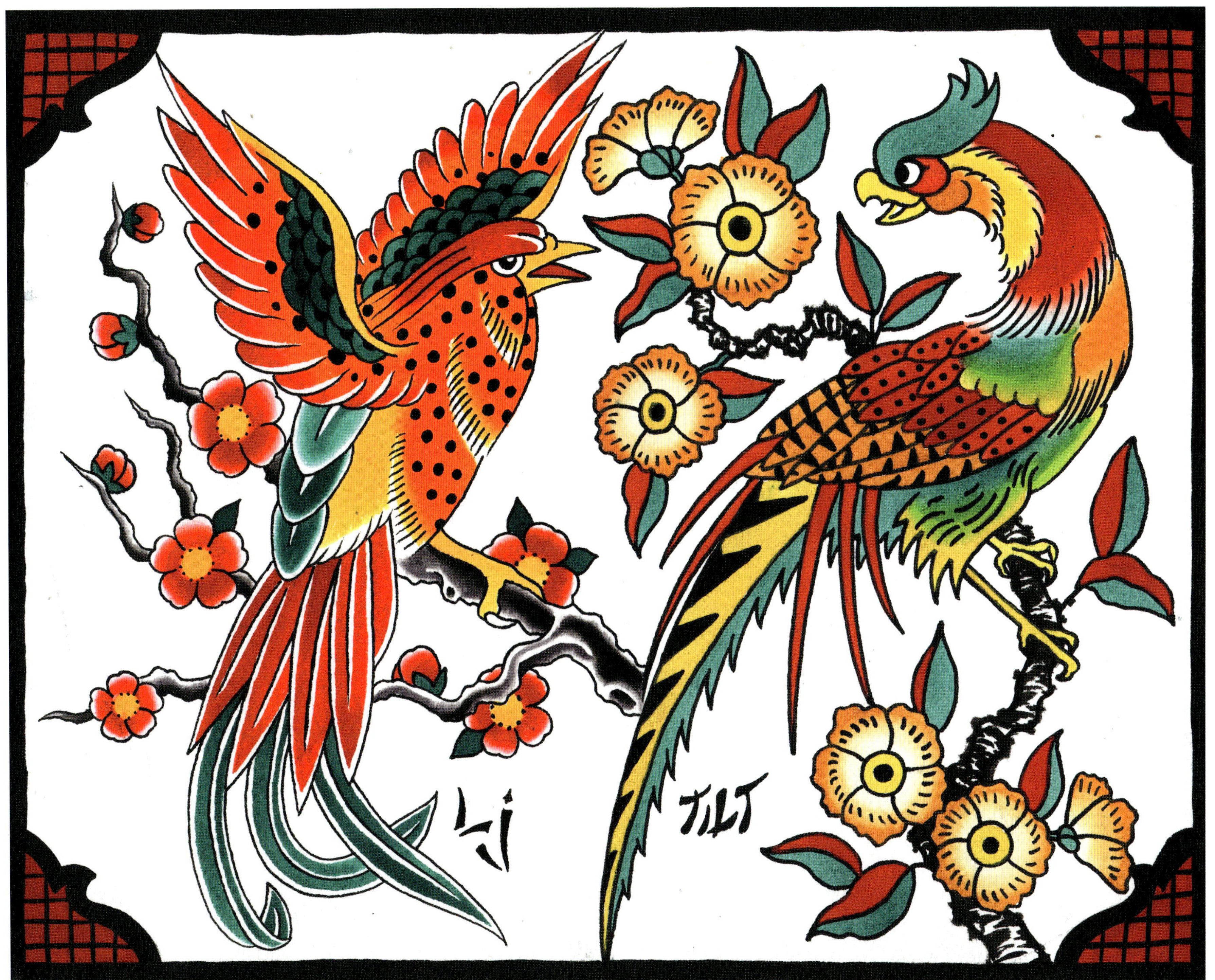
TILT

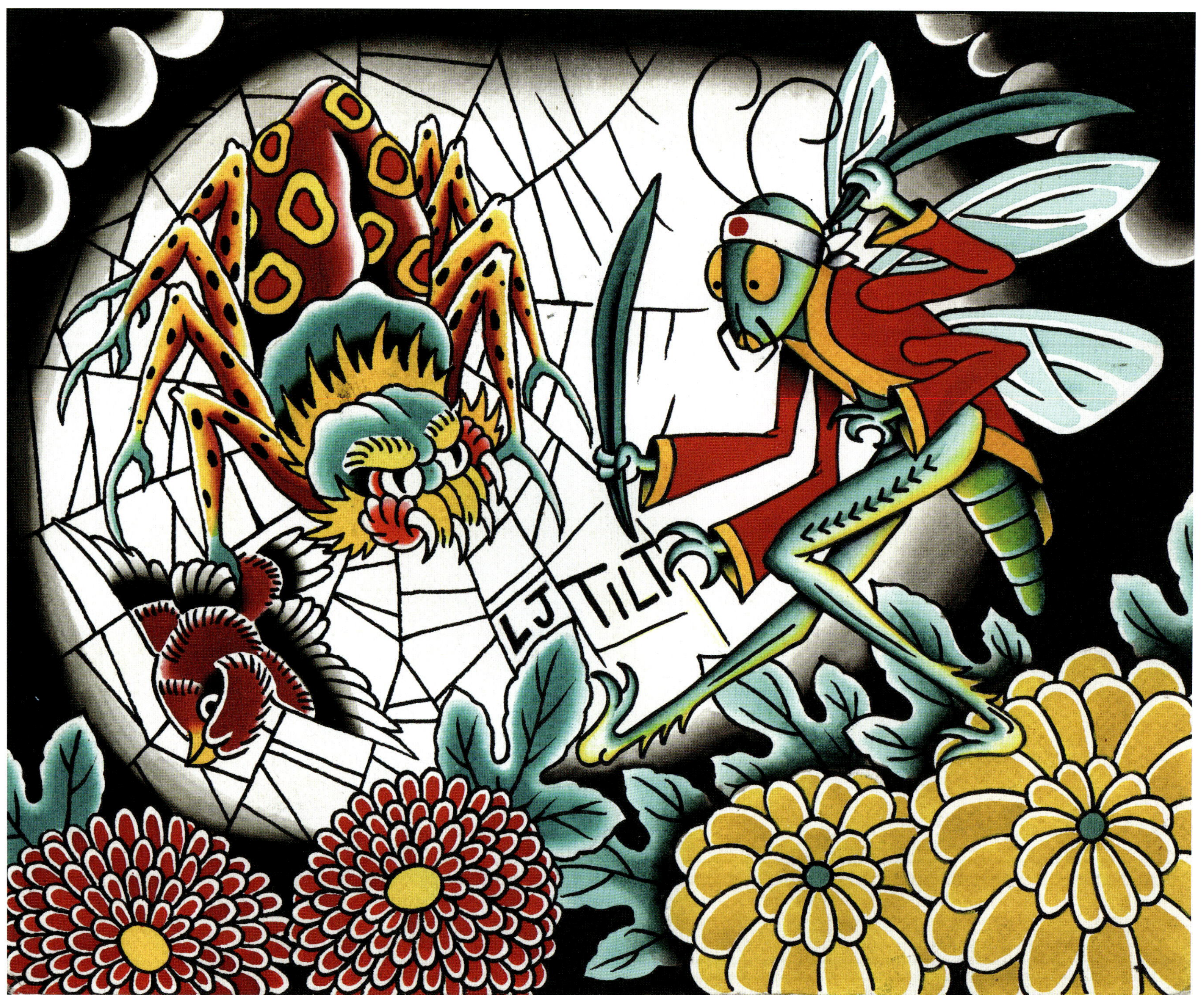
LJ TiLT

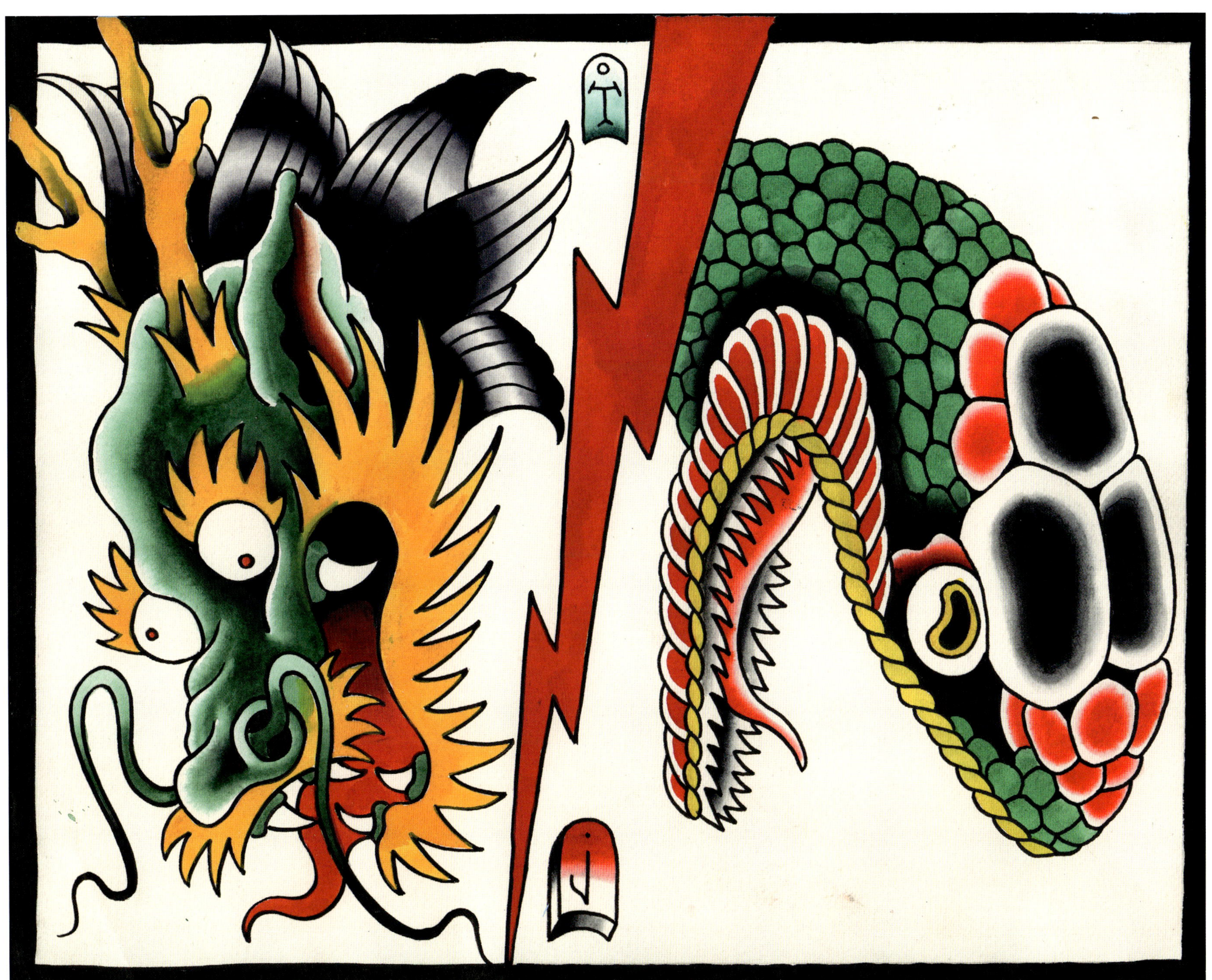

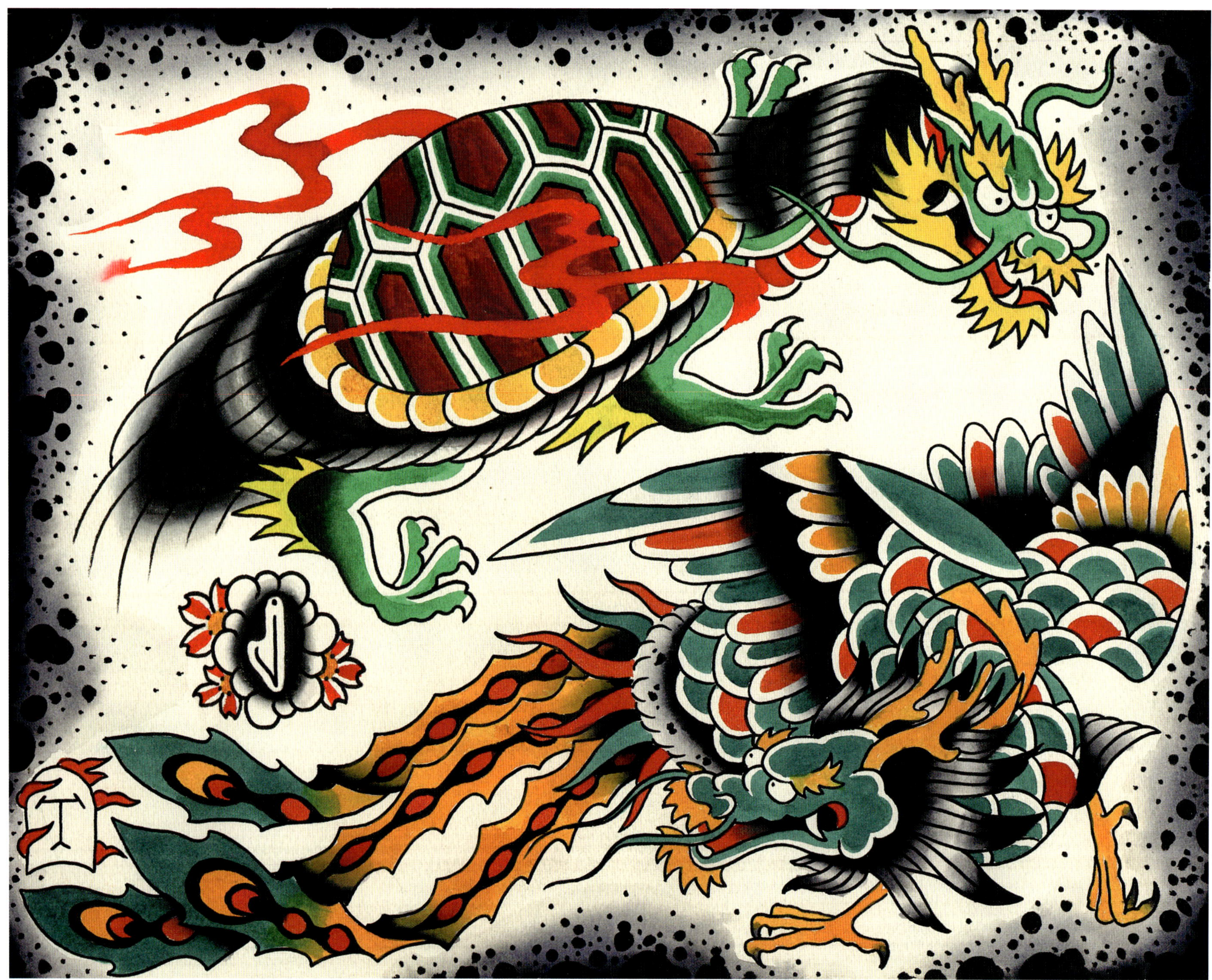

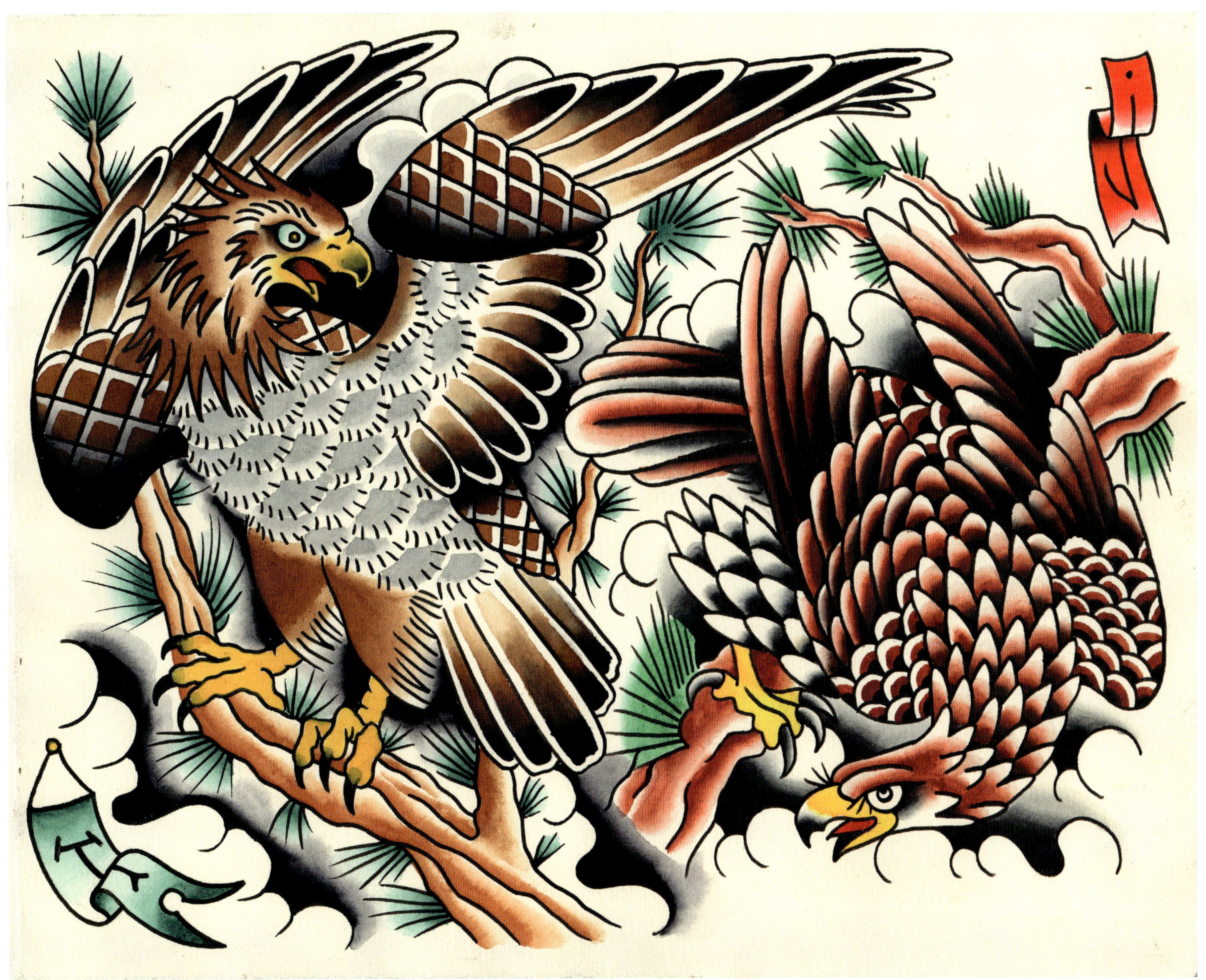

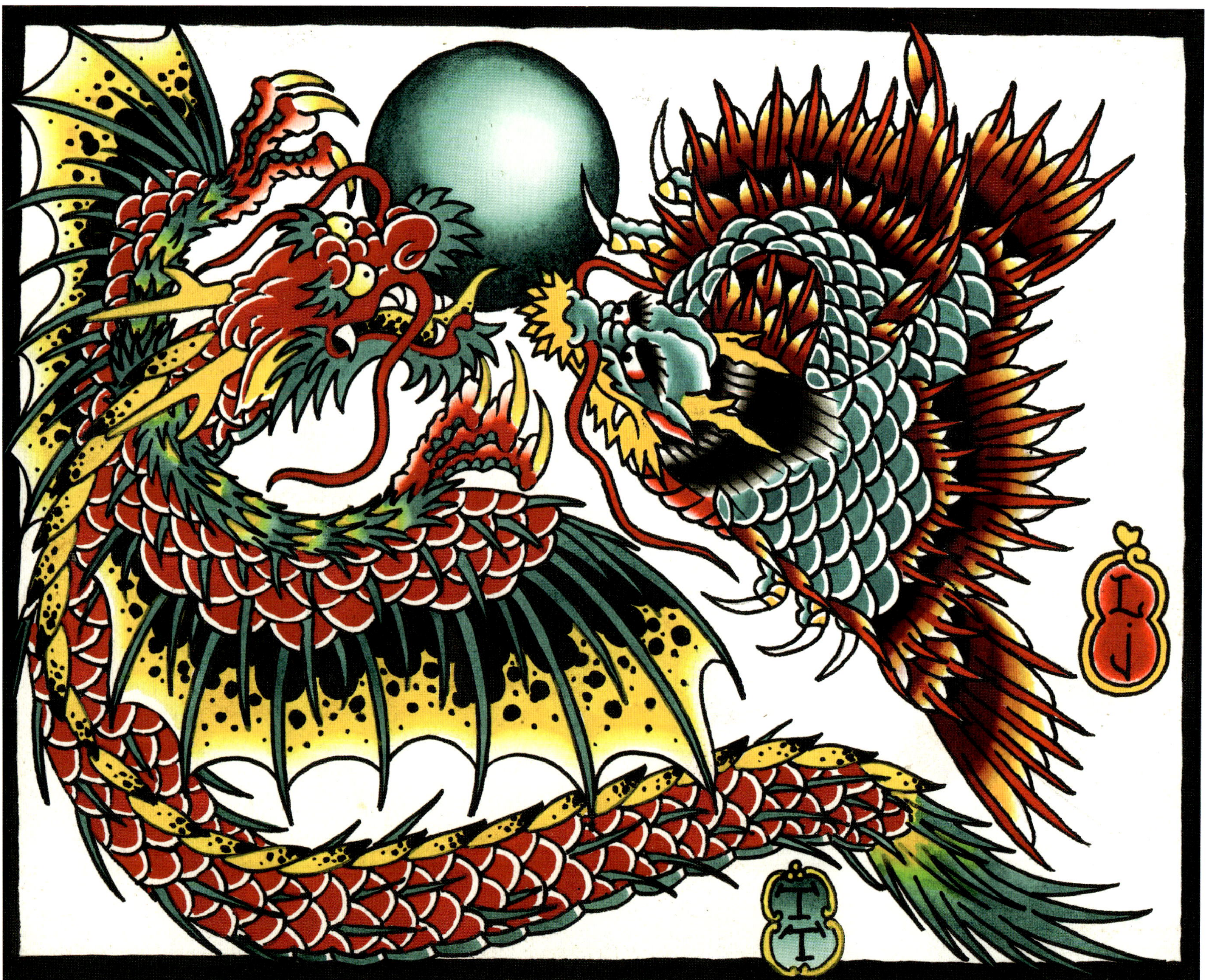

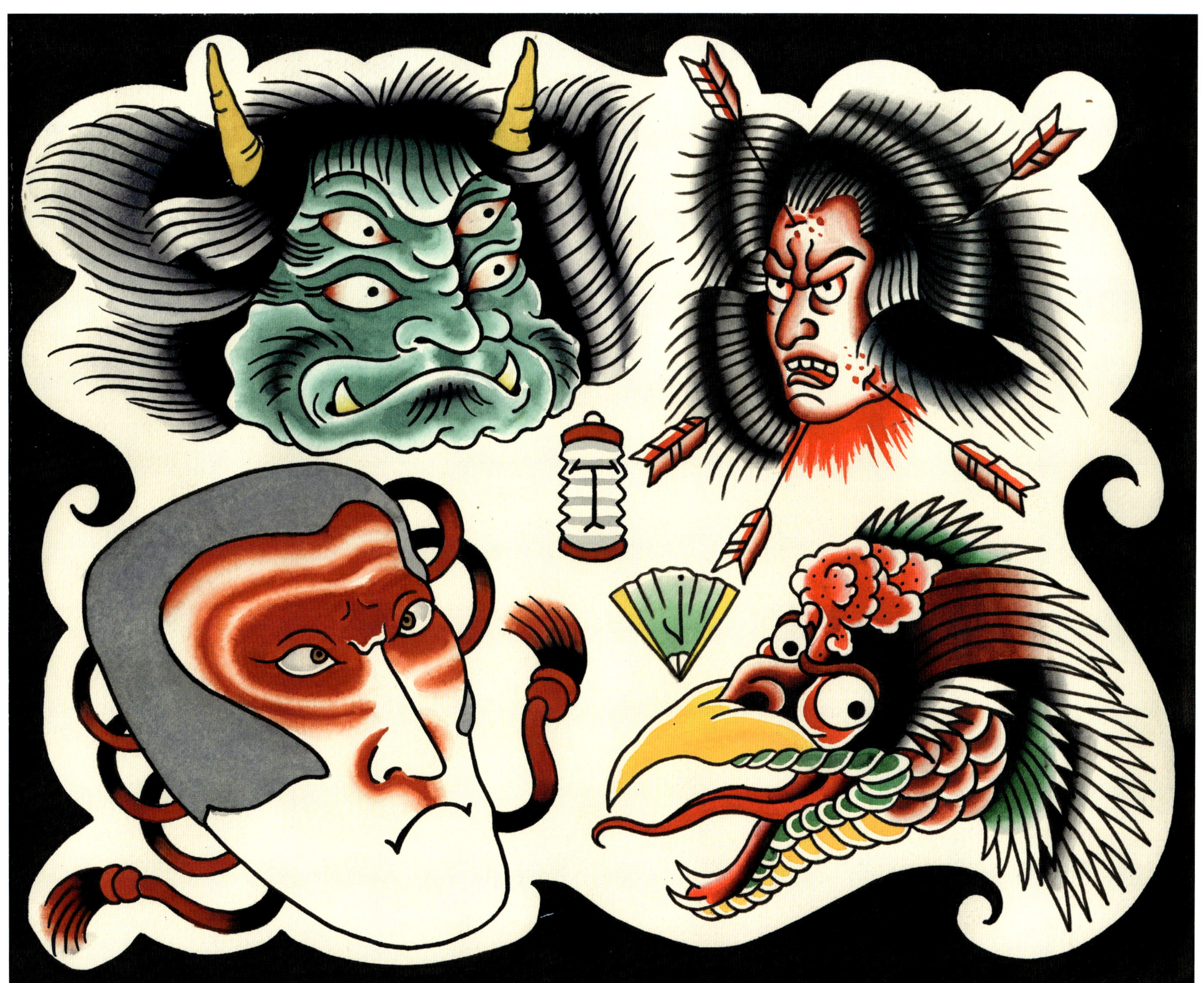

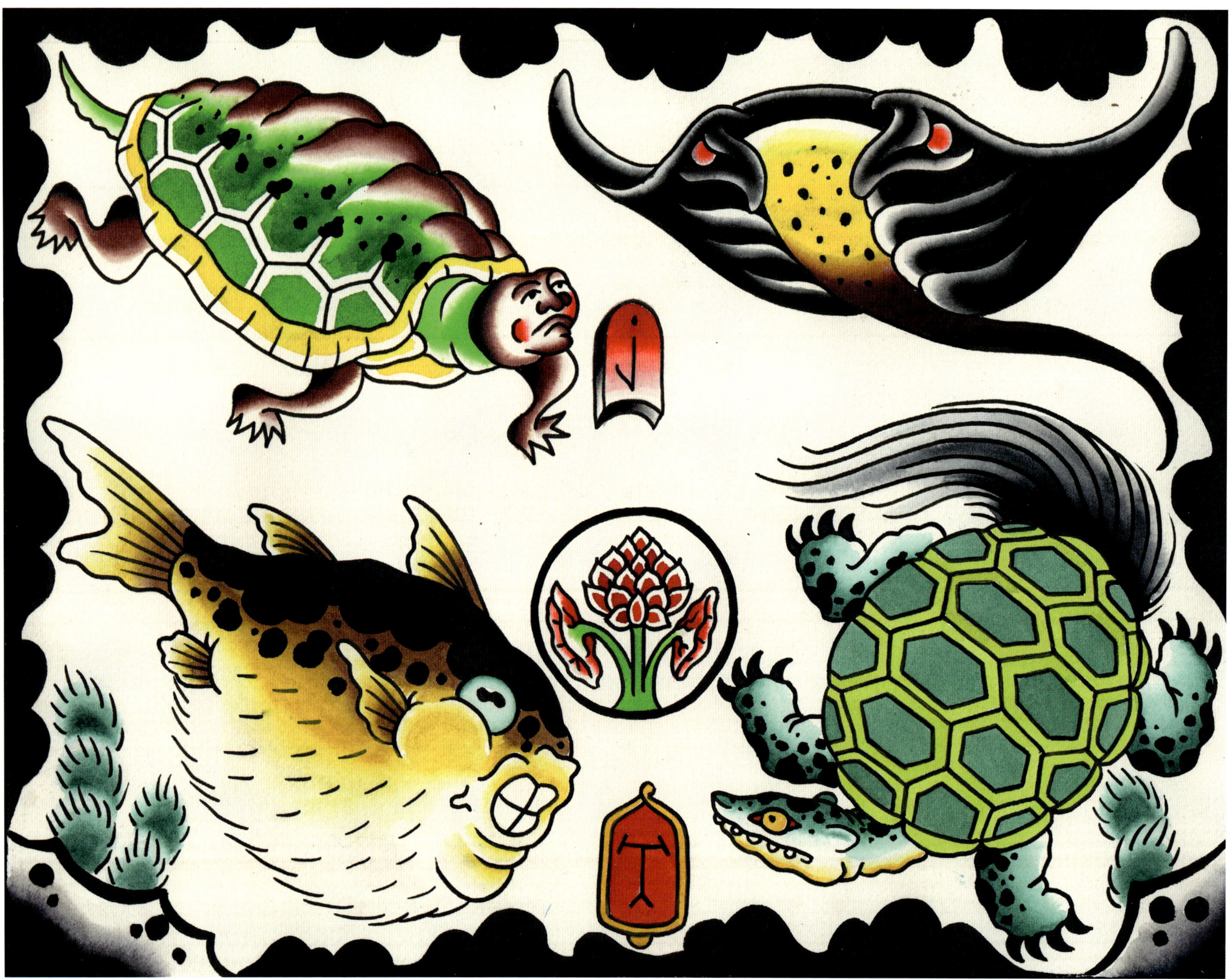

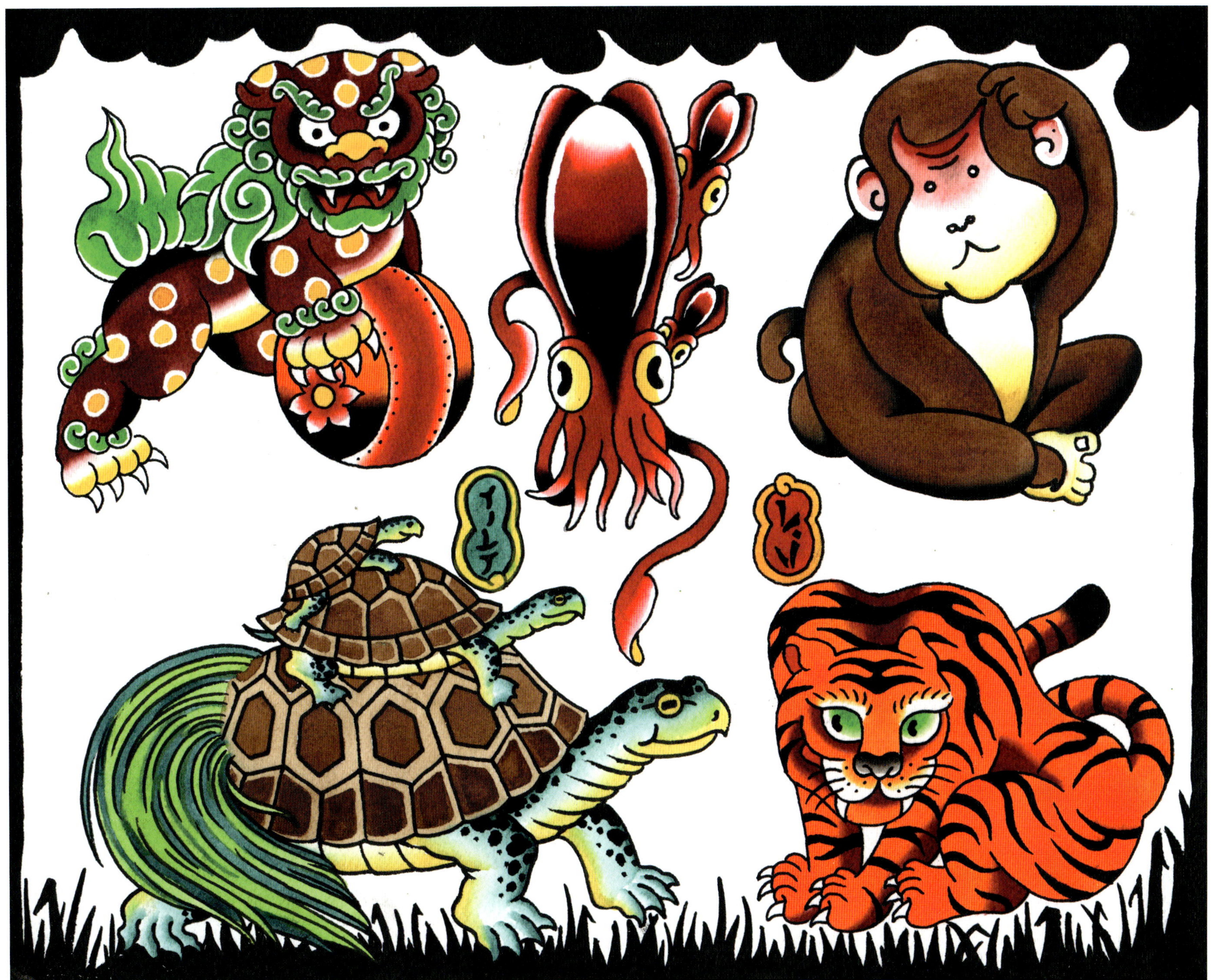

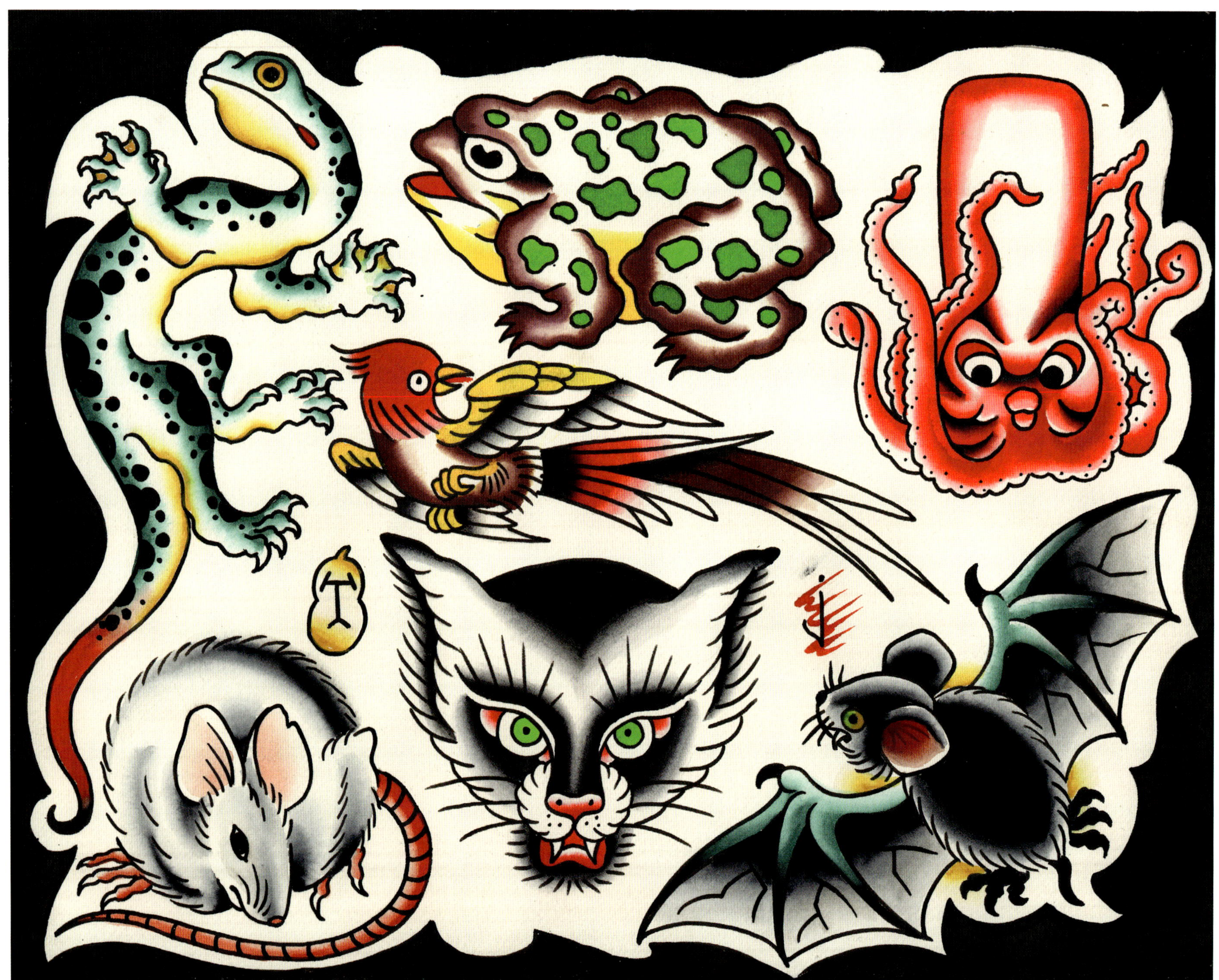

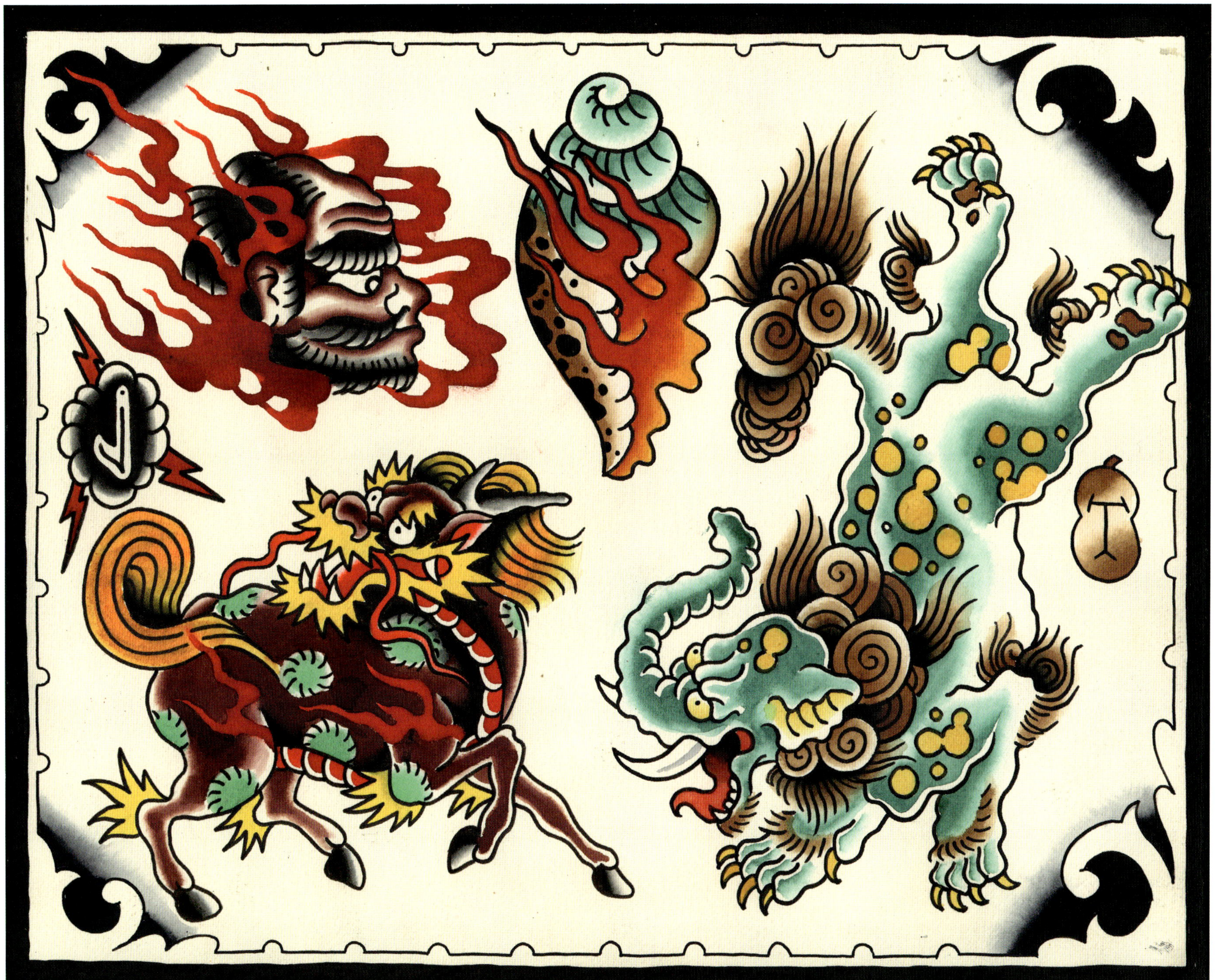

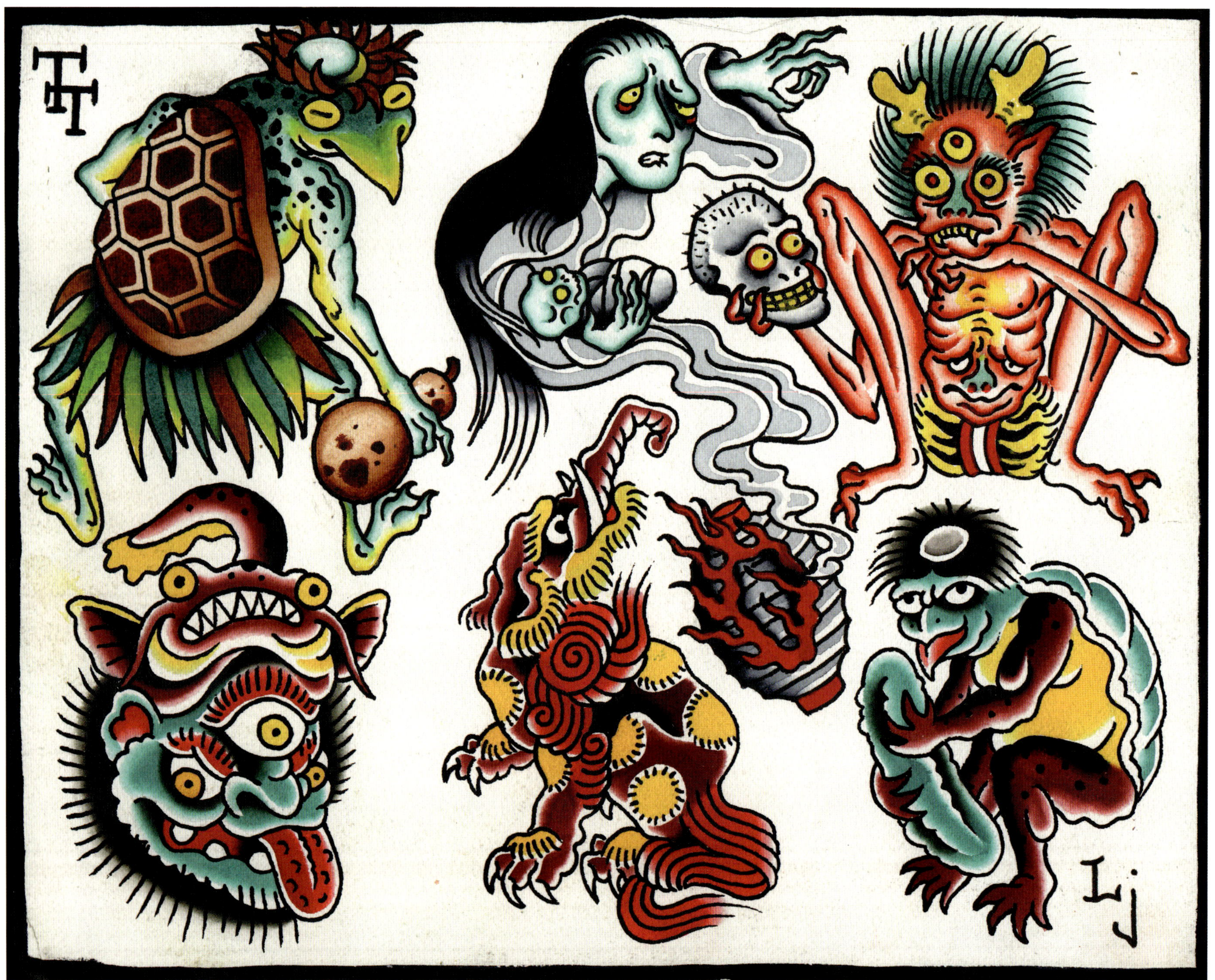

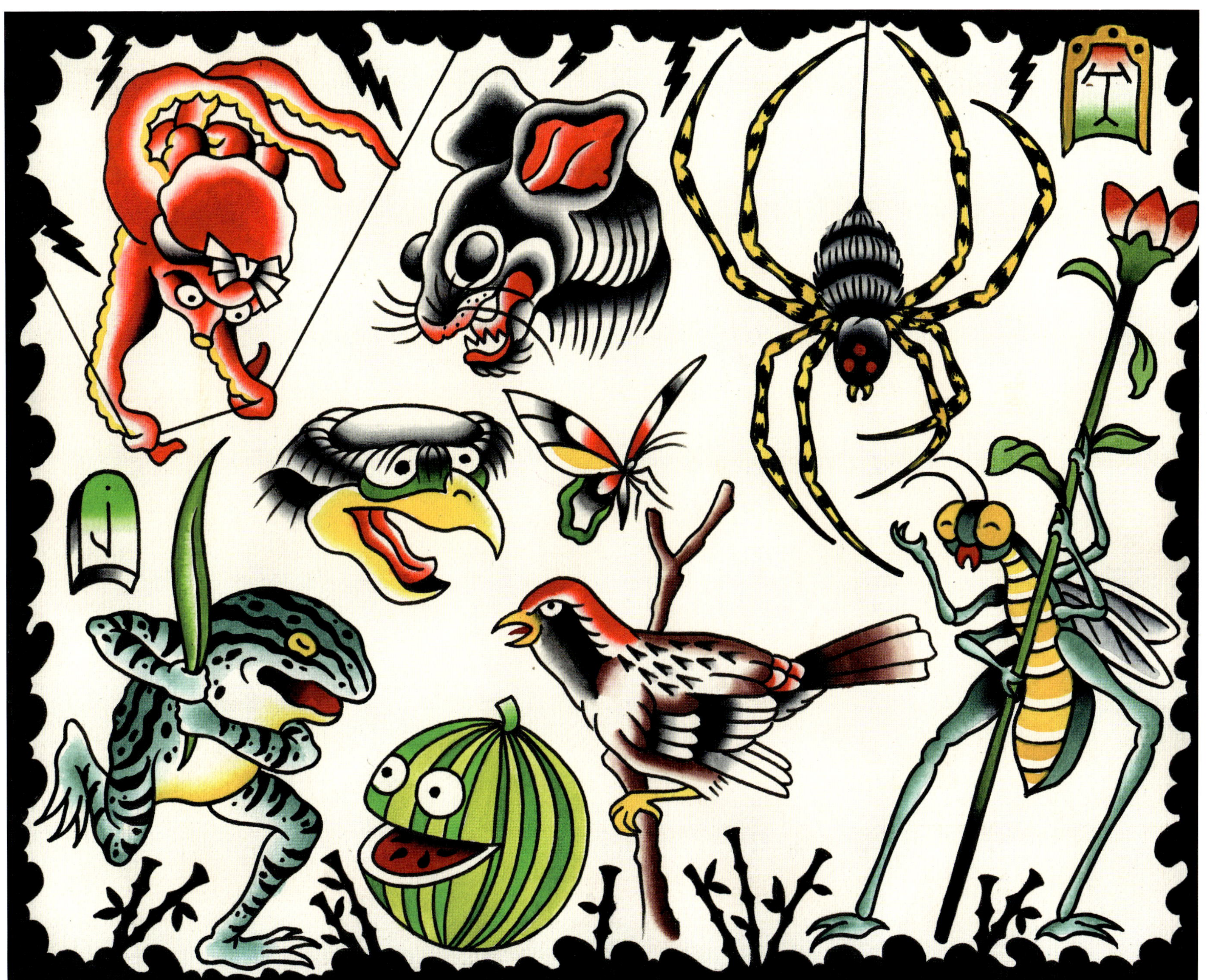

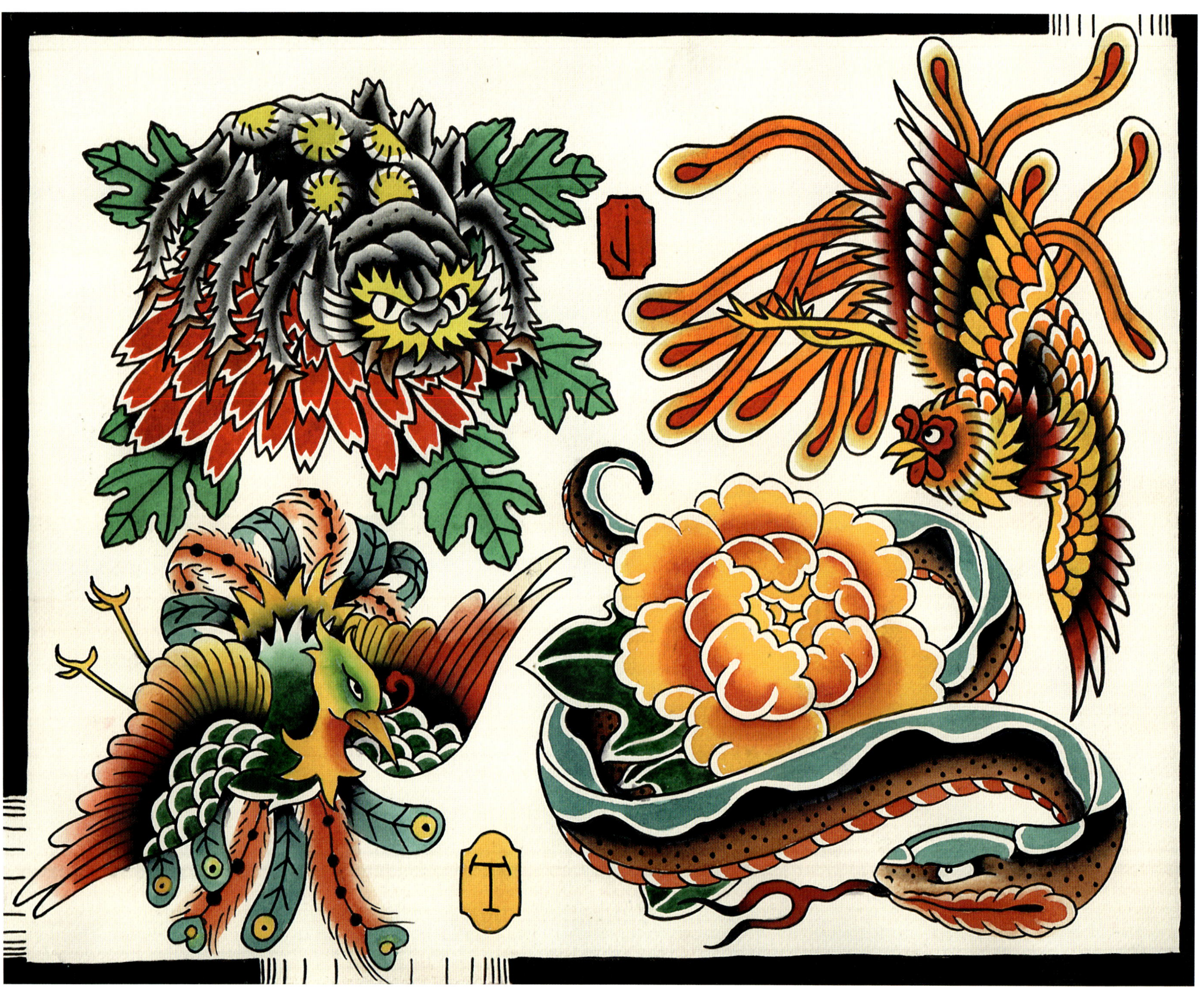
J
T

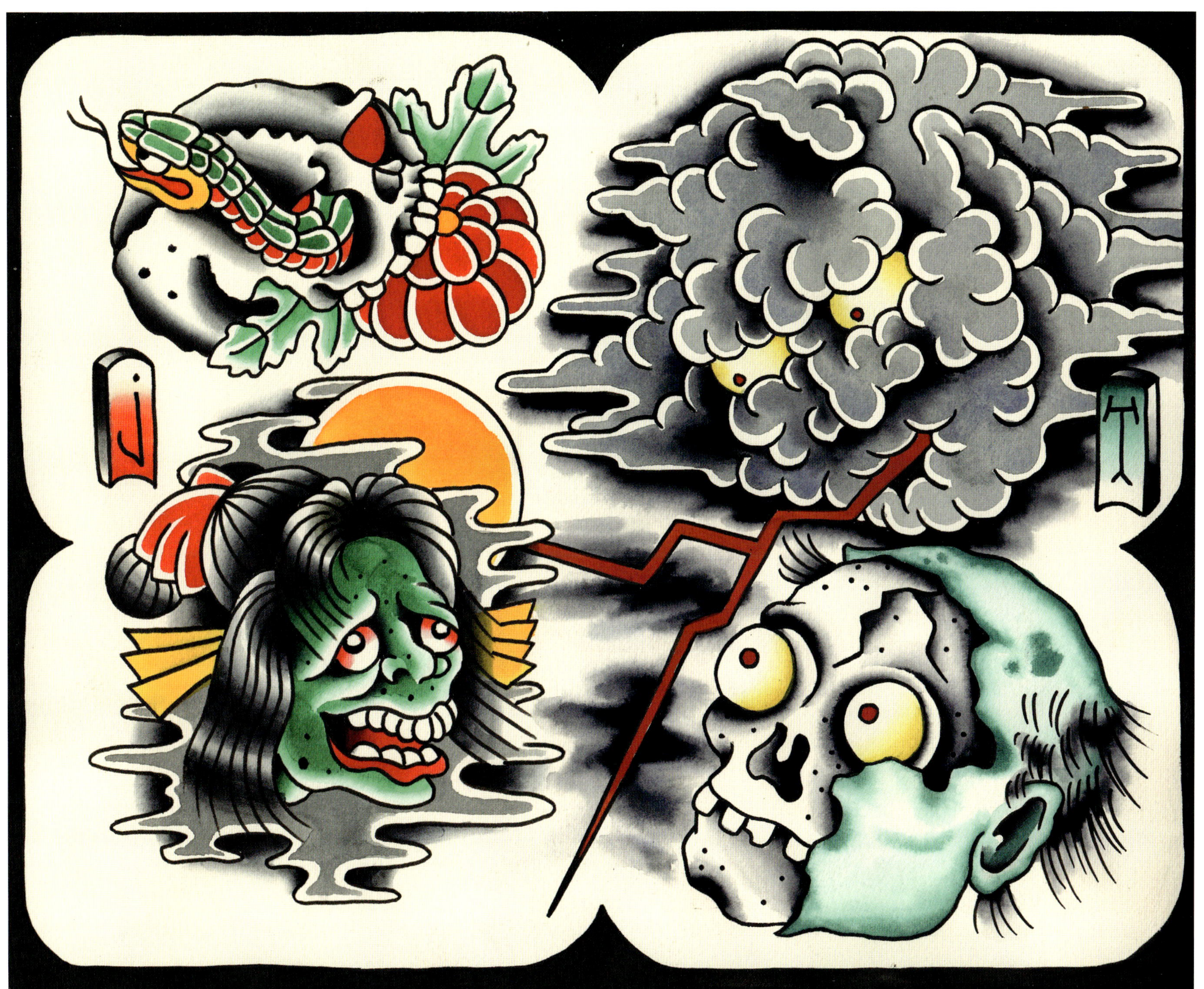

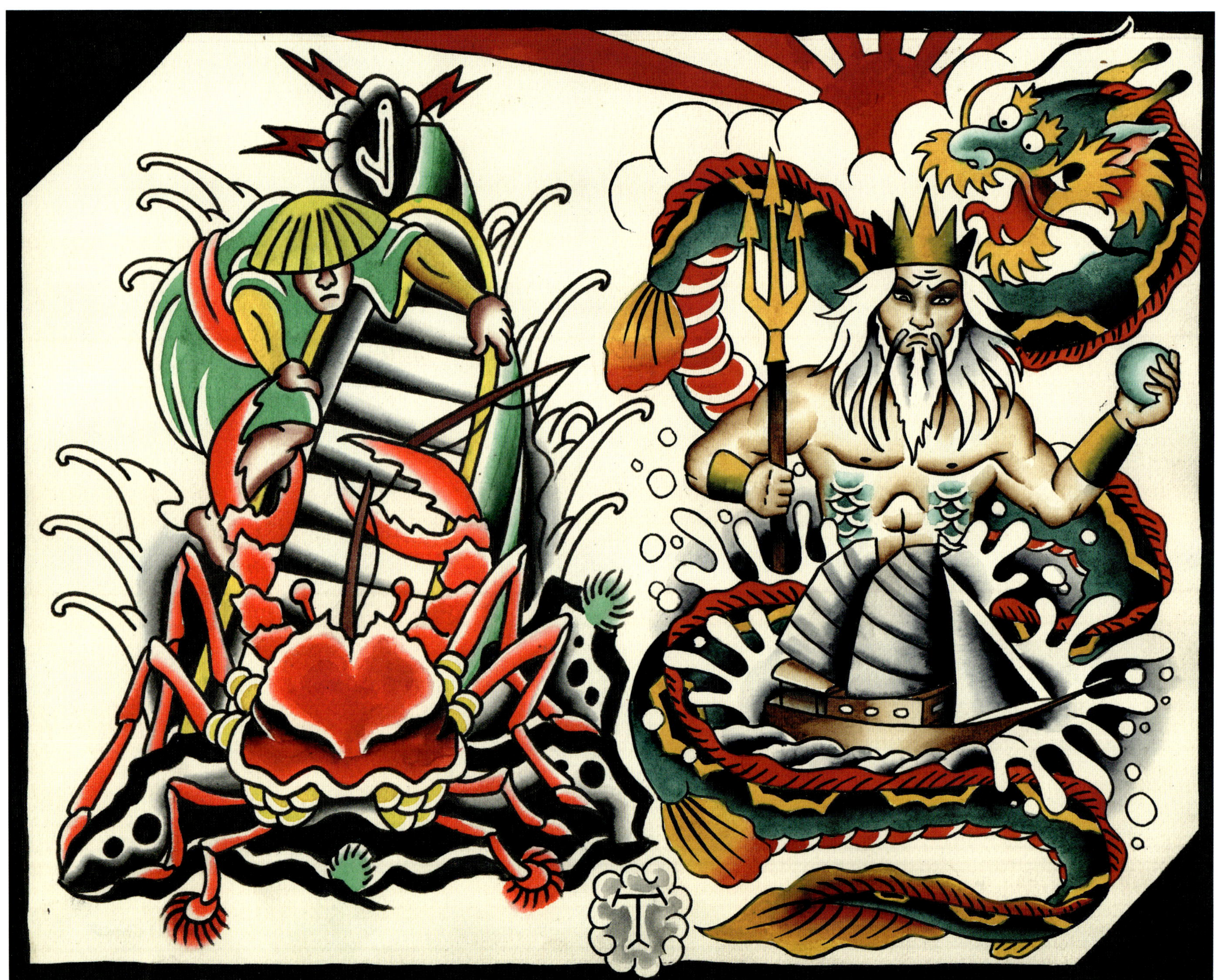

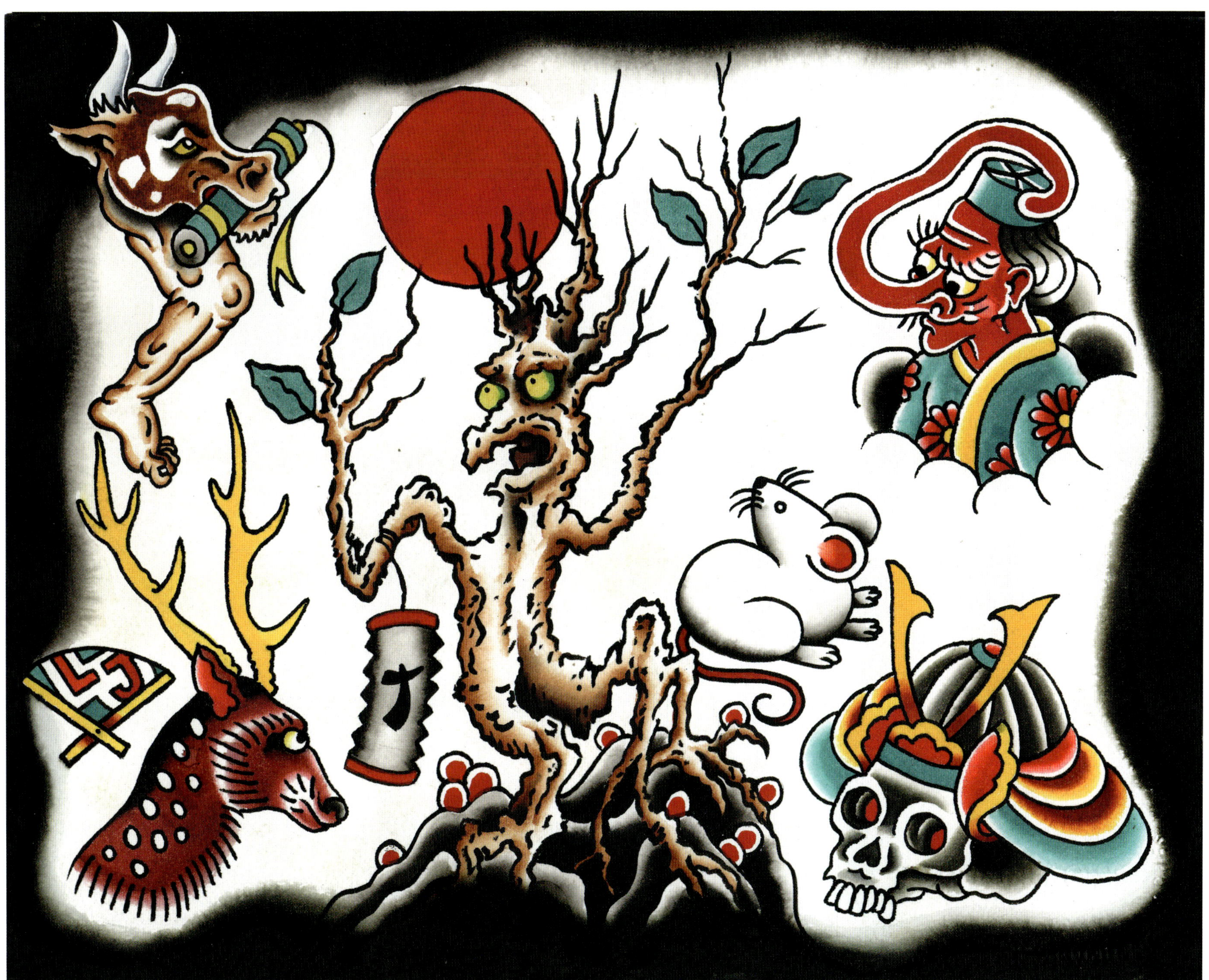

才

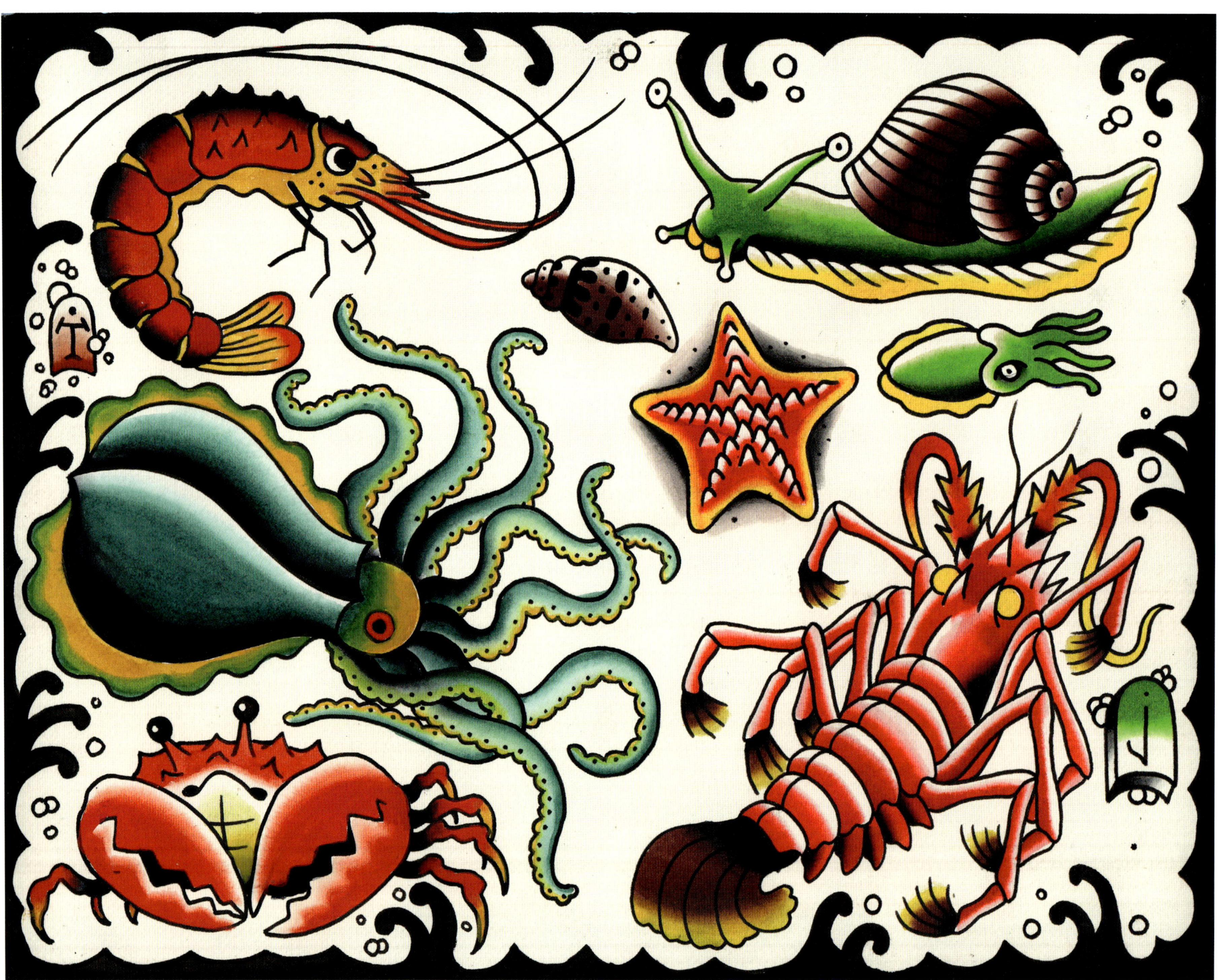

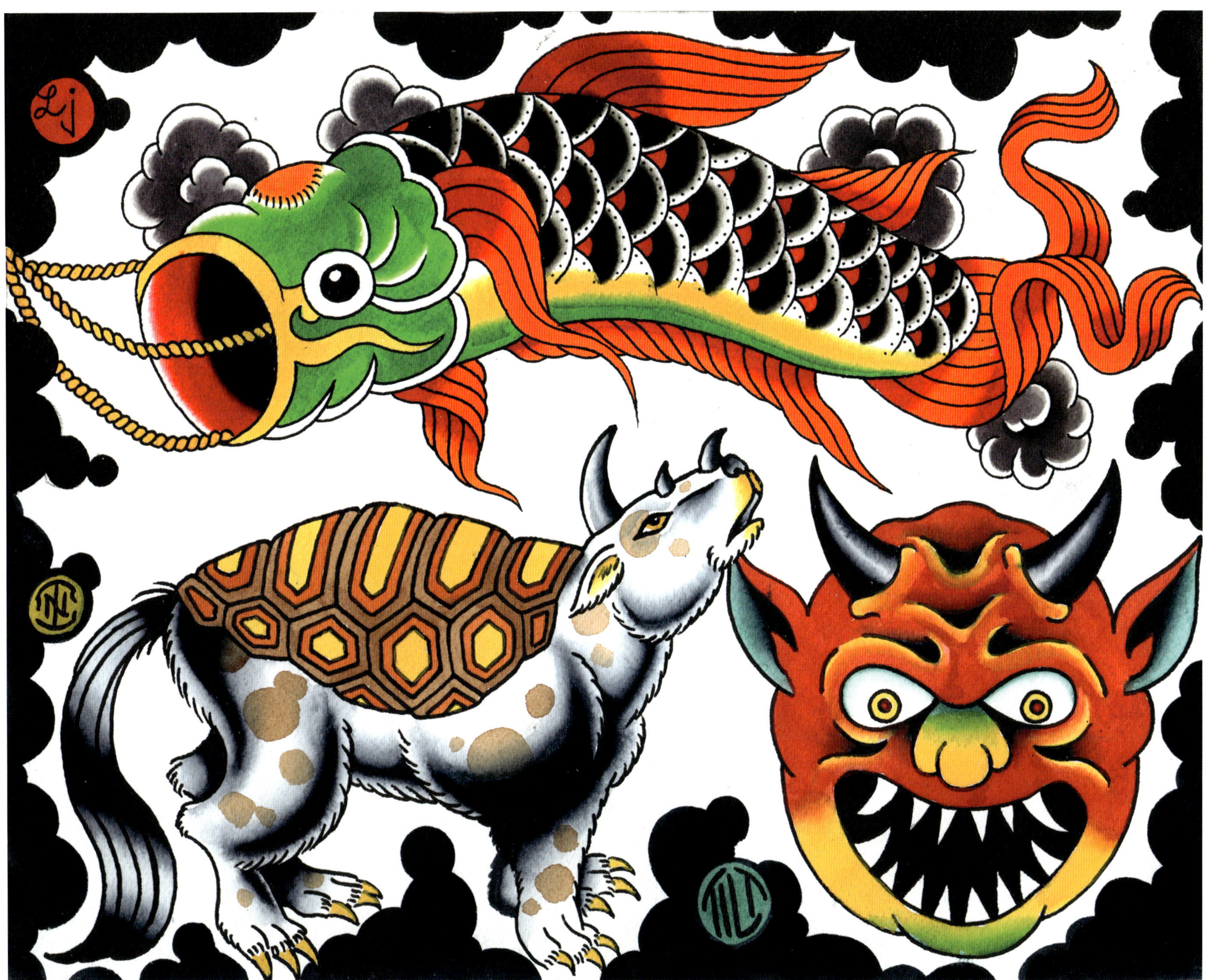

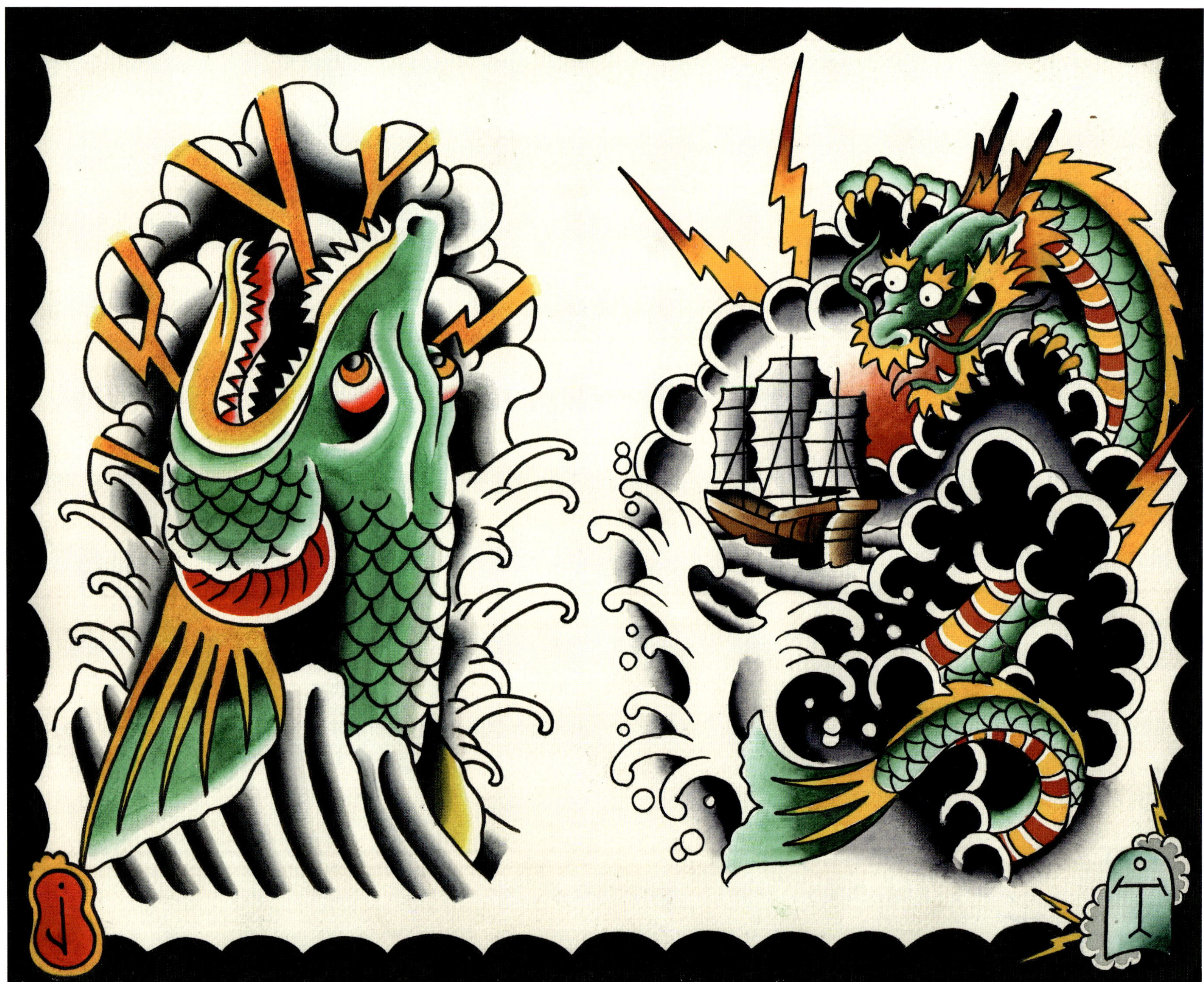

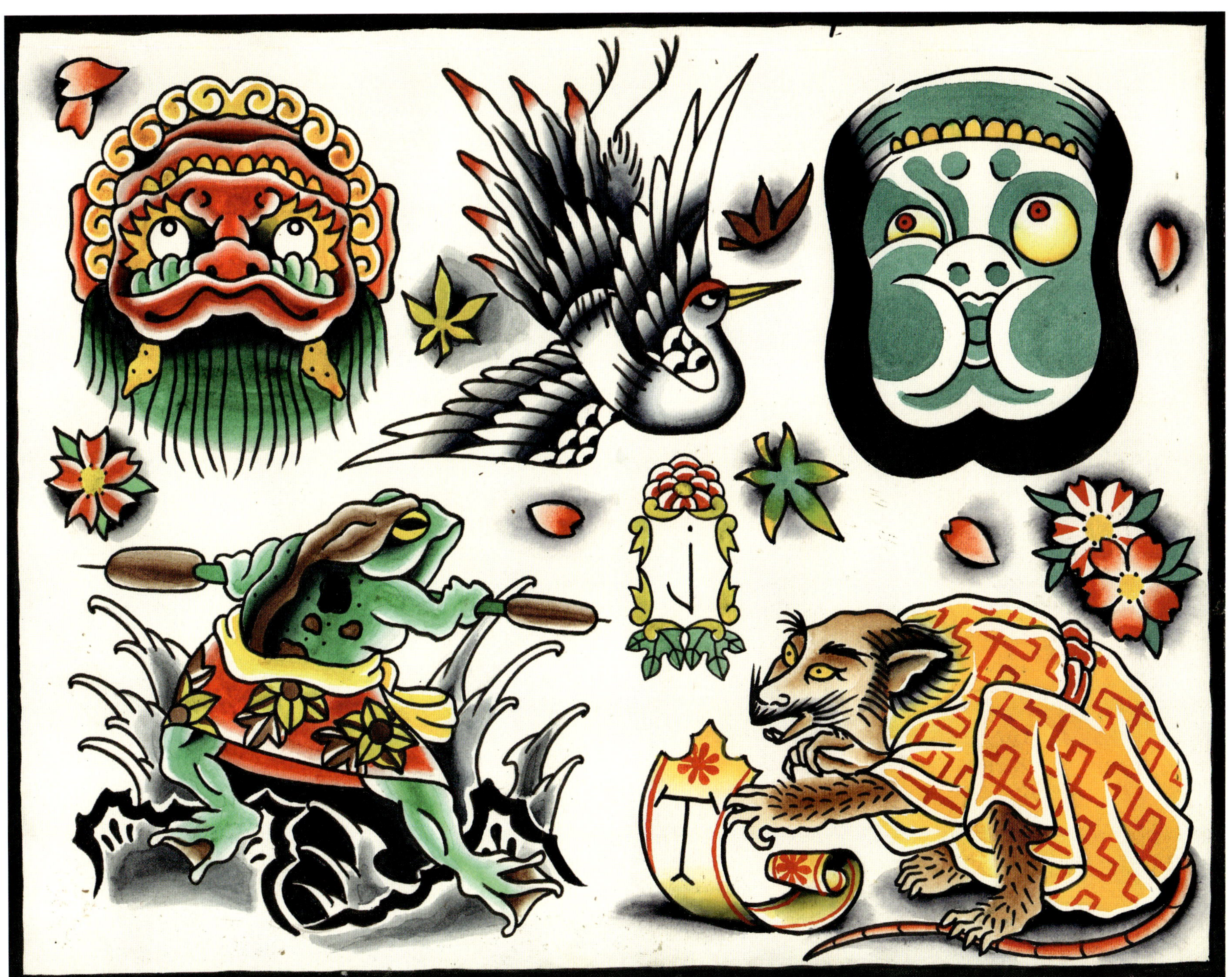

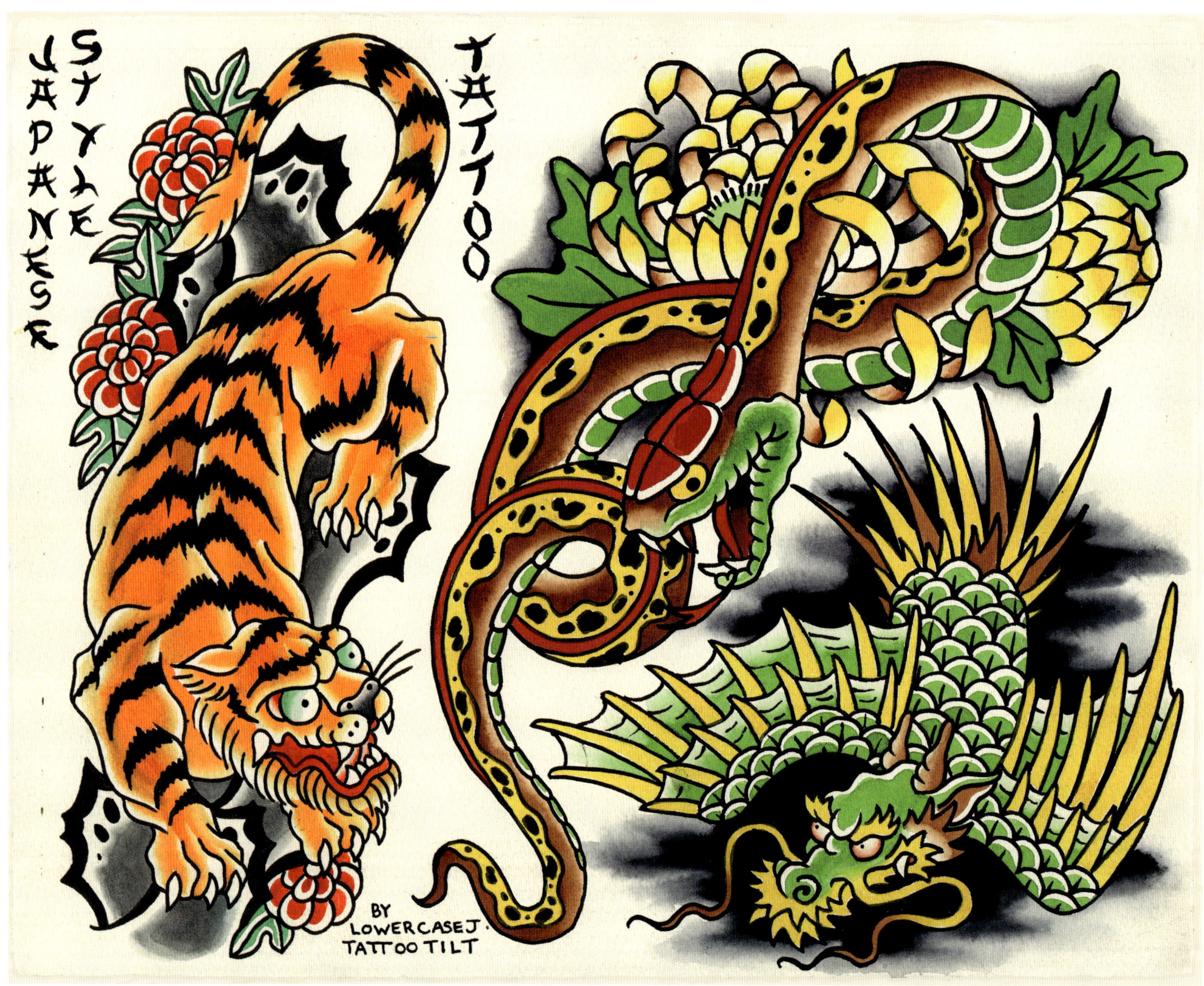
JAPANESE
STYLE
TATTOO
BY
LOWERCASEJ.
TATTOO TILT

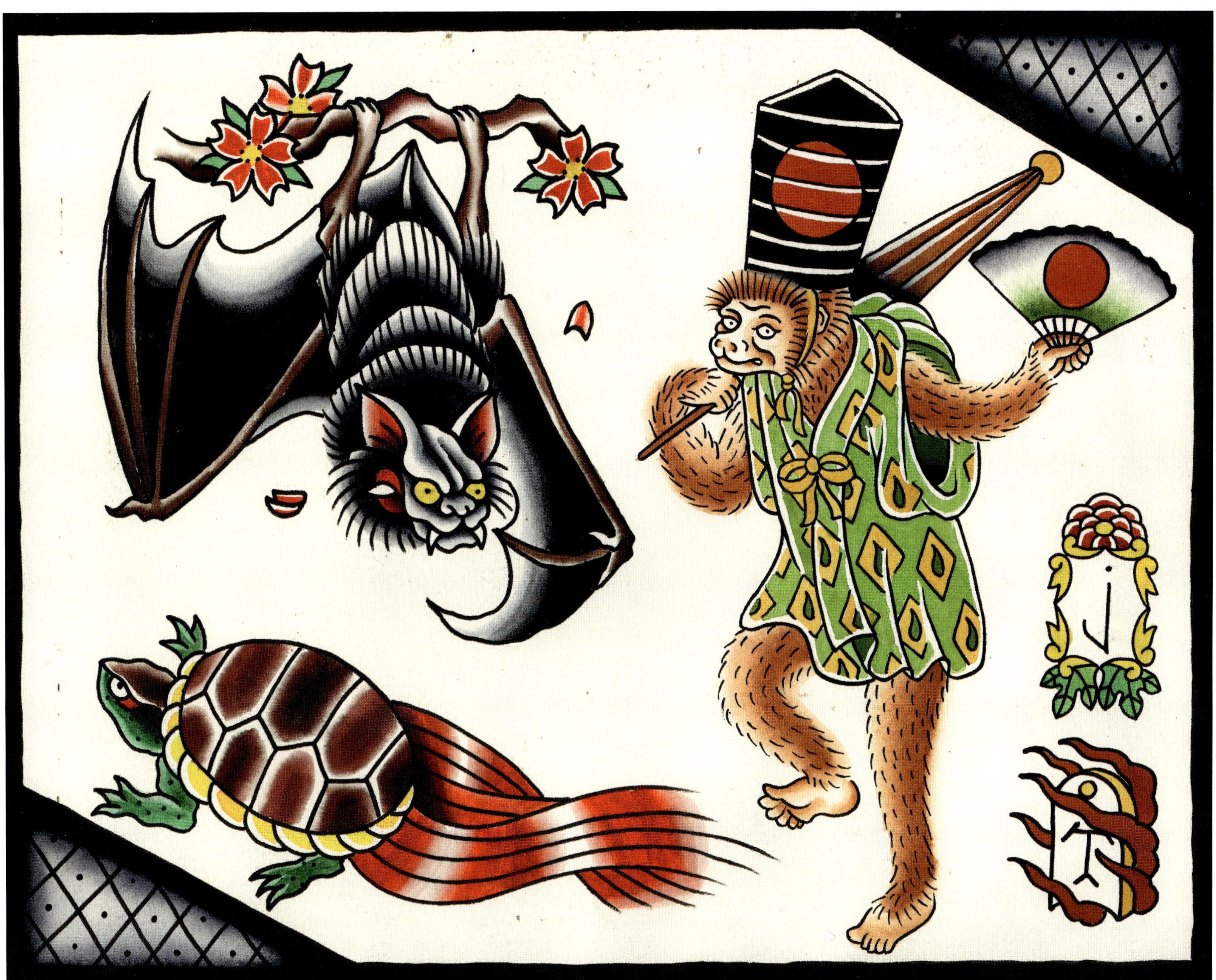

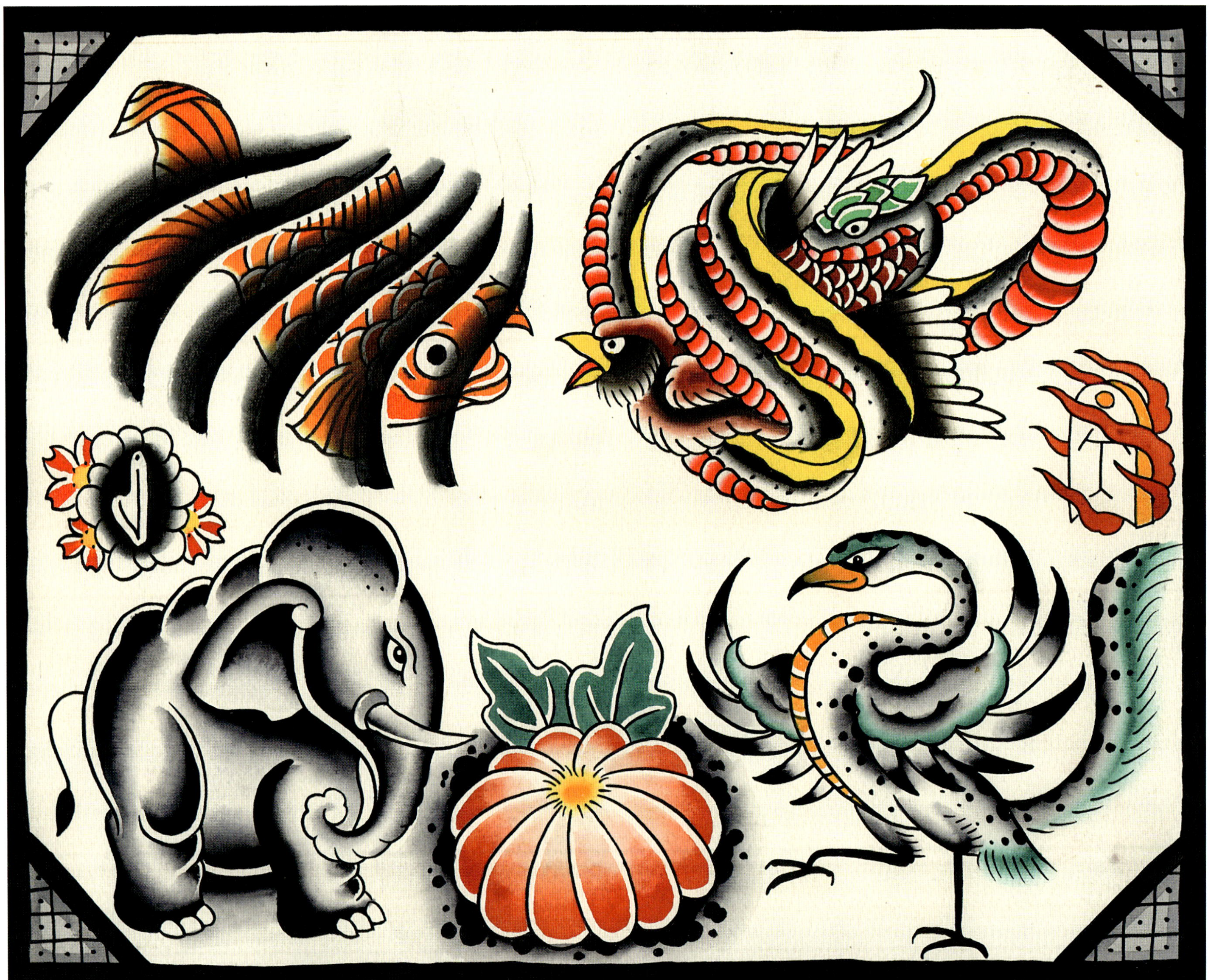

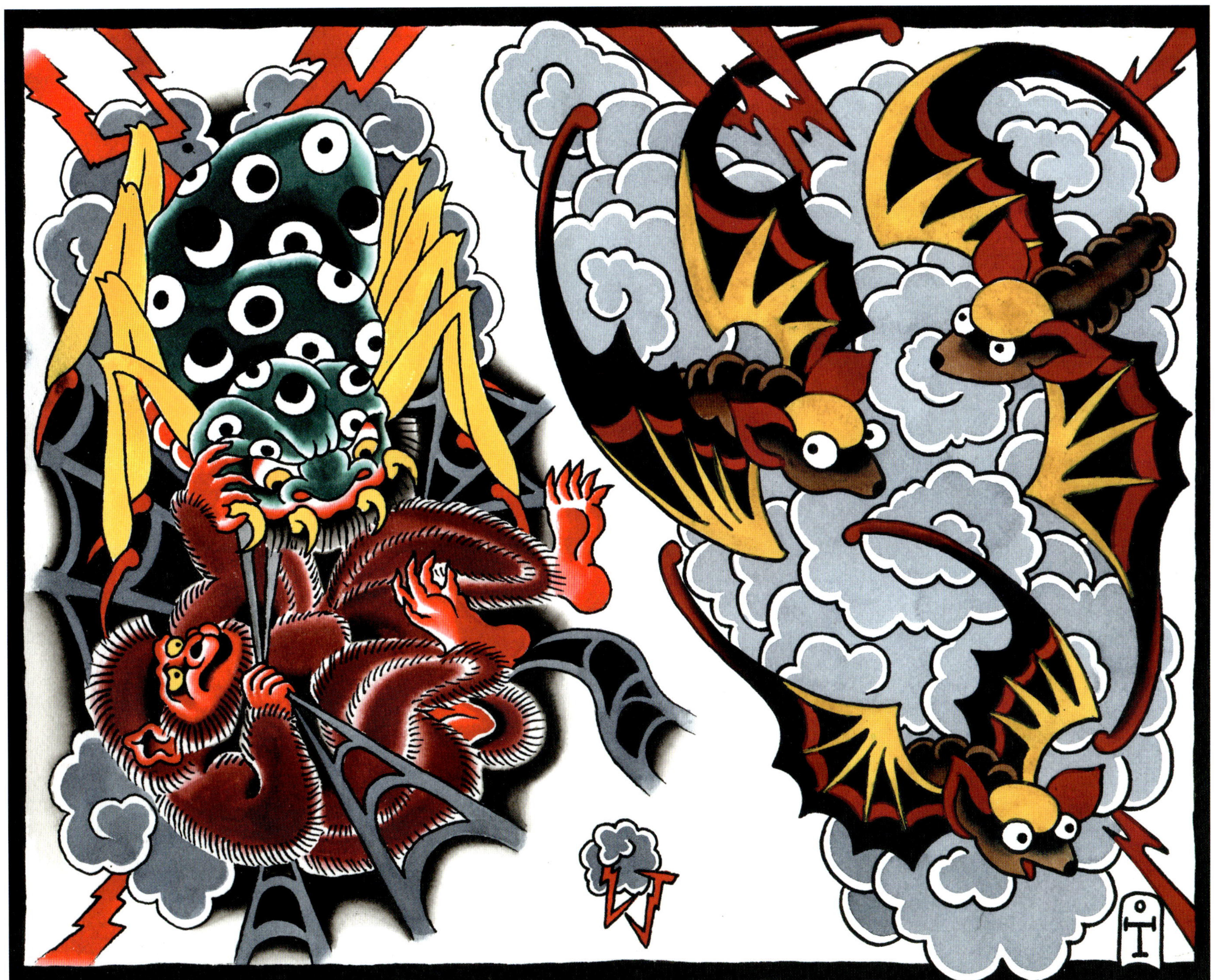

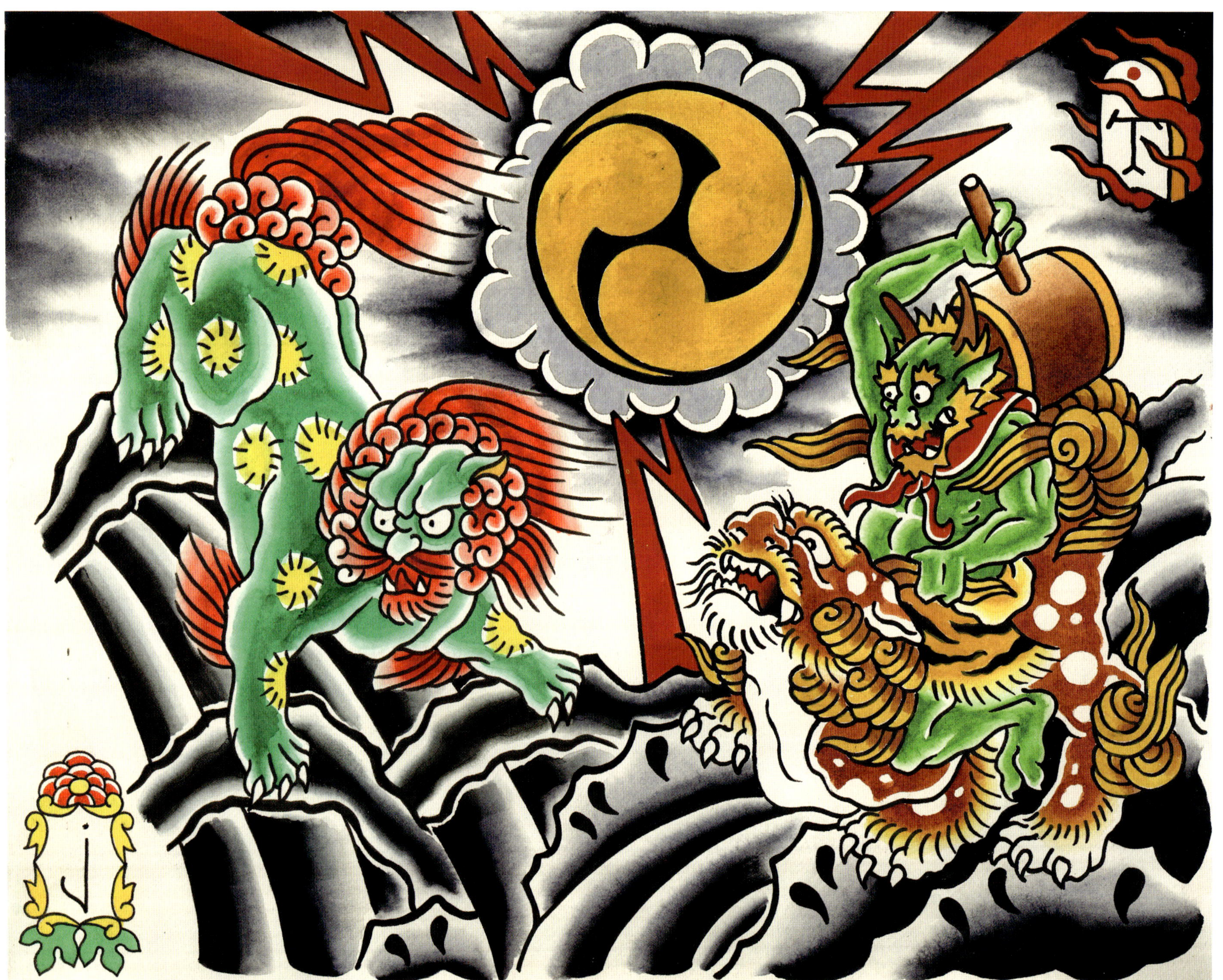

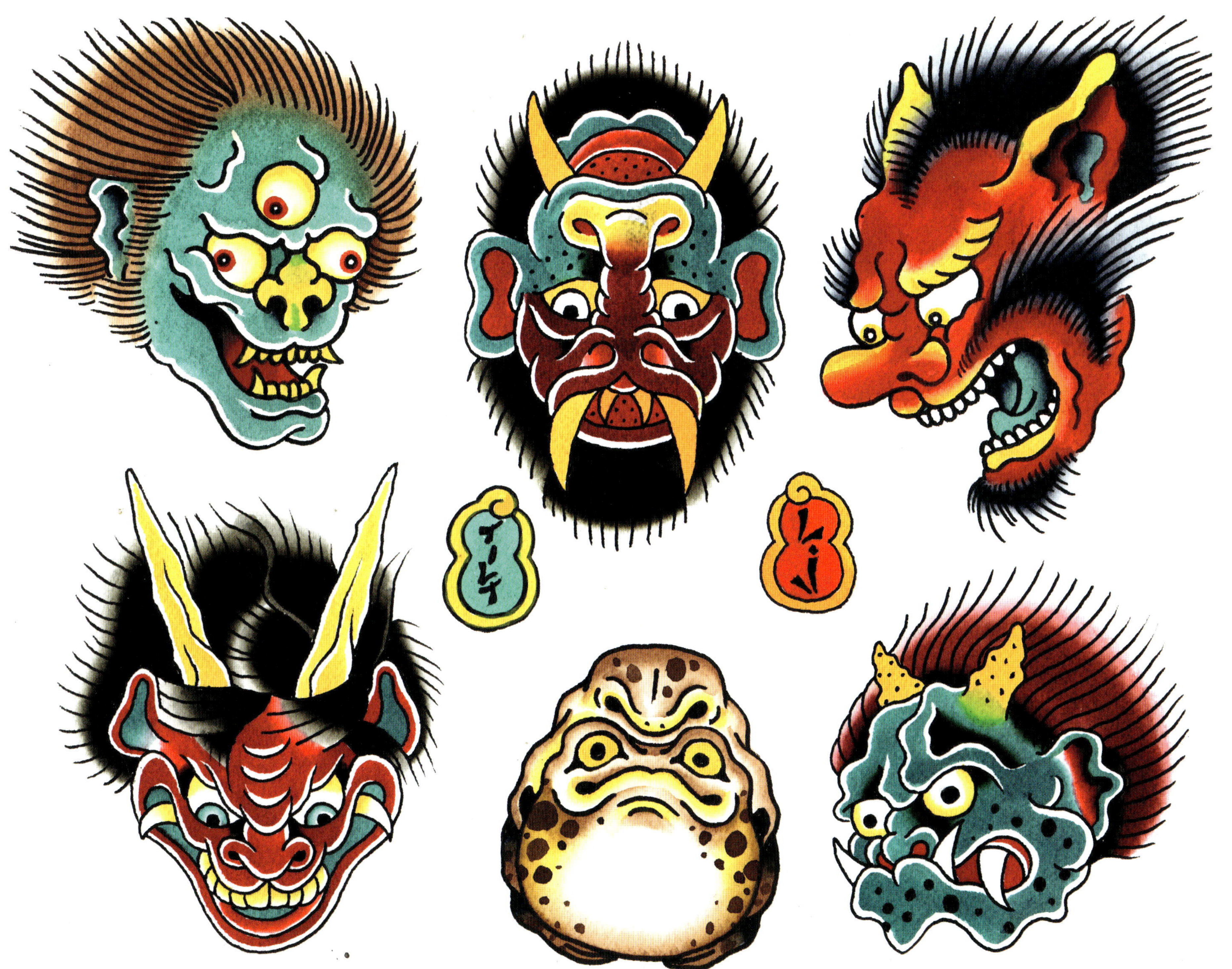

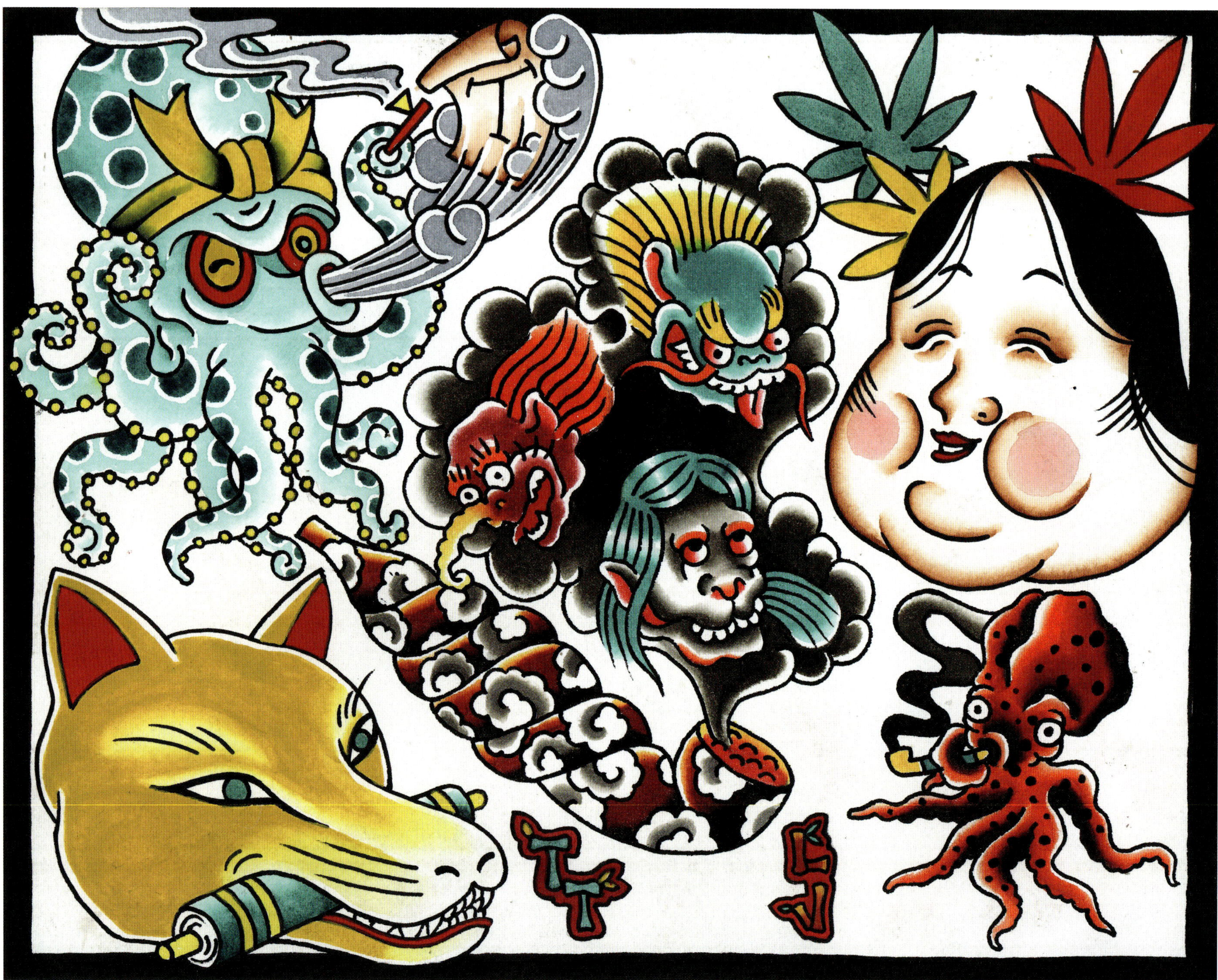

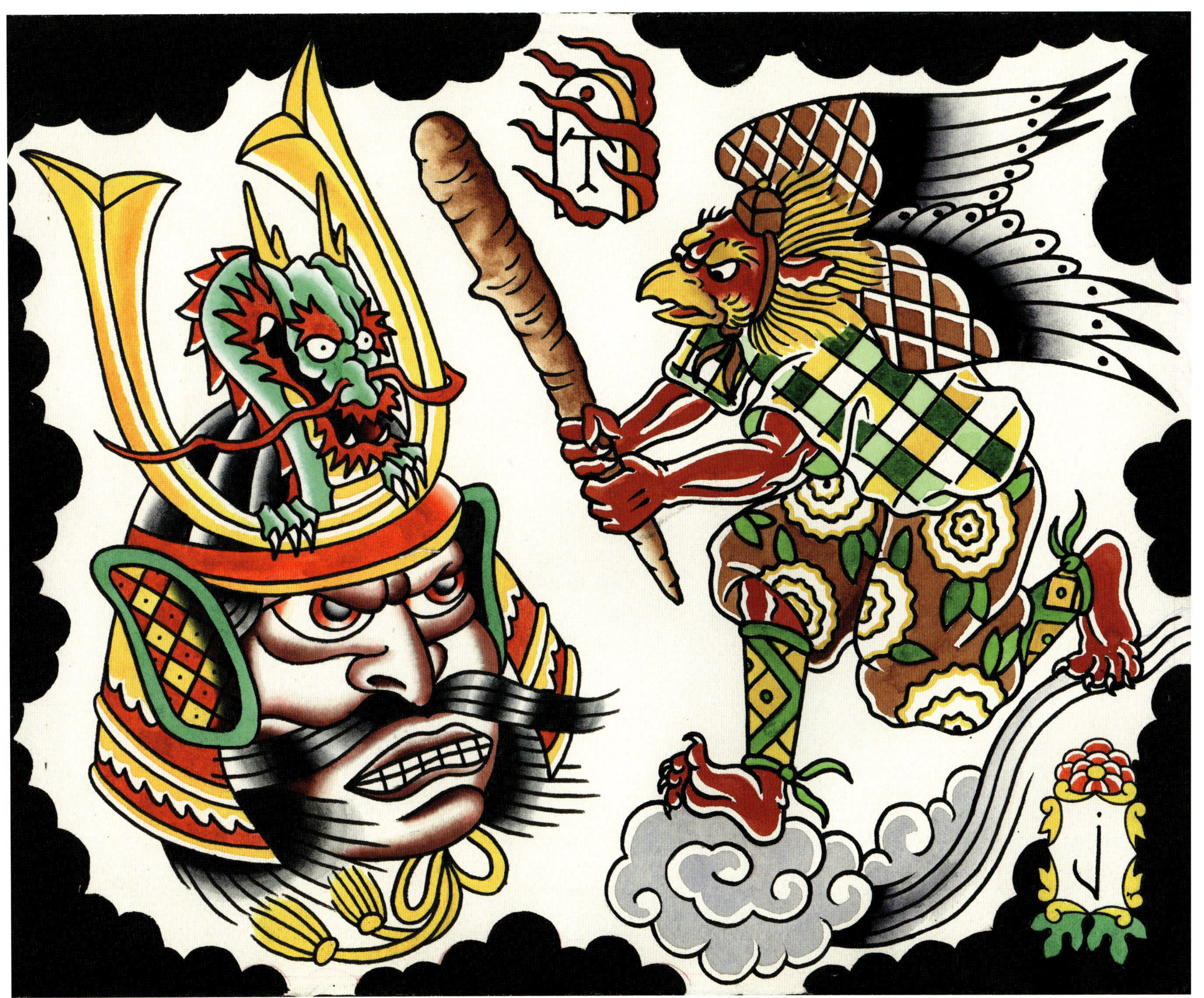

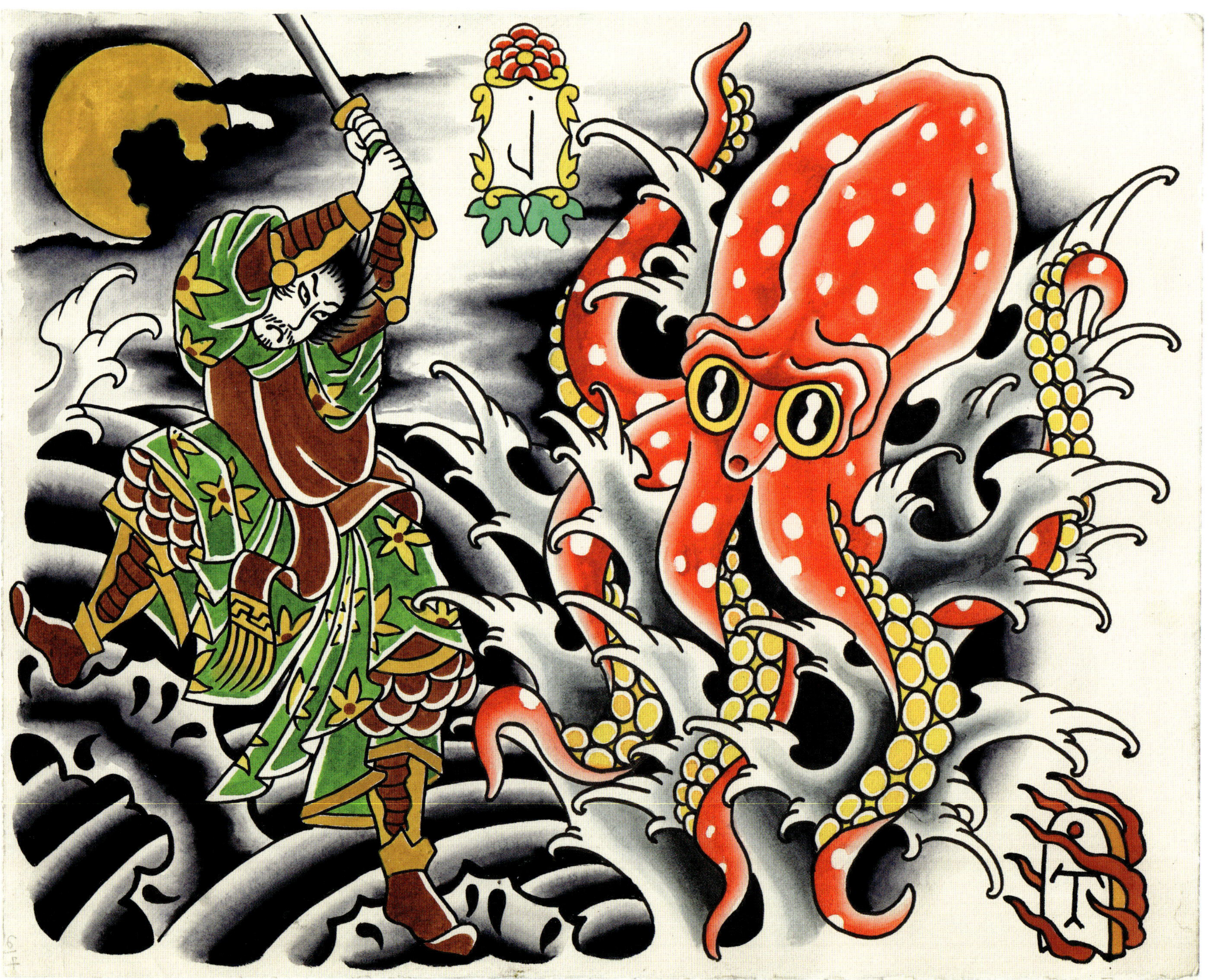

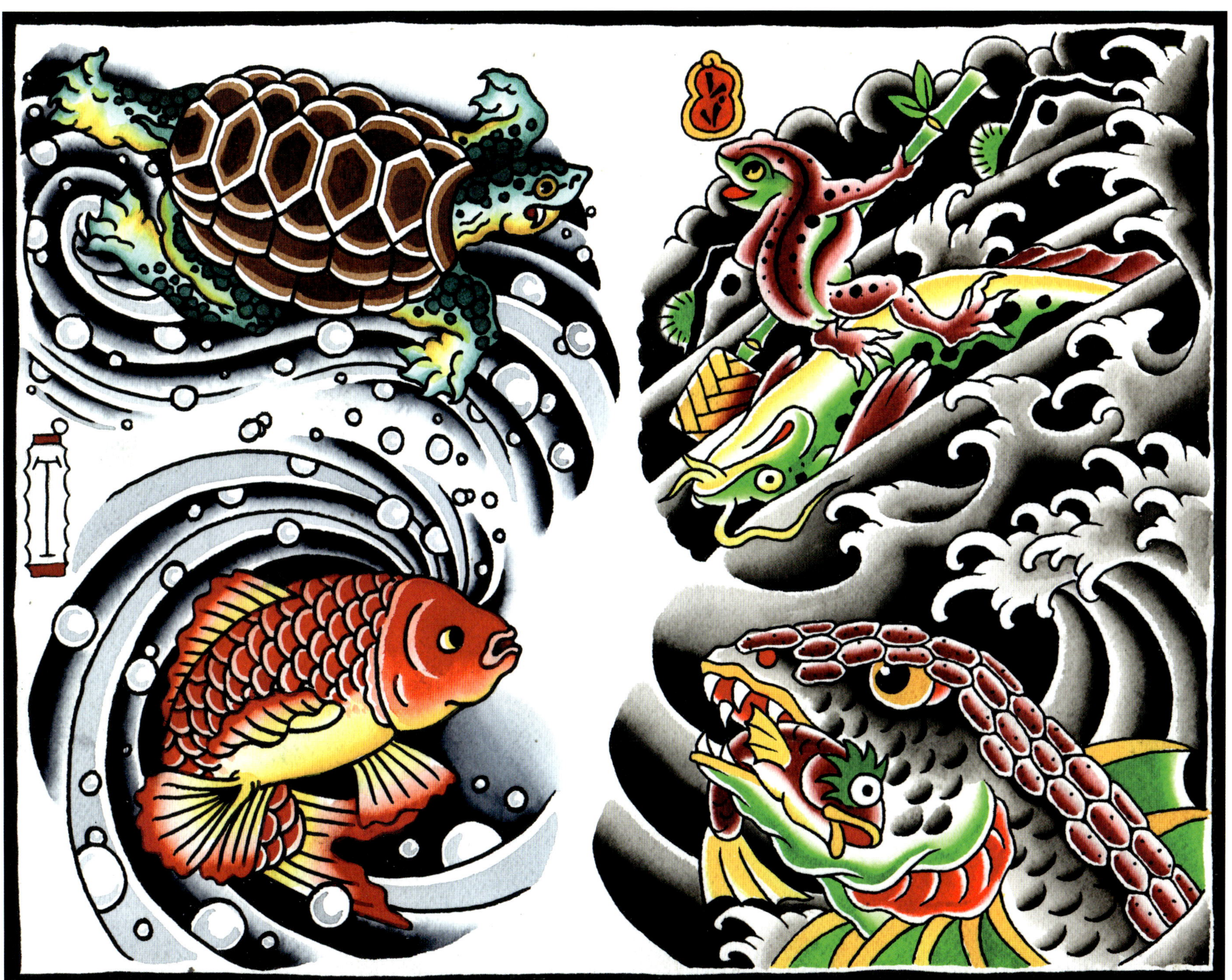

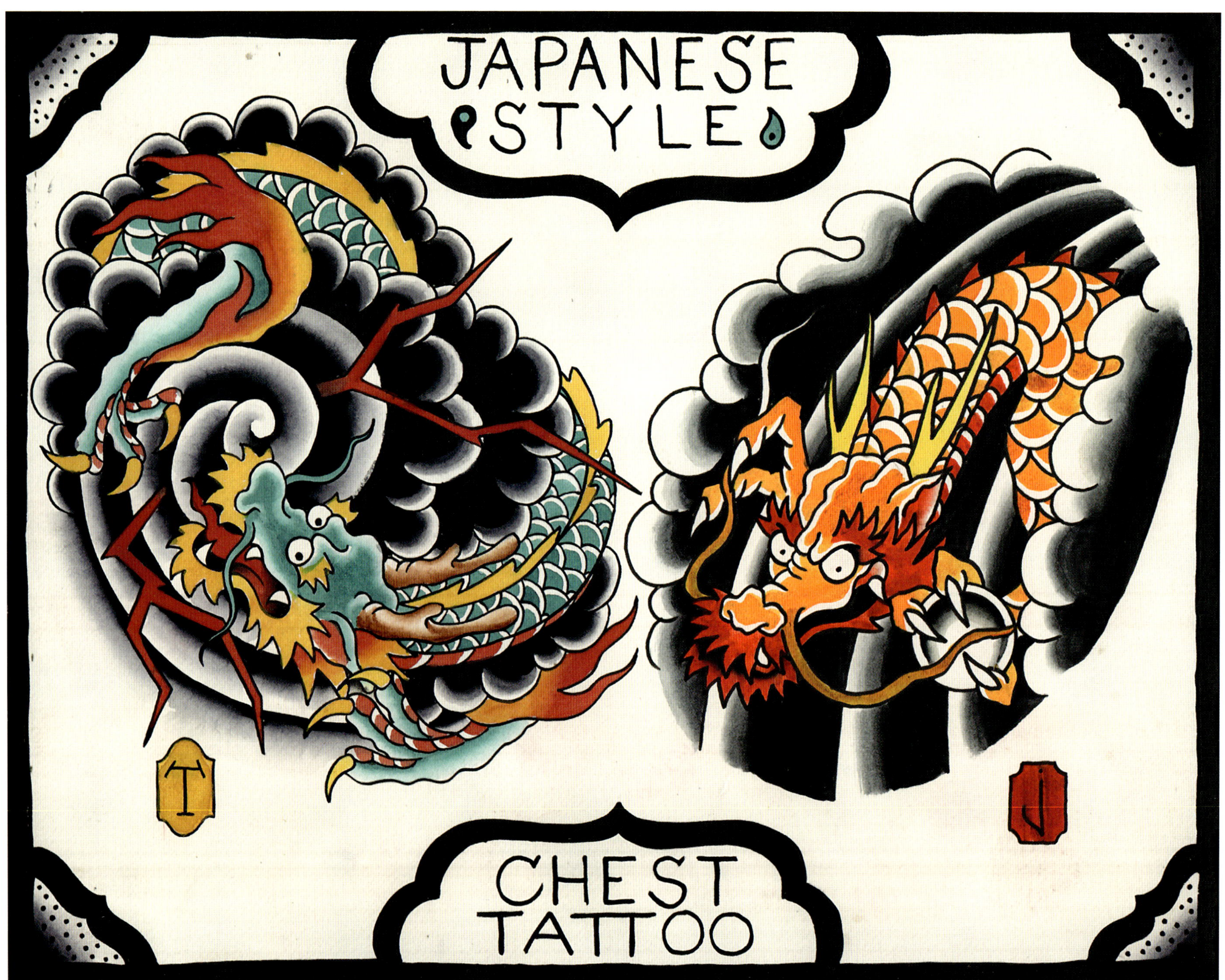
JAPANESE
STYLE
CHEST
TATTOO
T
J

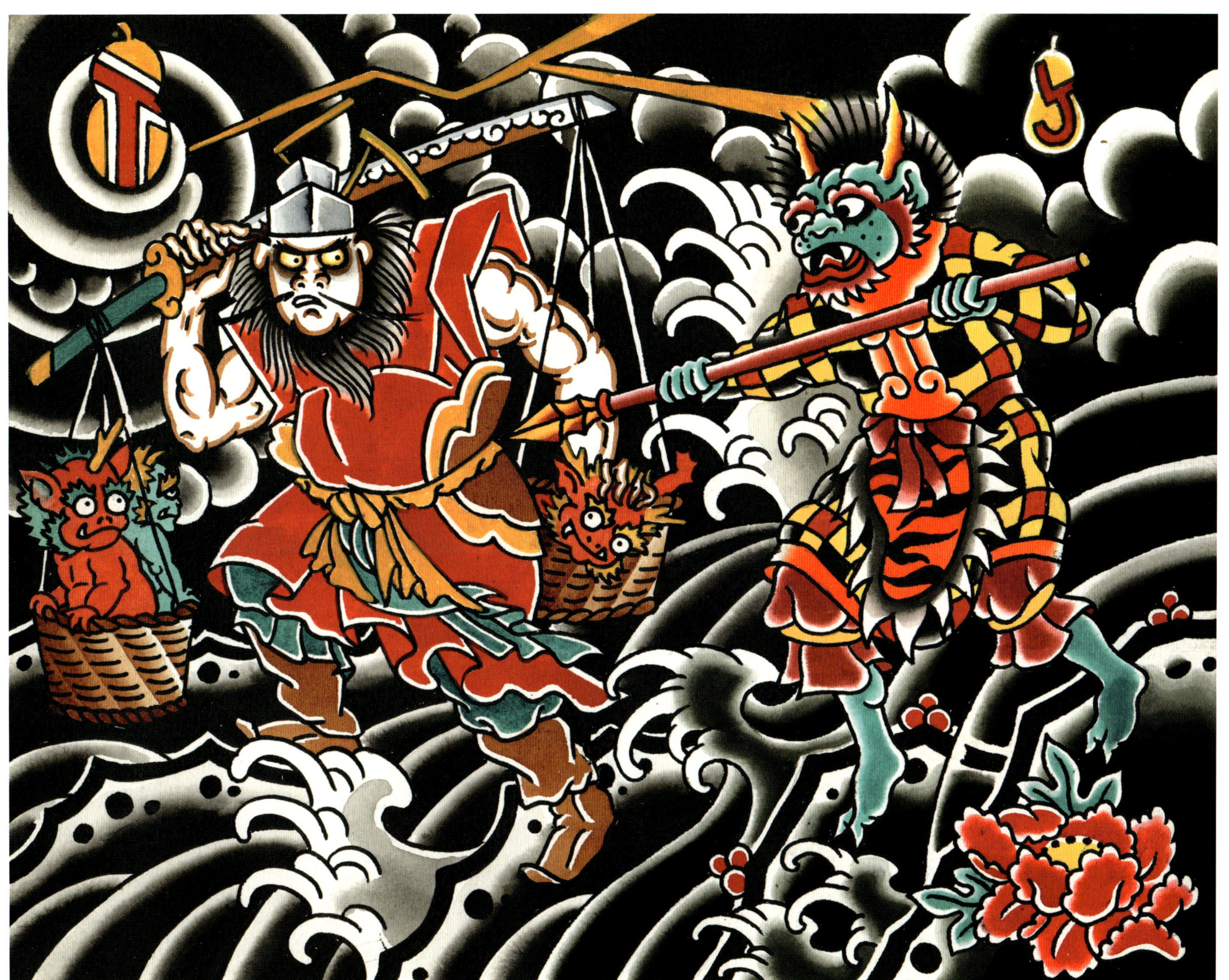

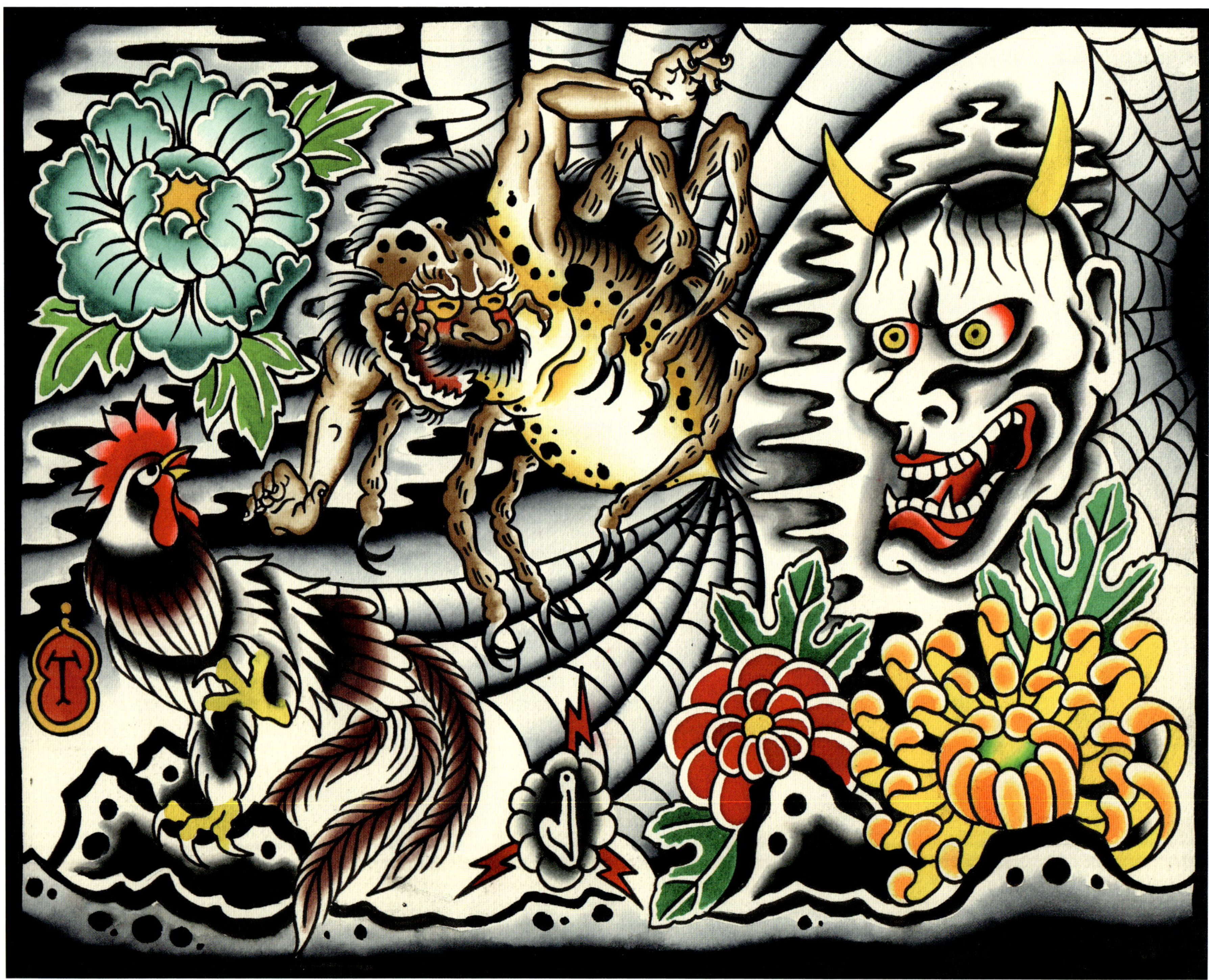

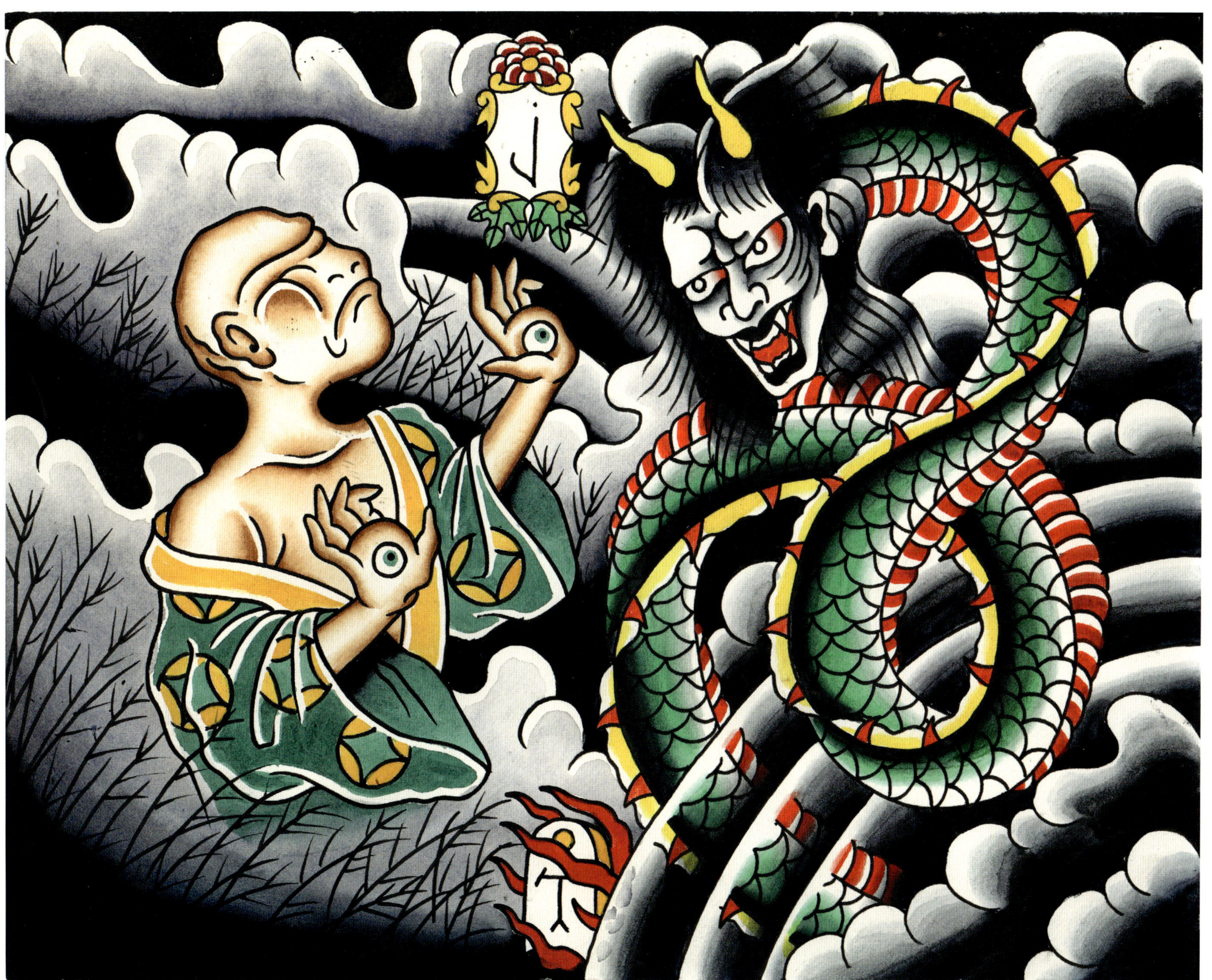

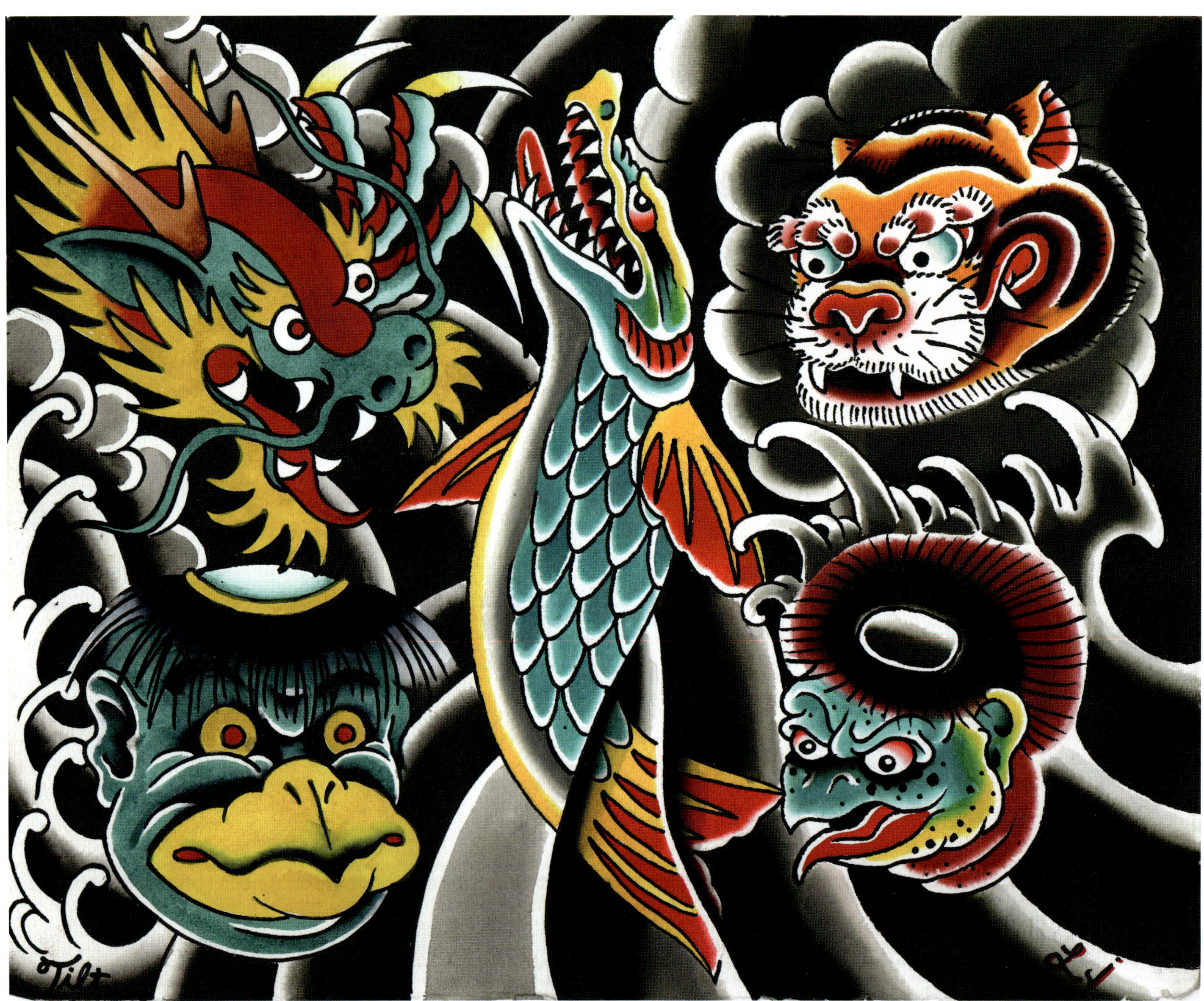
Tilt

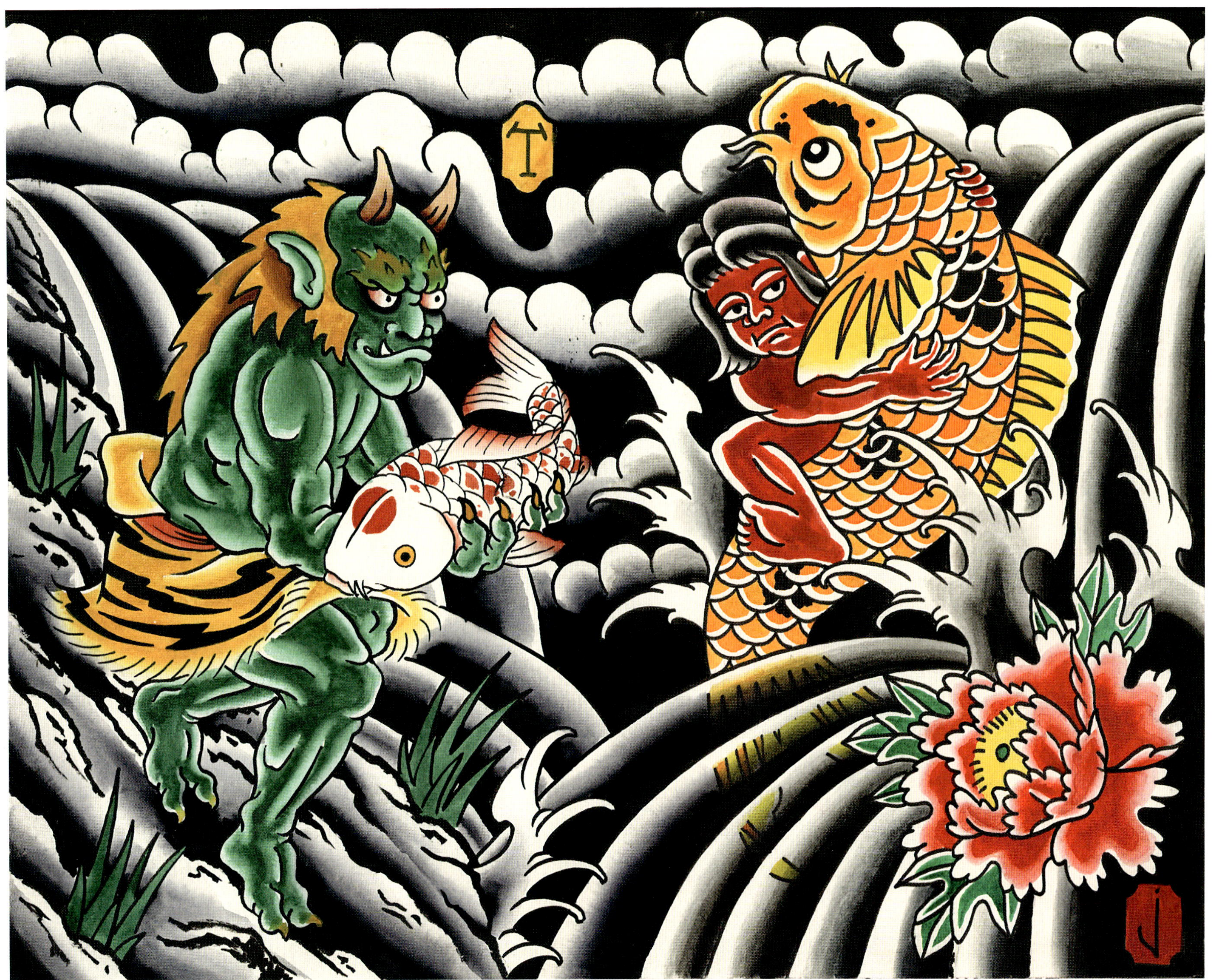

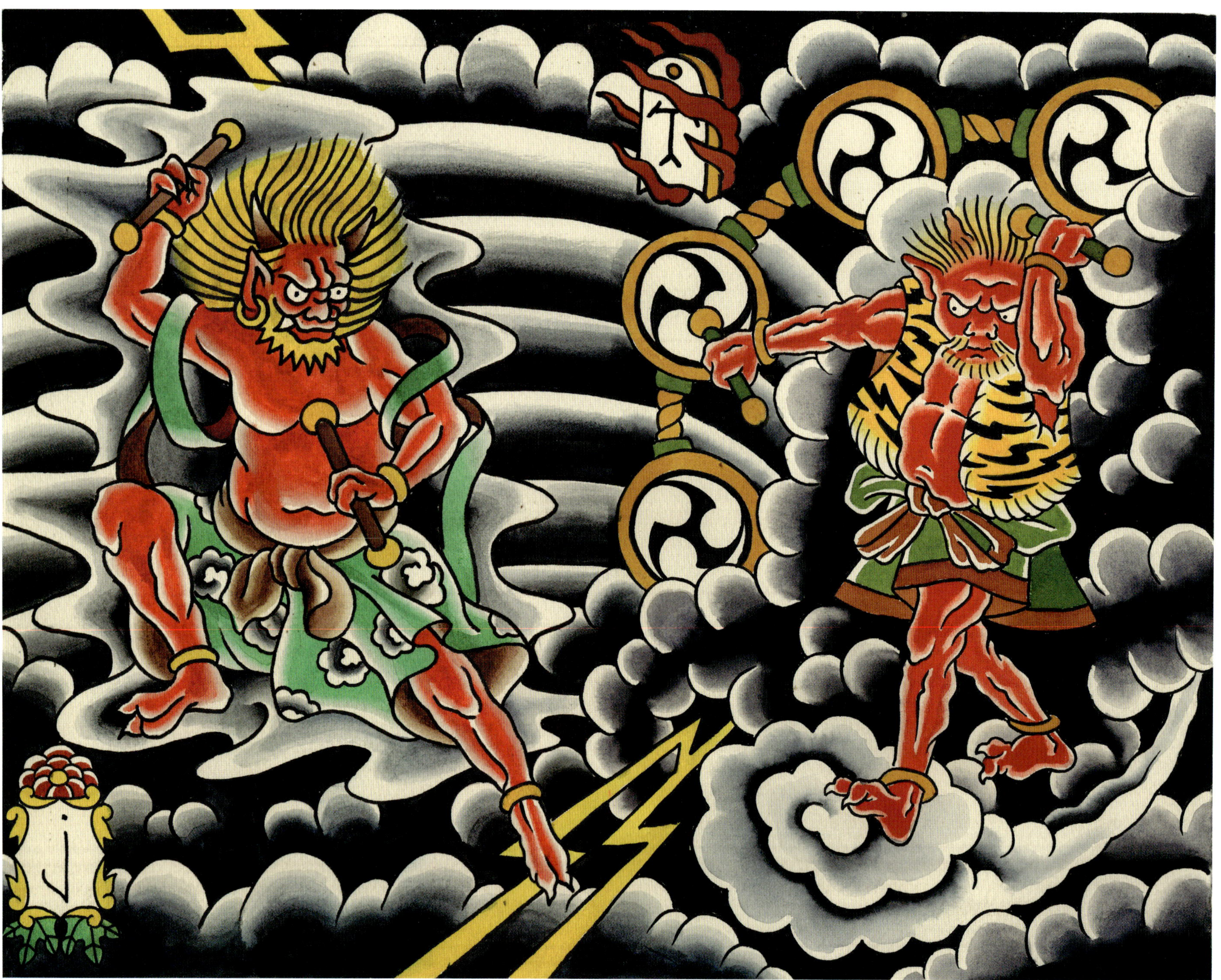

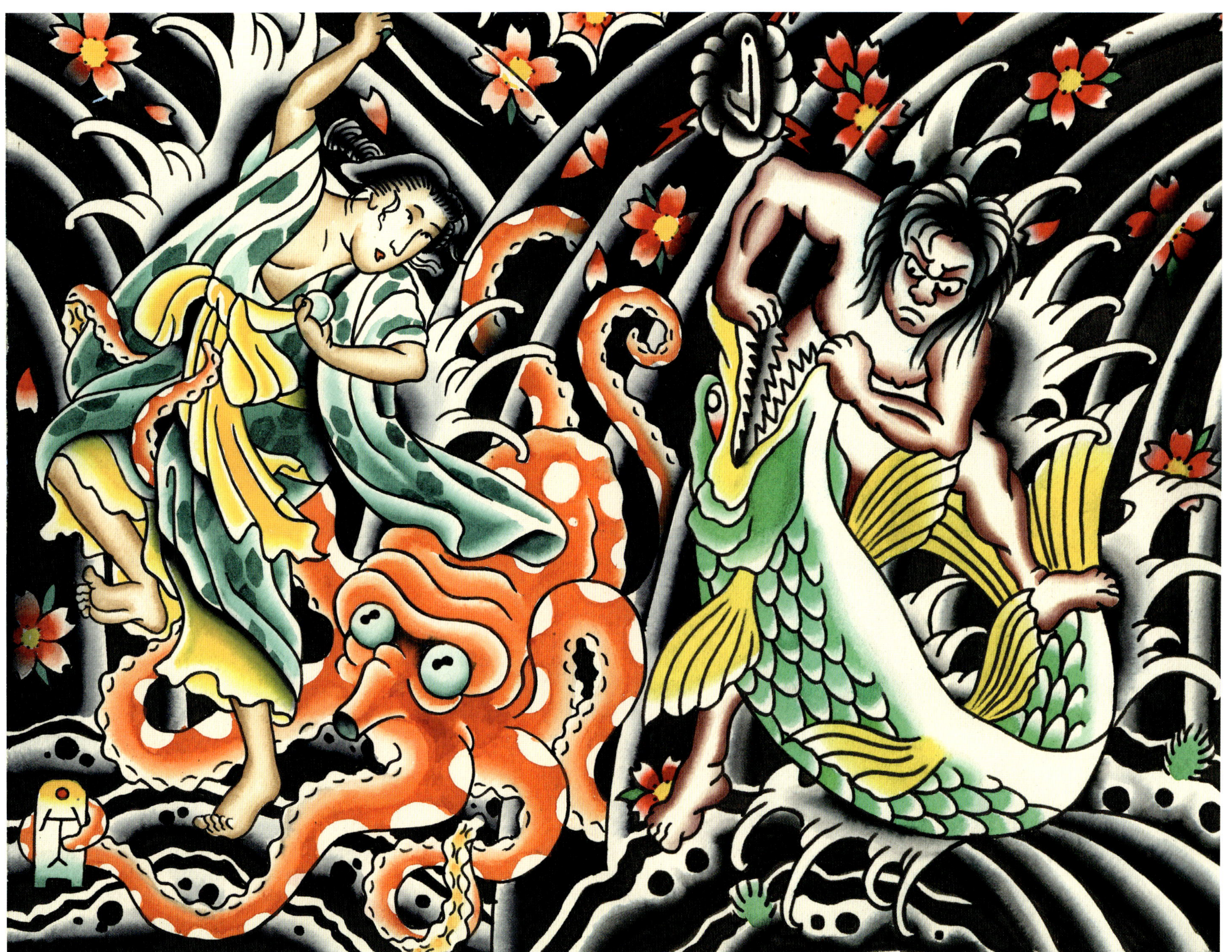

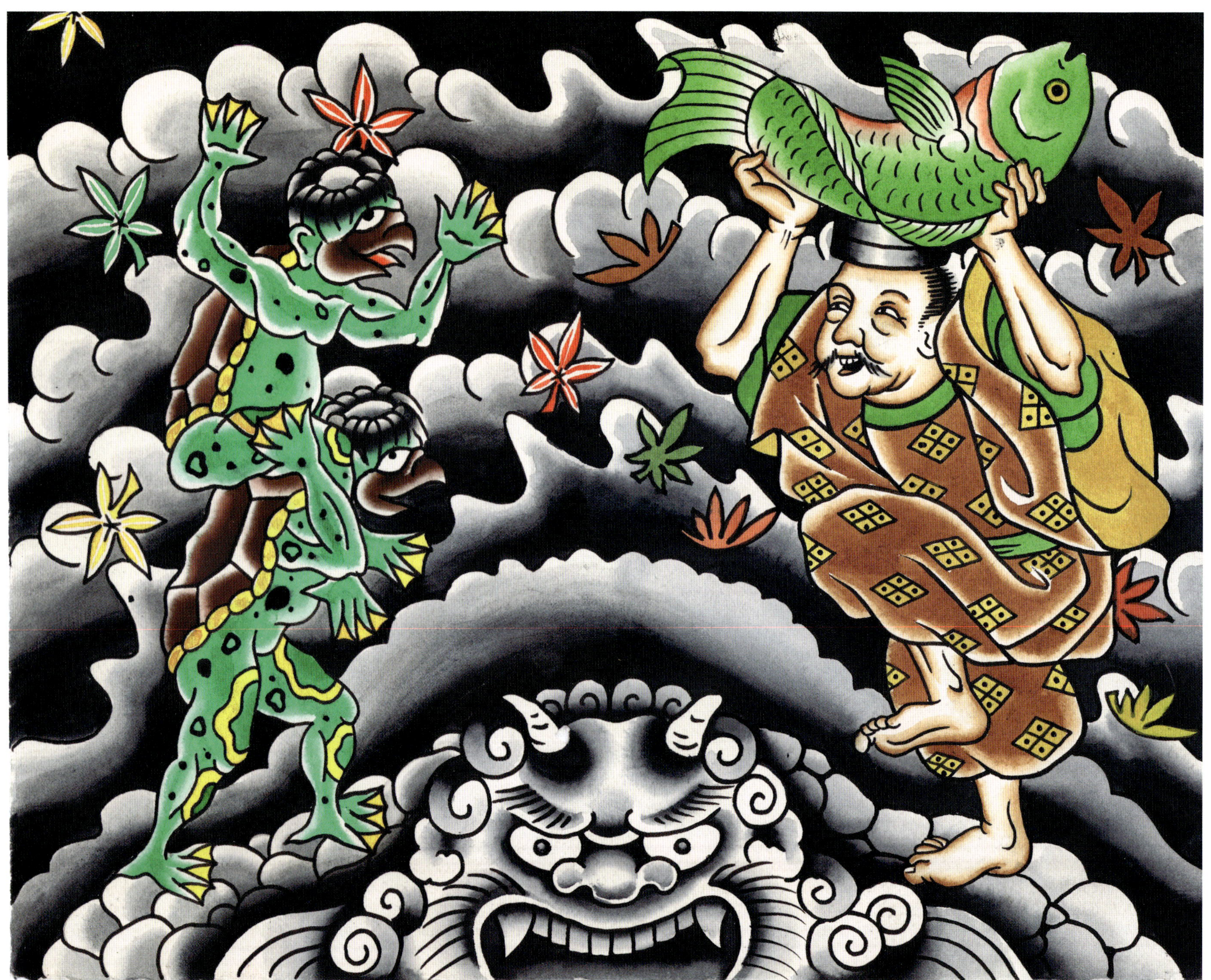

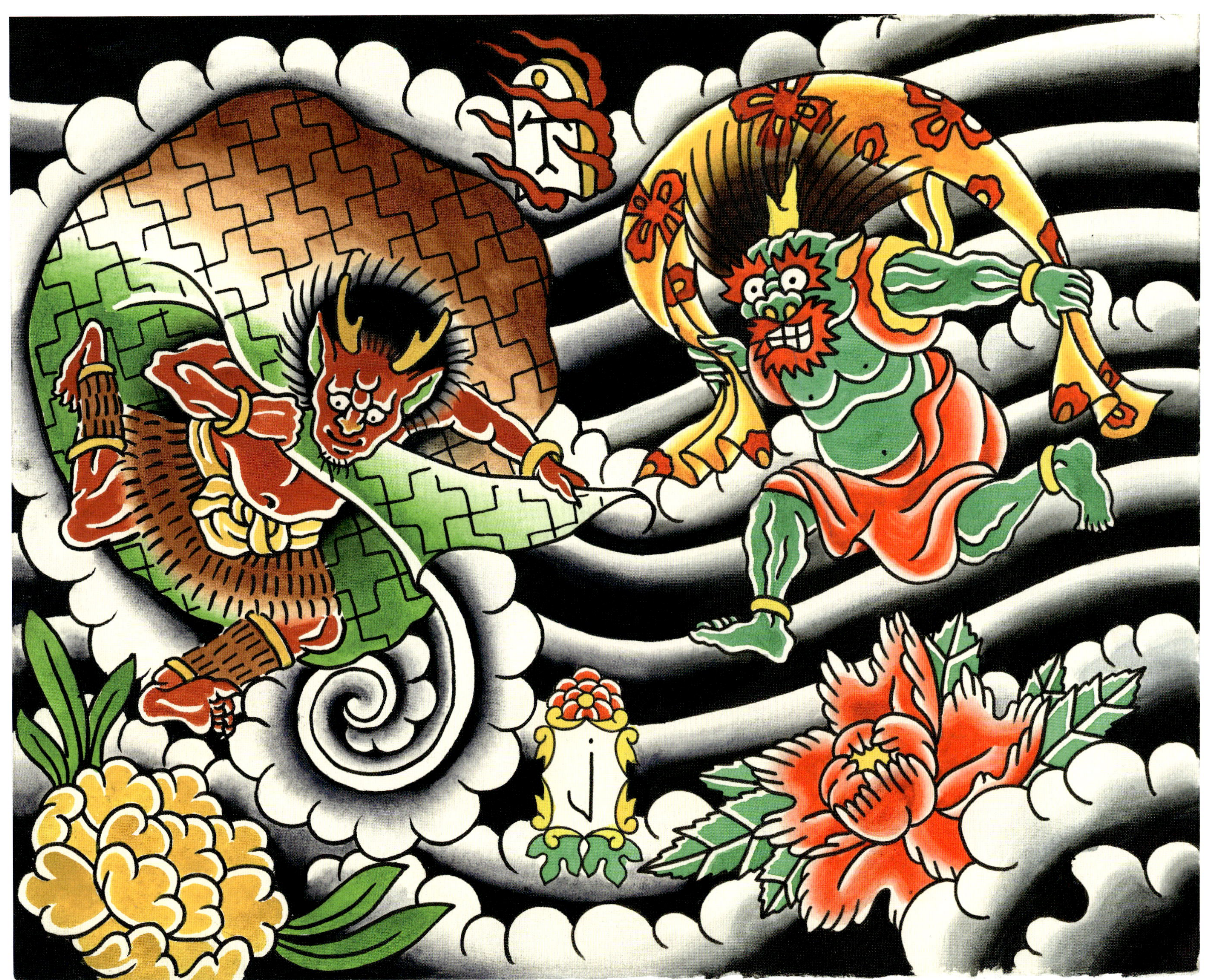

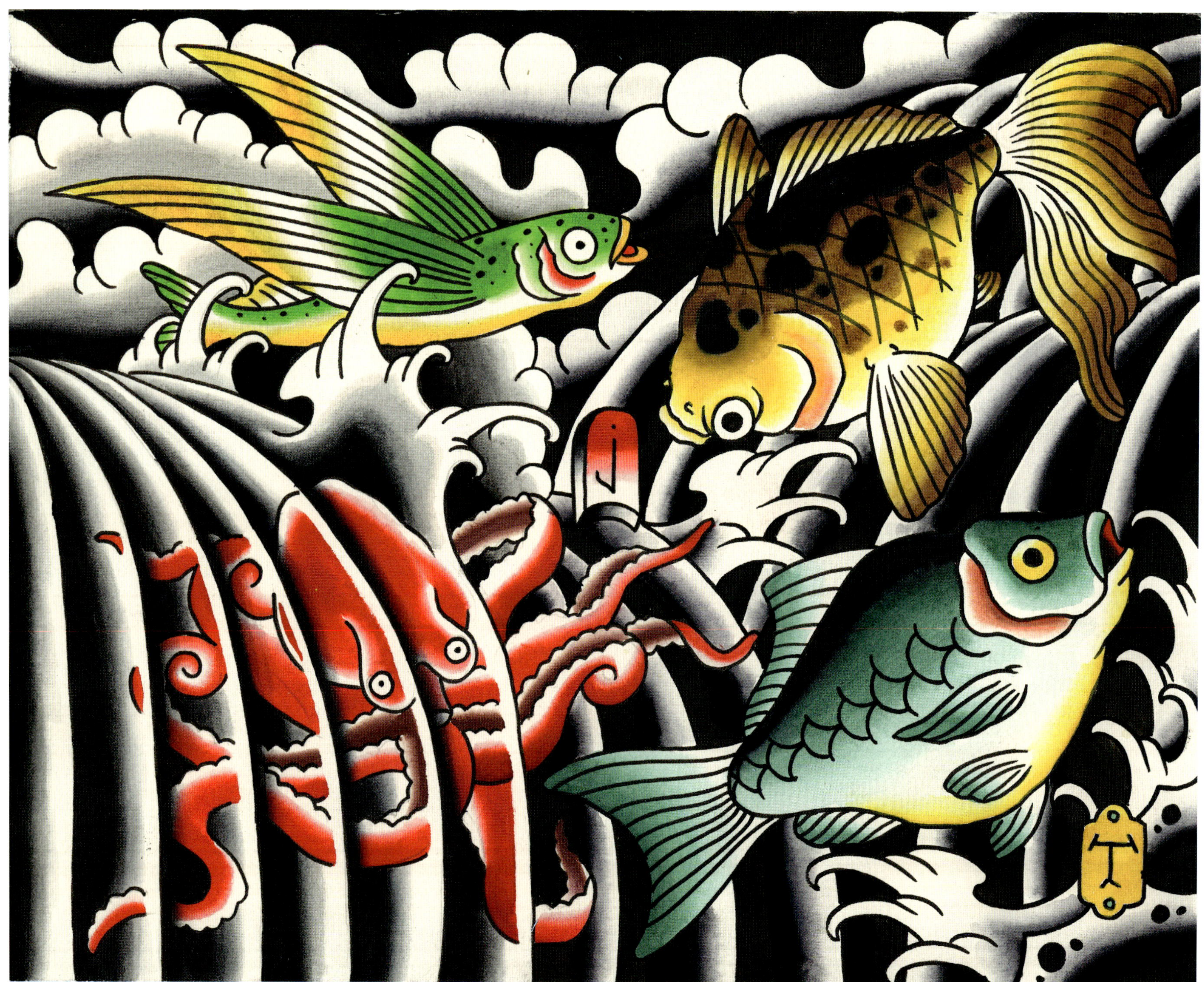

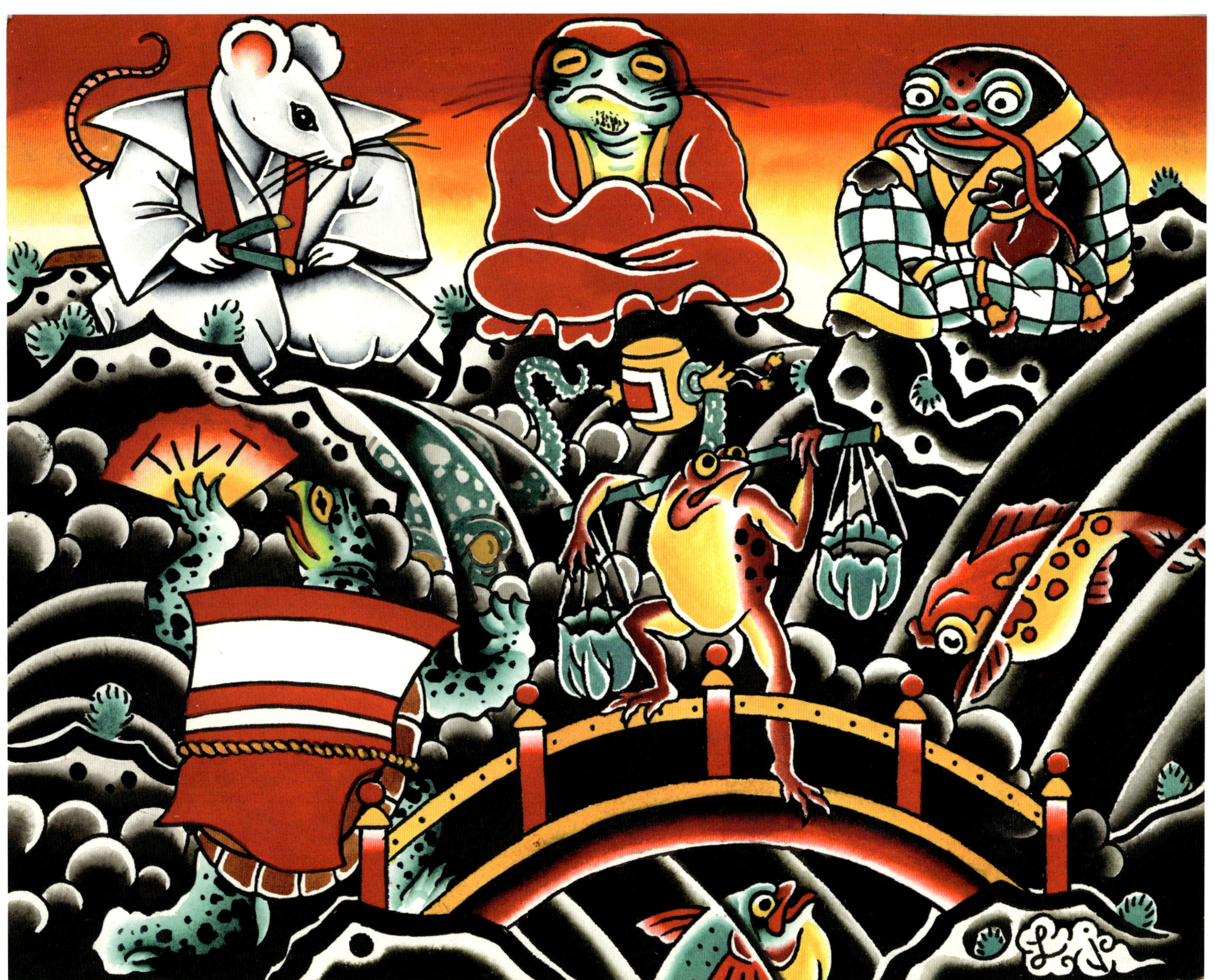
TILT

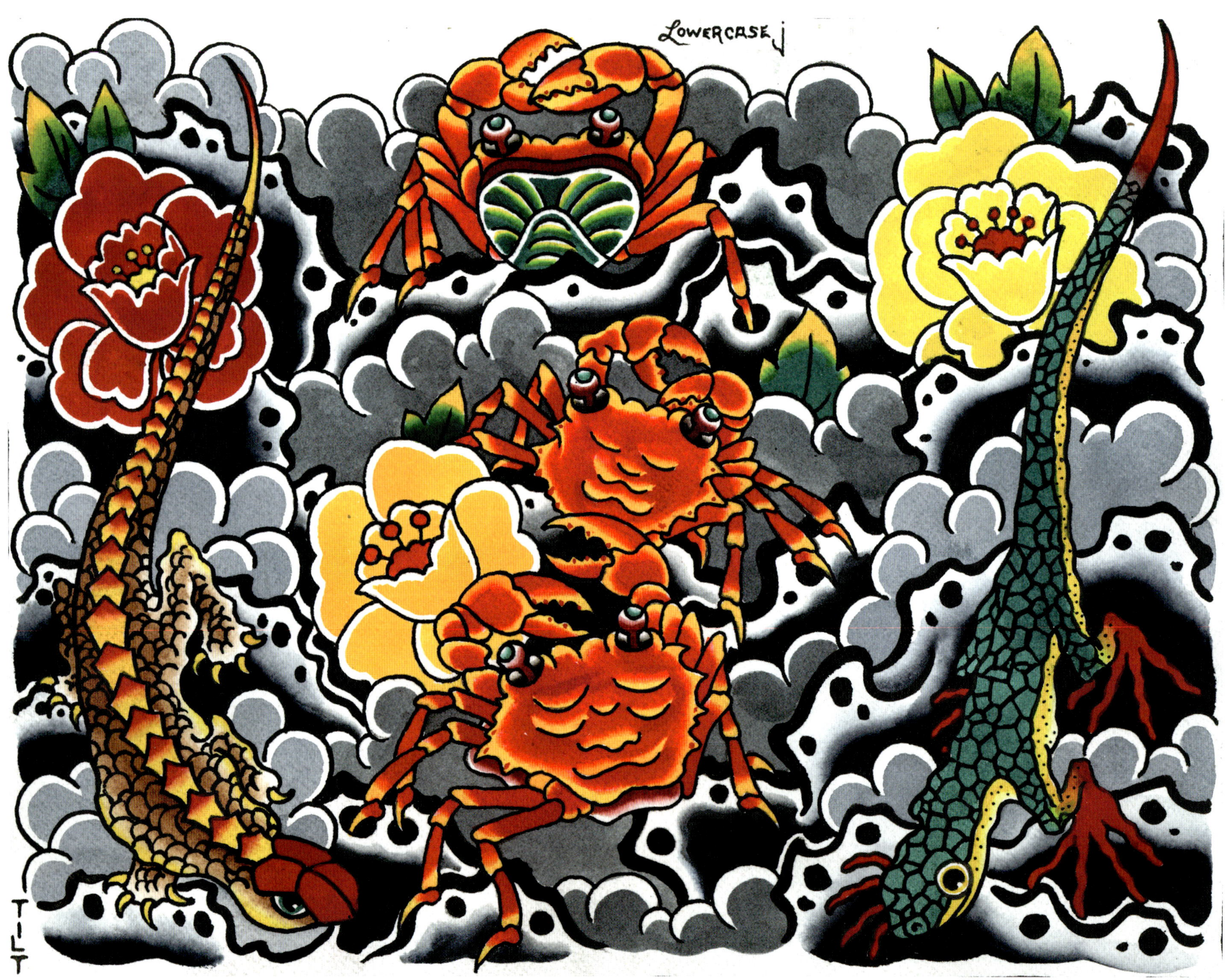
LOWERCASE j
TILT

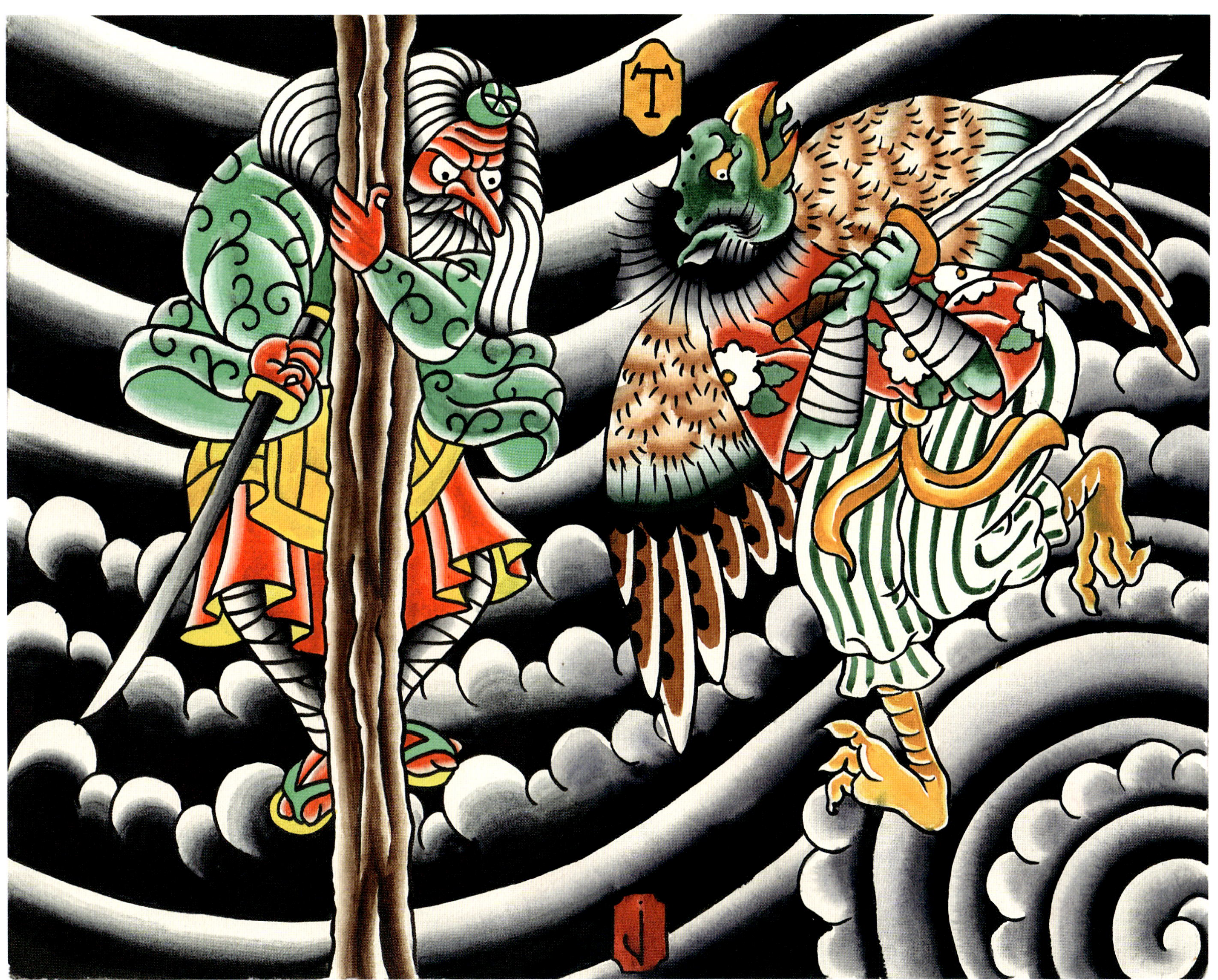
T
J

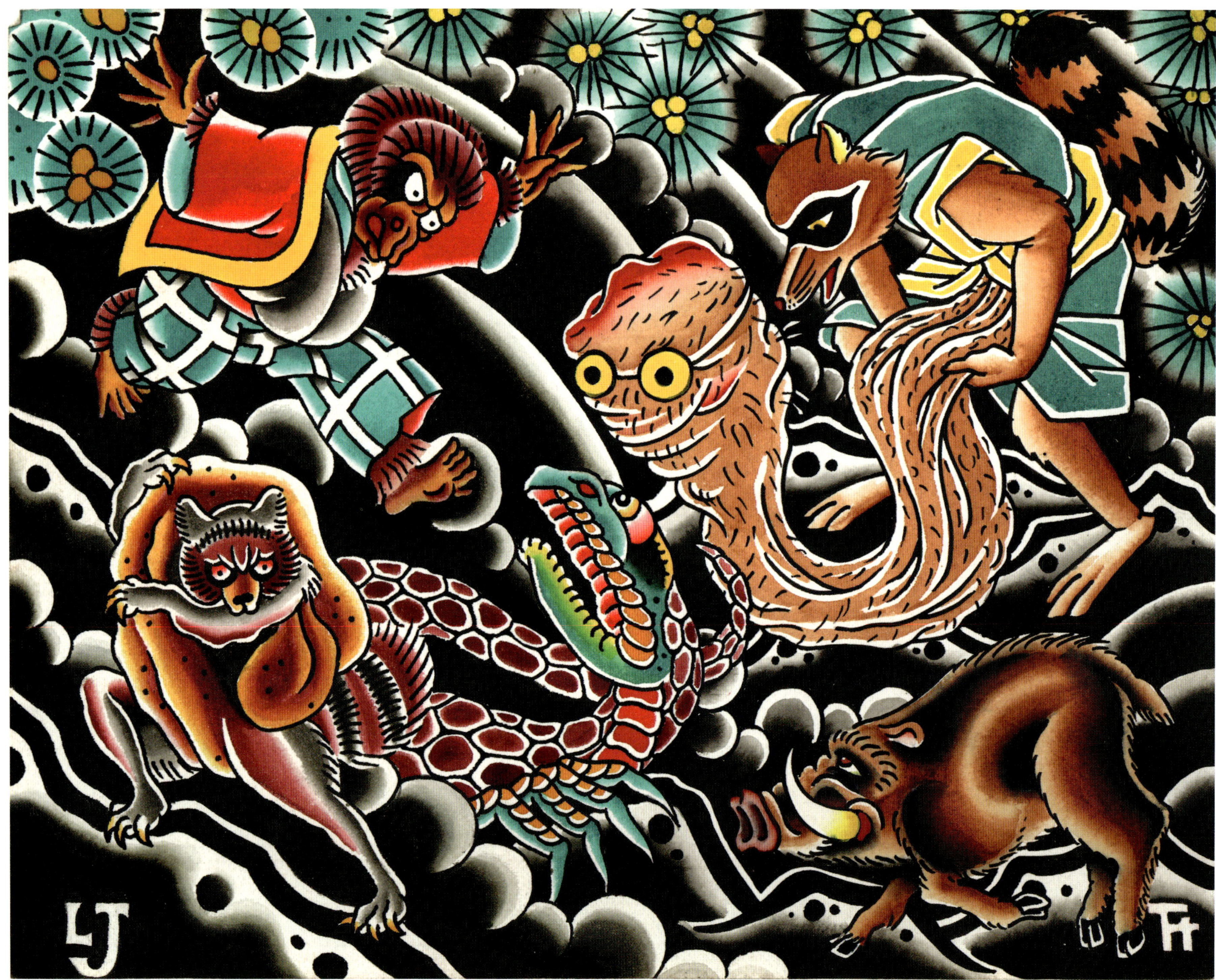

TILT

Tattooing has deep roots in the Japanese aesthetic, something I've been drawn to since I was a child. My first memory of Japanese traditions came from watching G. I. Joe. "Snake Eyes" was my favorite character; he wore a black suit, was incredible with a katana, and had a mysterious Japanese backstory. Japan seemed like a magical, far-away island that I would never see. And I was drawn to toys decorated with dragons and other Japanese images. They are playful because of their roots in manga (early Japanese ink-drawn illustrations, kind of like newspaper comics), but also fierce and strong.

Japanese tattooing is a collection of many aspects of the culture, including symbolism from Shintoism and Buddhism. There are layers to the Japanese tradition that we can't begin to comprehend. We can only try to interpret it through study, and it's taken a few hundred years to work out how the images flow with and fit on the body. One characteristic of this style is a strong black background that makes bright foregrounds pop off the skin.

Lowercase j and I thought it would be nice to see more people "collecting" Japanese-style tattoos, which is why we decided to create more single-sitting tattoos. Some pages have no background, as we felt that the art and its boldness would be more easily understood as a stand-alone tattoo. The pages grow progressively more intricate to show how the images can interact with a bold background. Every tattooer who cares about the history of this art should spend some time studying Japanese tattoo.

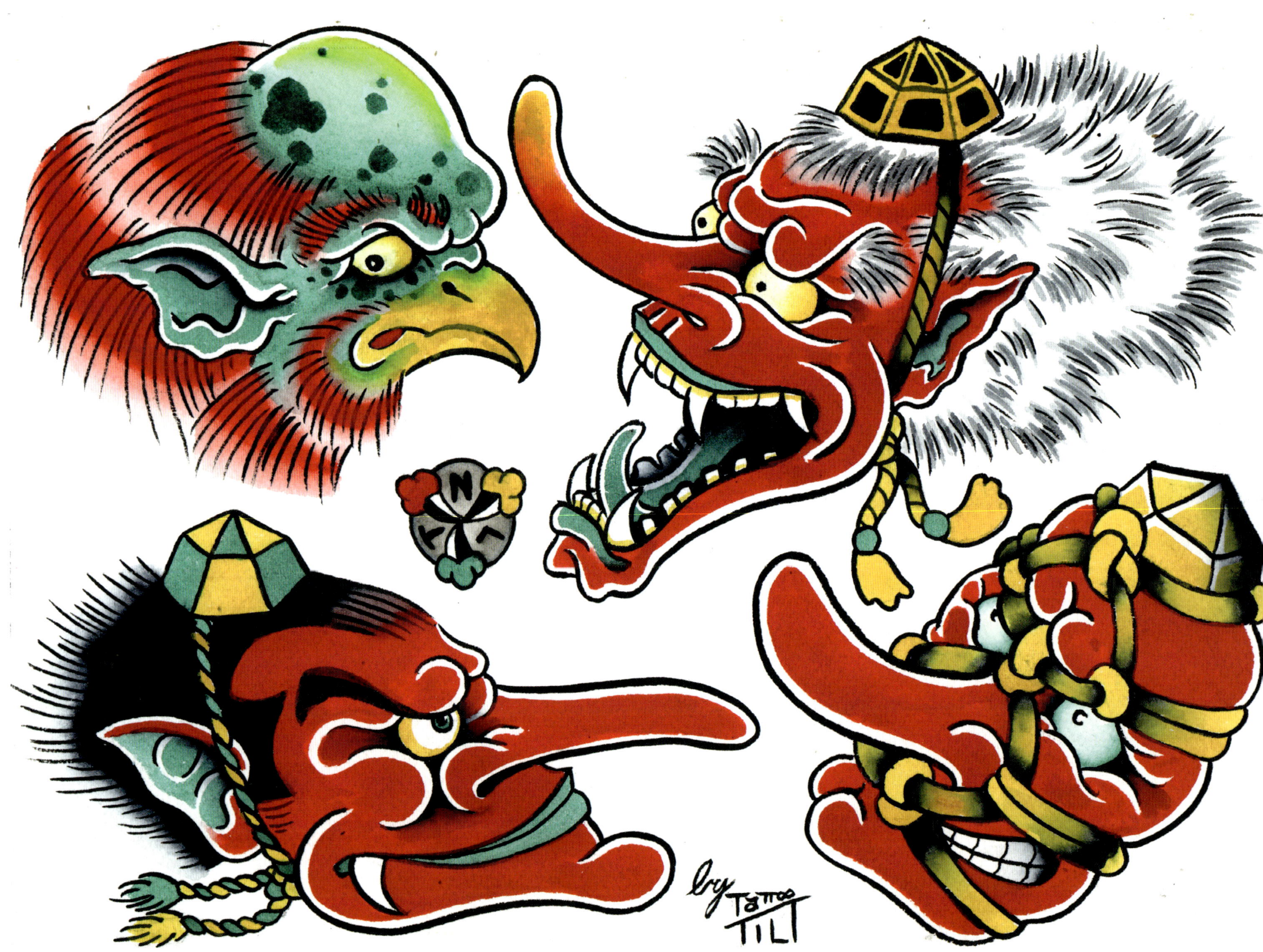
N
by Tattoo TILT

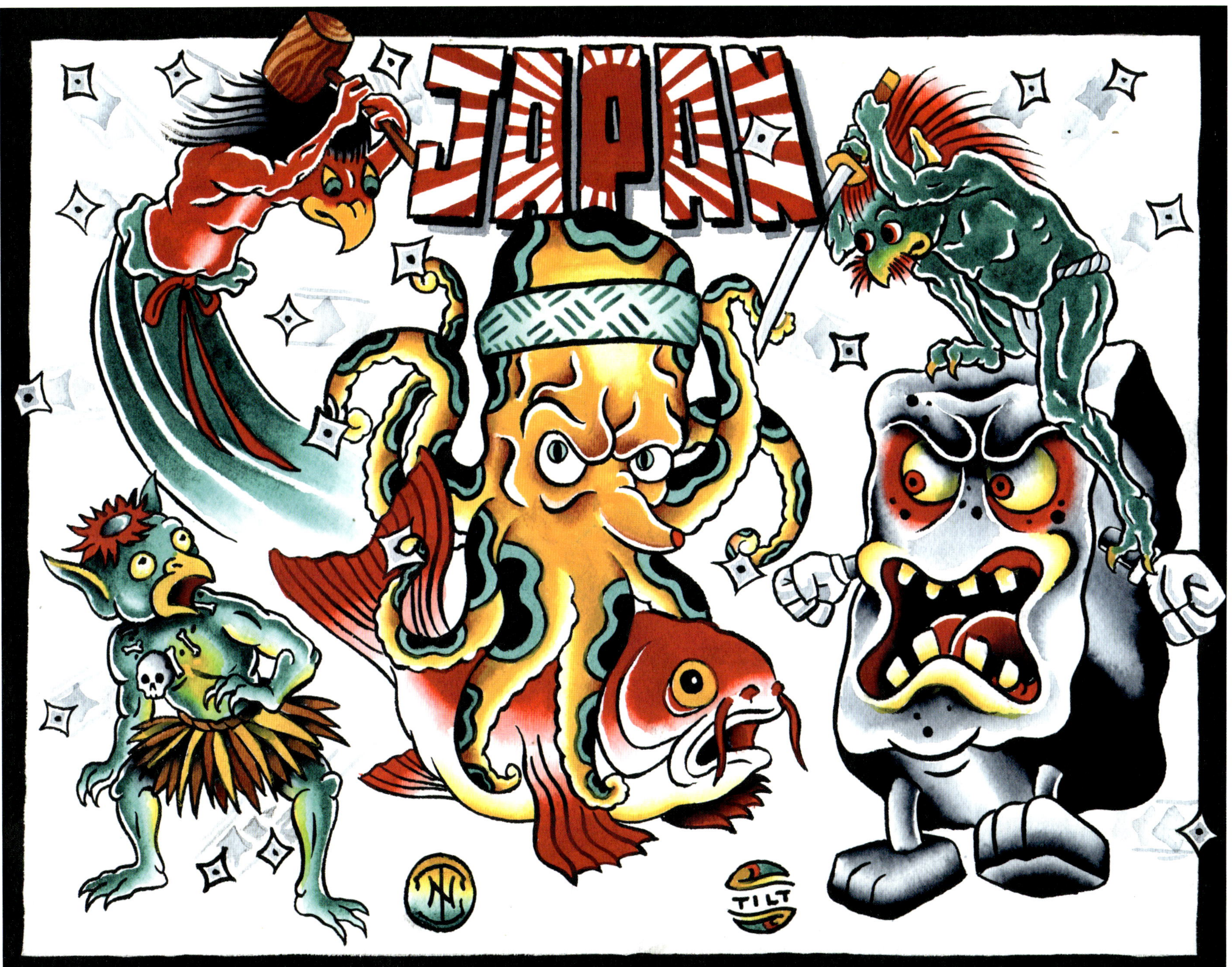
JAPAN
TILT

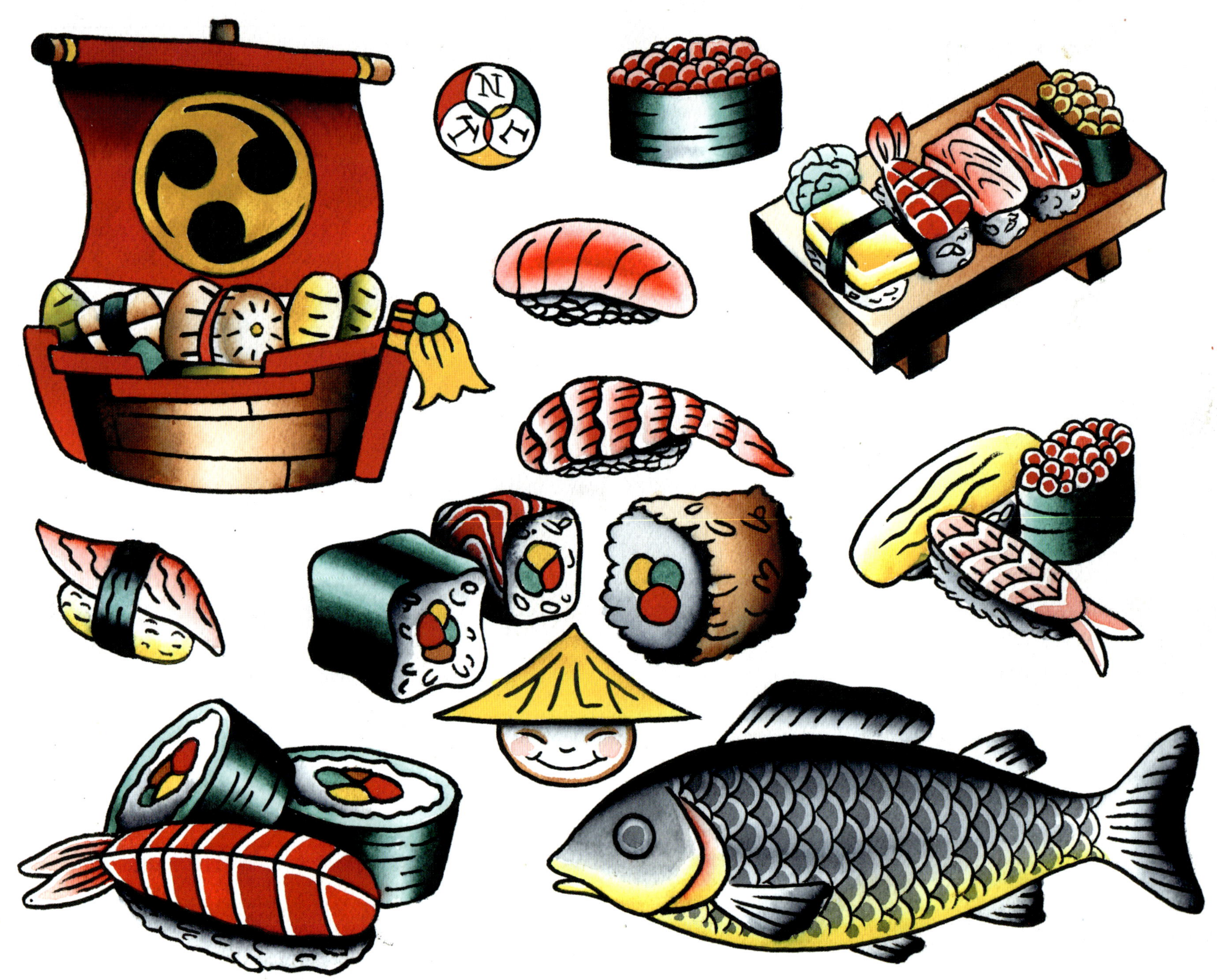

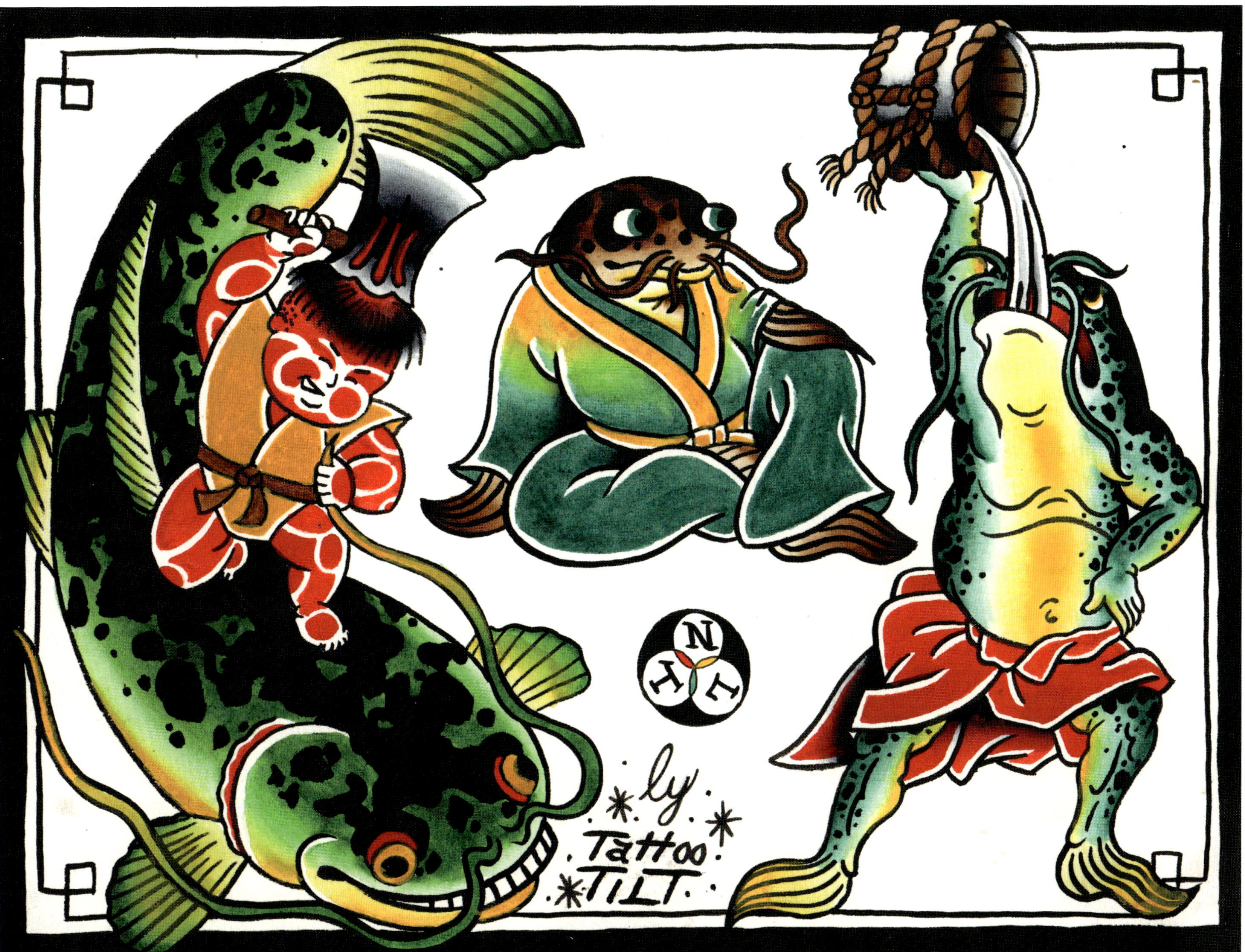
N
T
T
ly
Tattoo
TILT

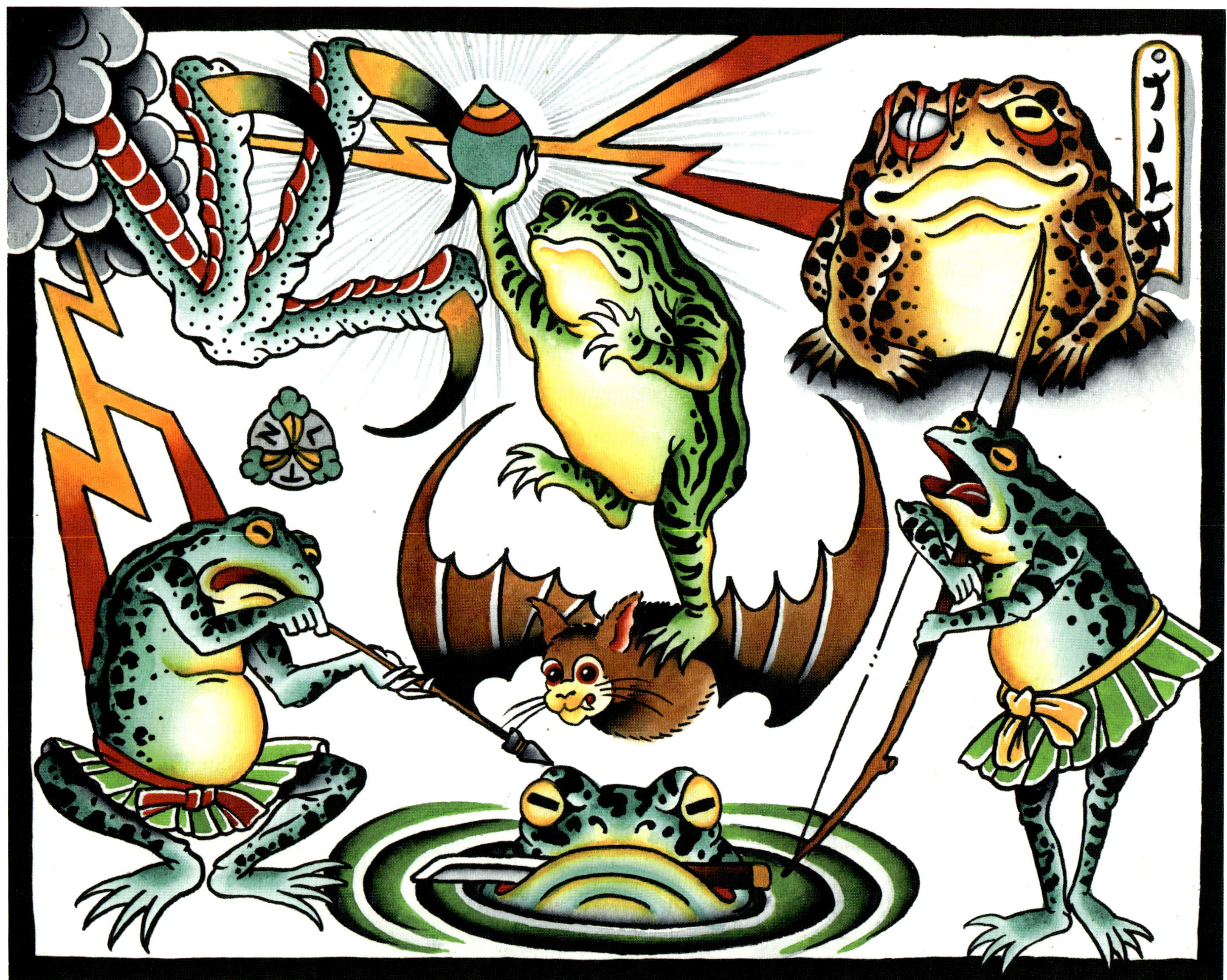

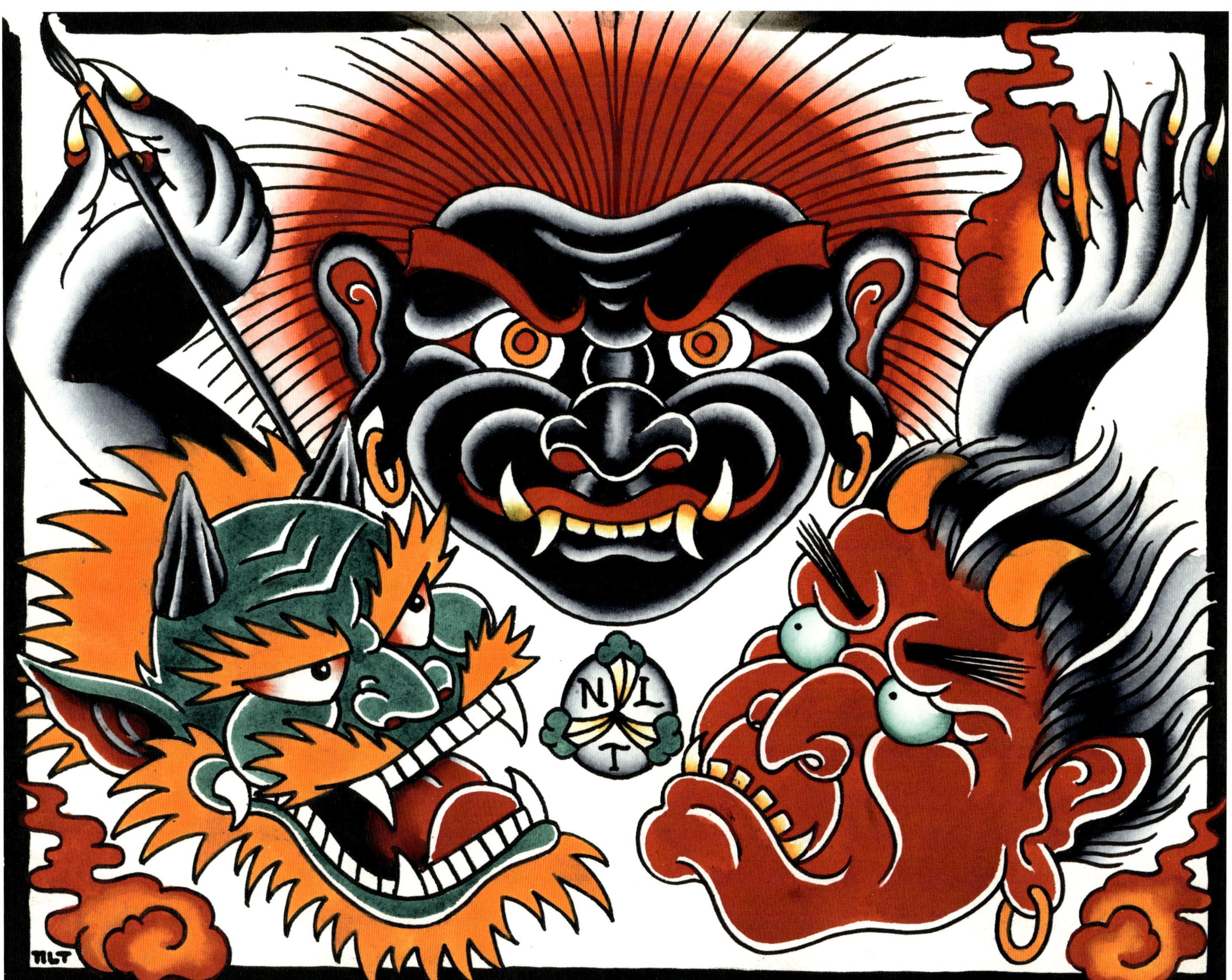
N
L
T
TILT

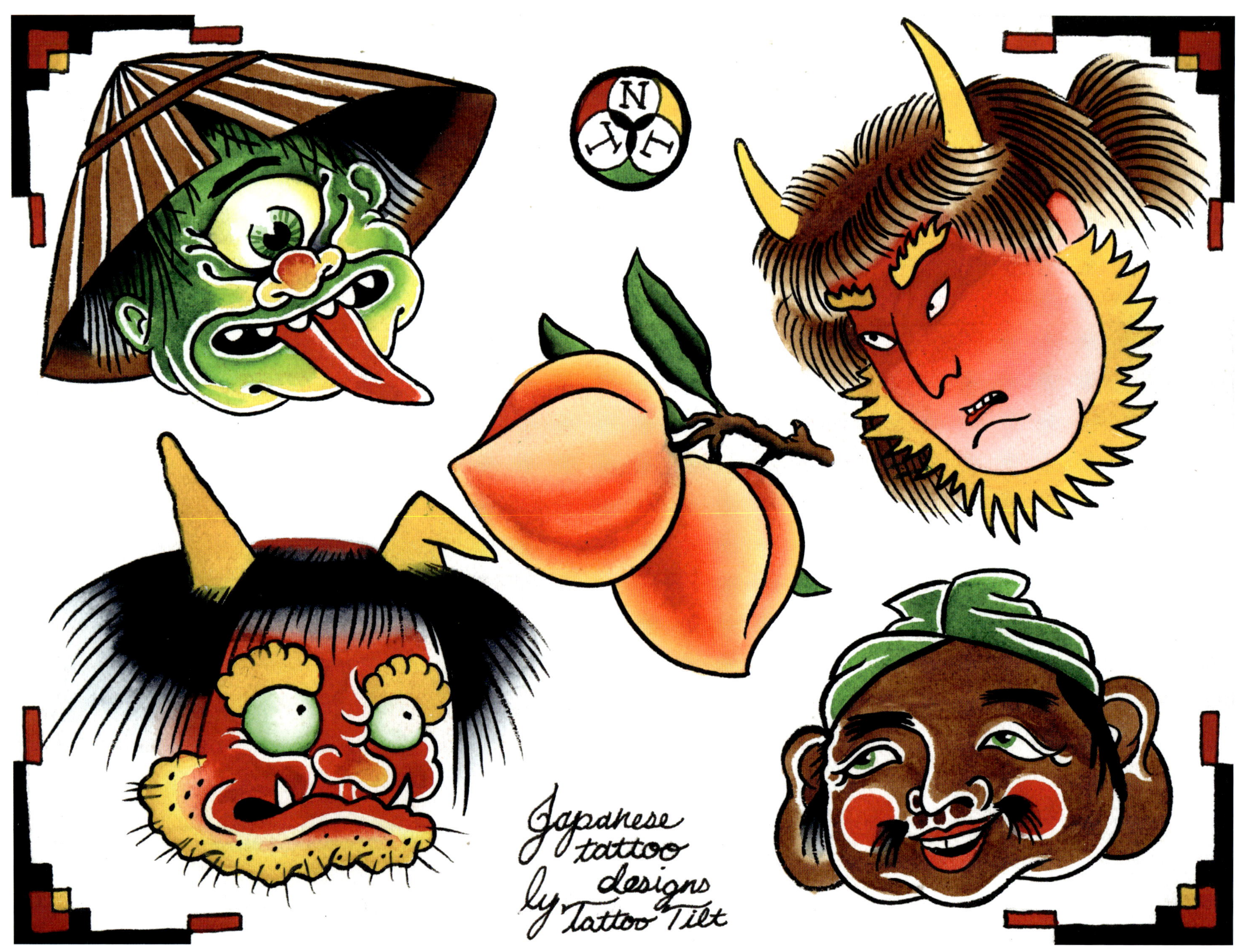
N
T
K
Japanese
tattoo
designs
by Tattoo Tilt

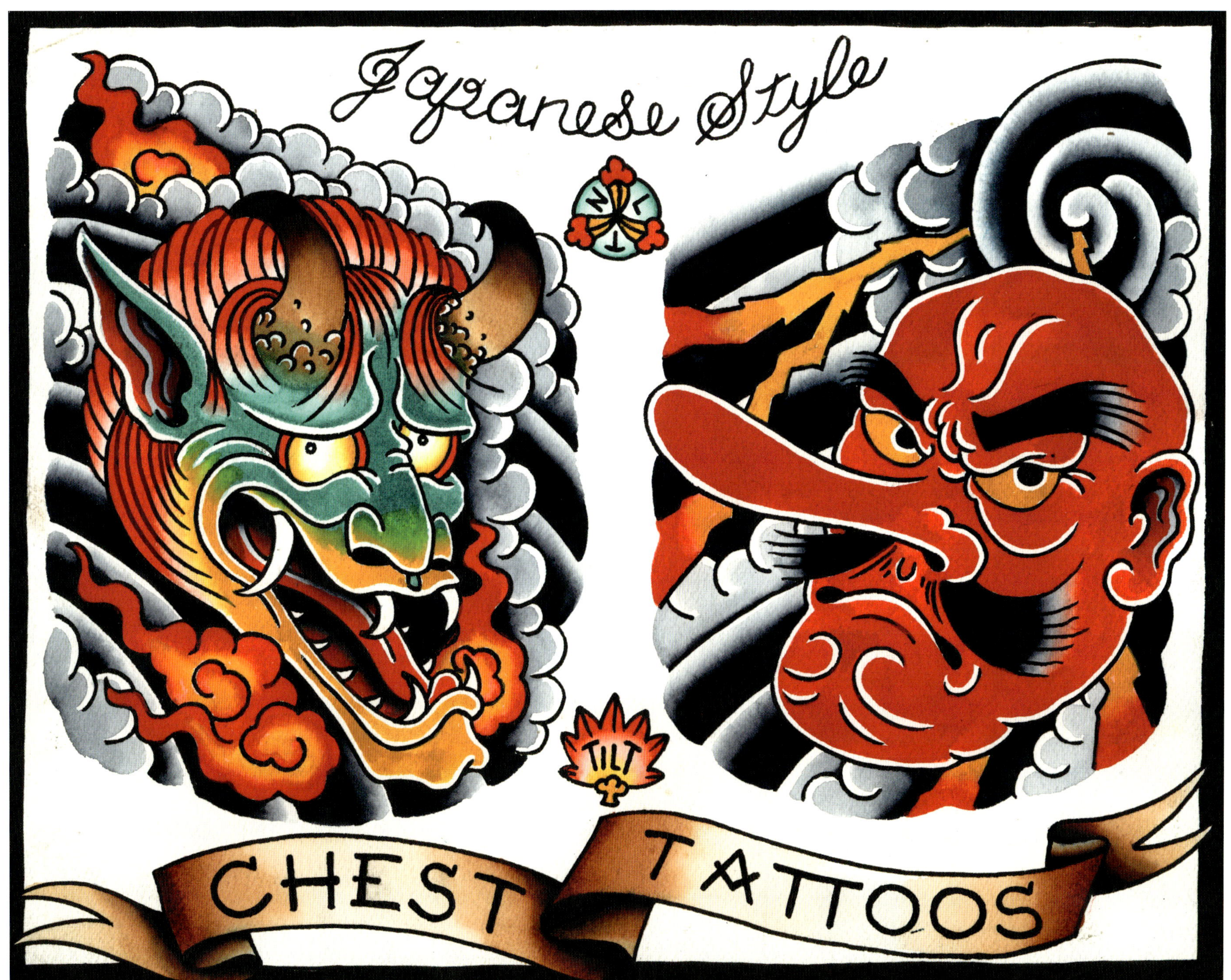
Japanese Style
TILT
CHEST TATTOOS

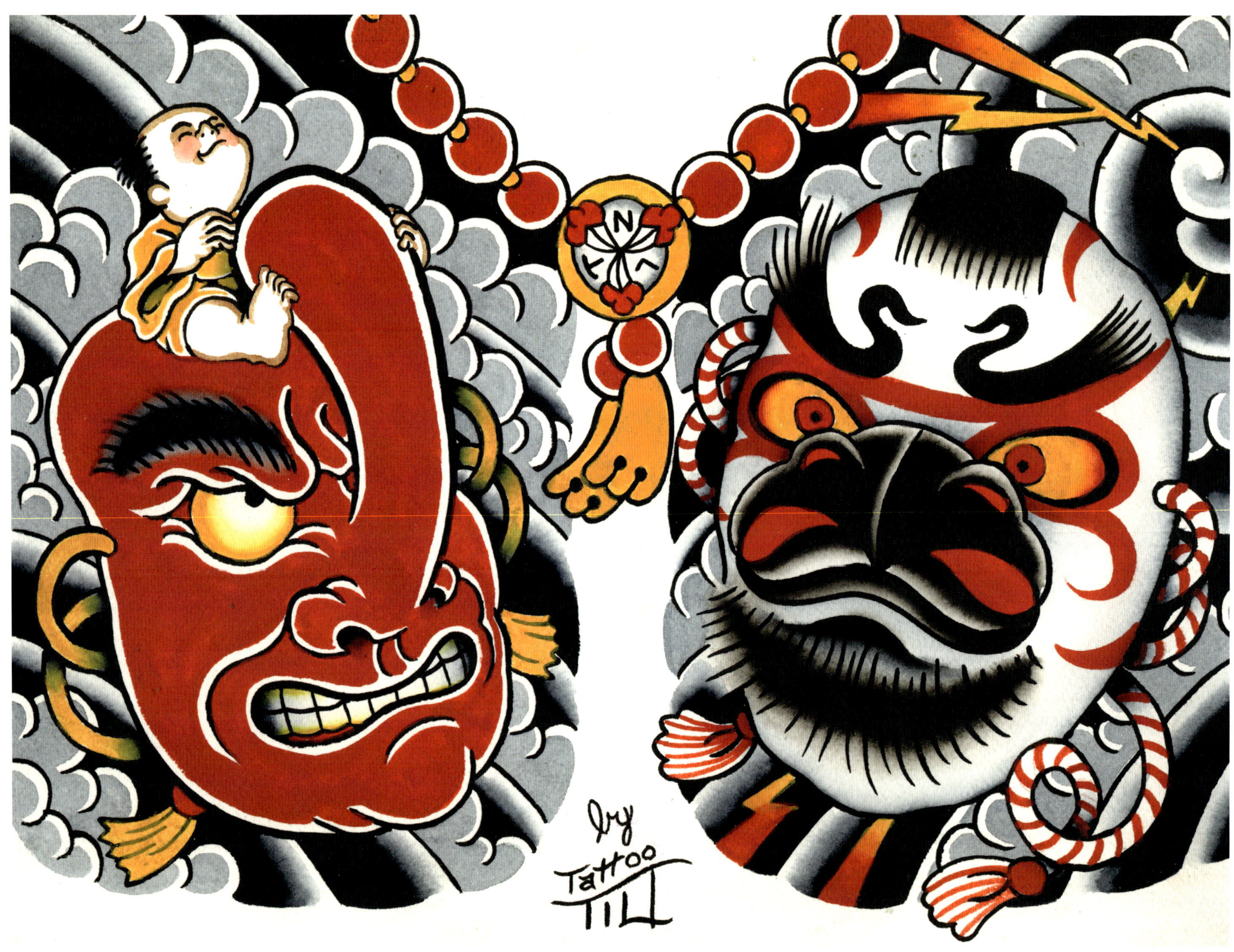
by
Tattoo
Till

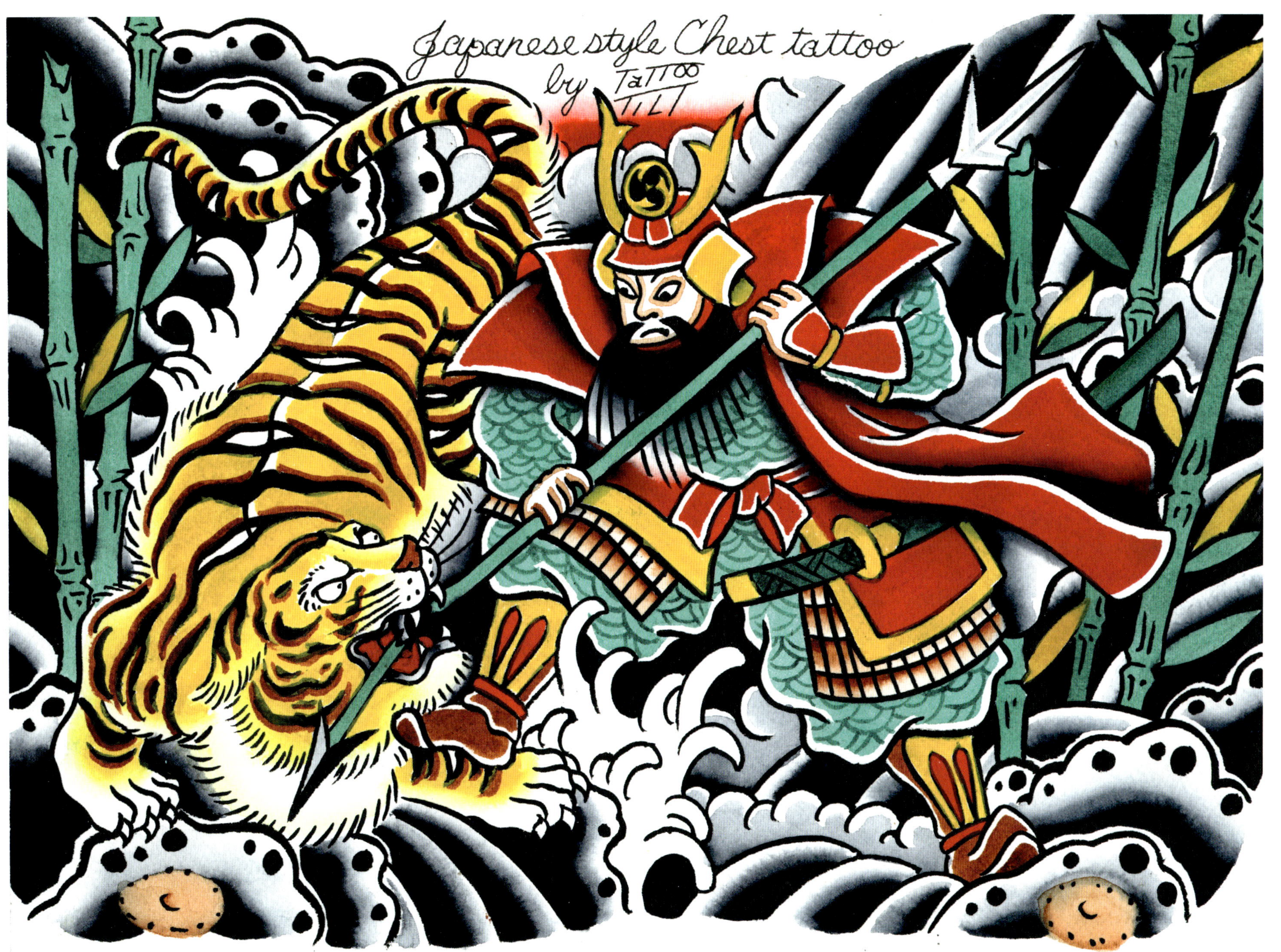
Japanese style Chest tattoo
by TaTTOO TILT

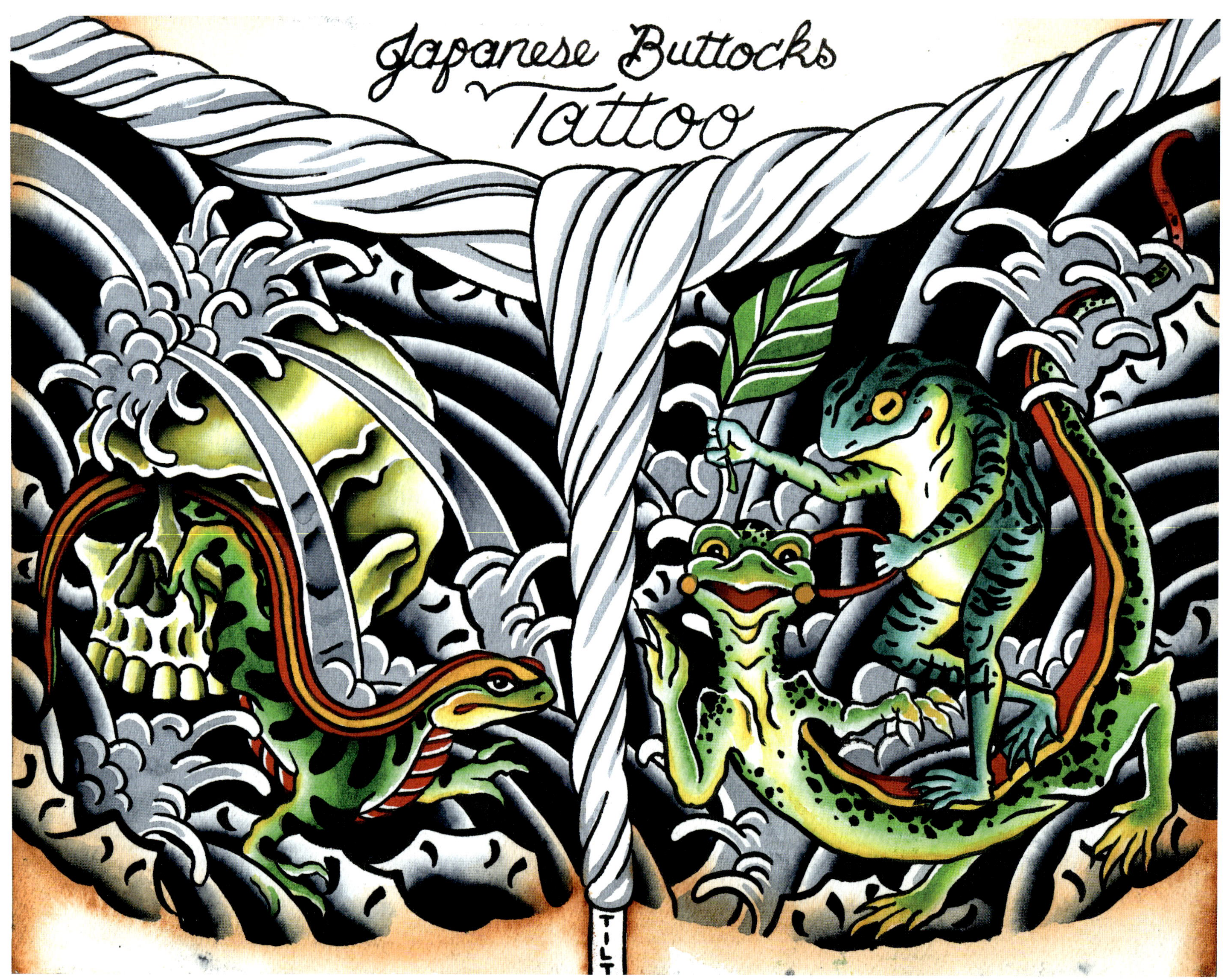
Japanese Buttocks
Tattoo
TILT

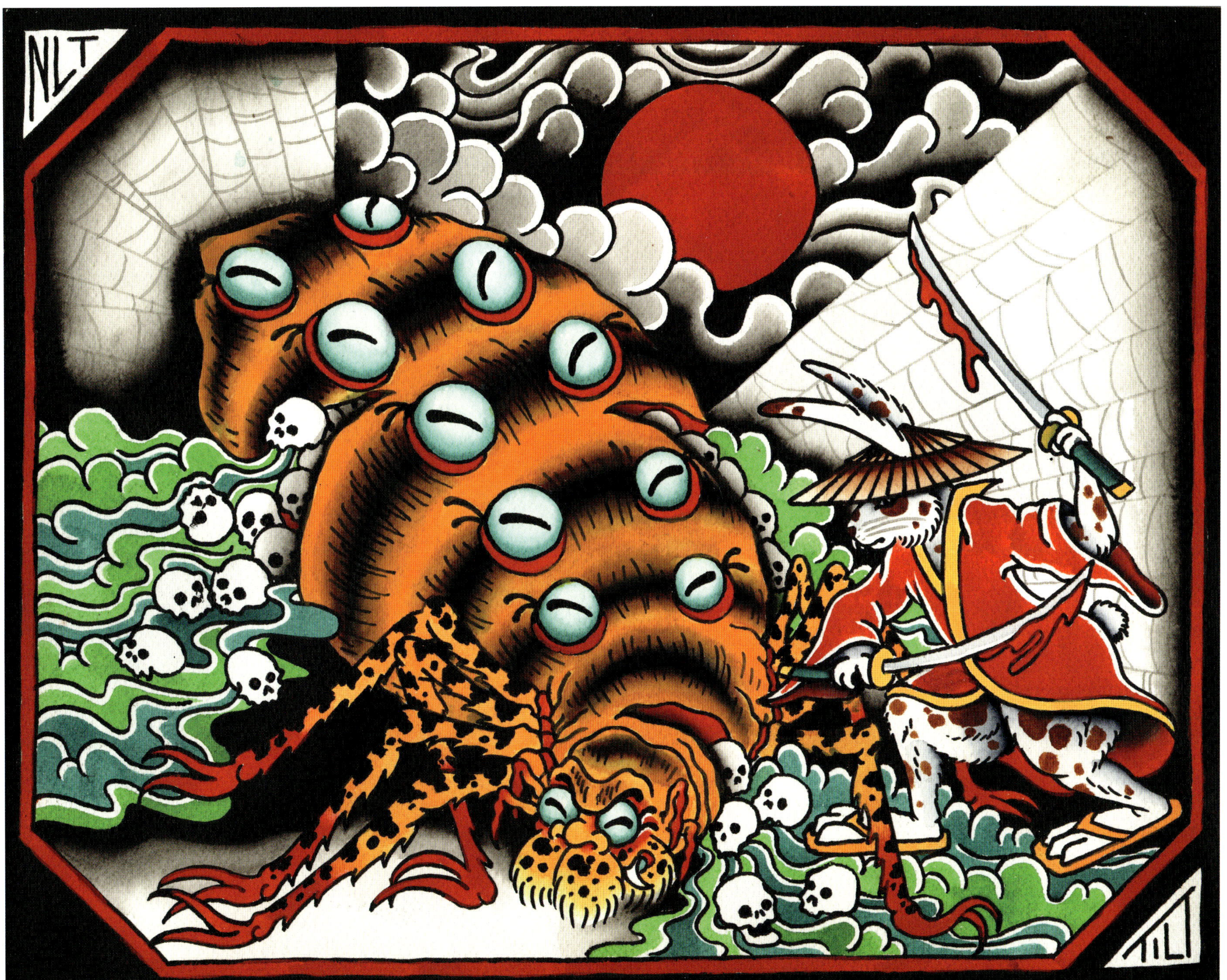
NLT
TILT

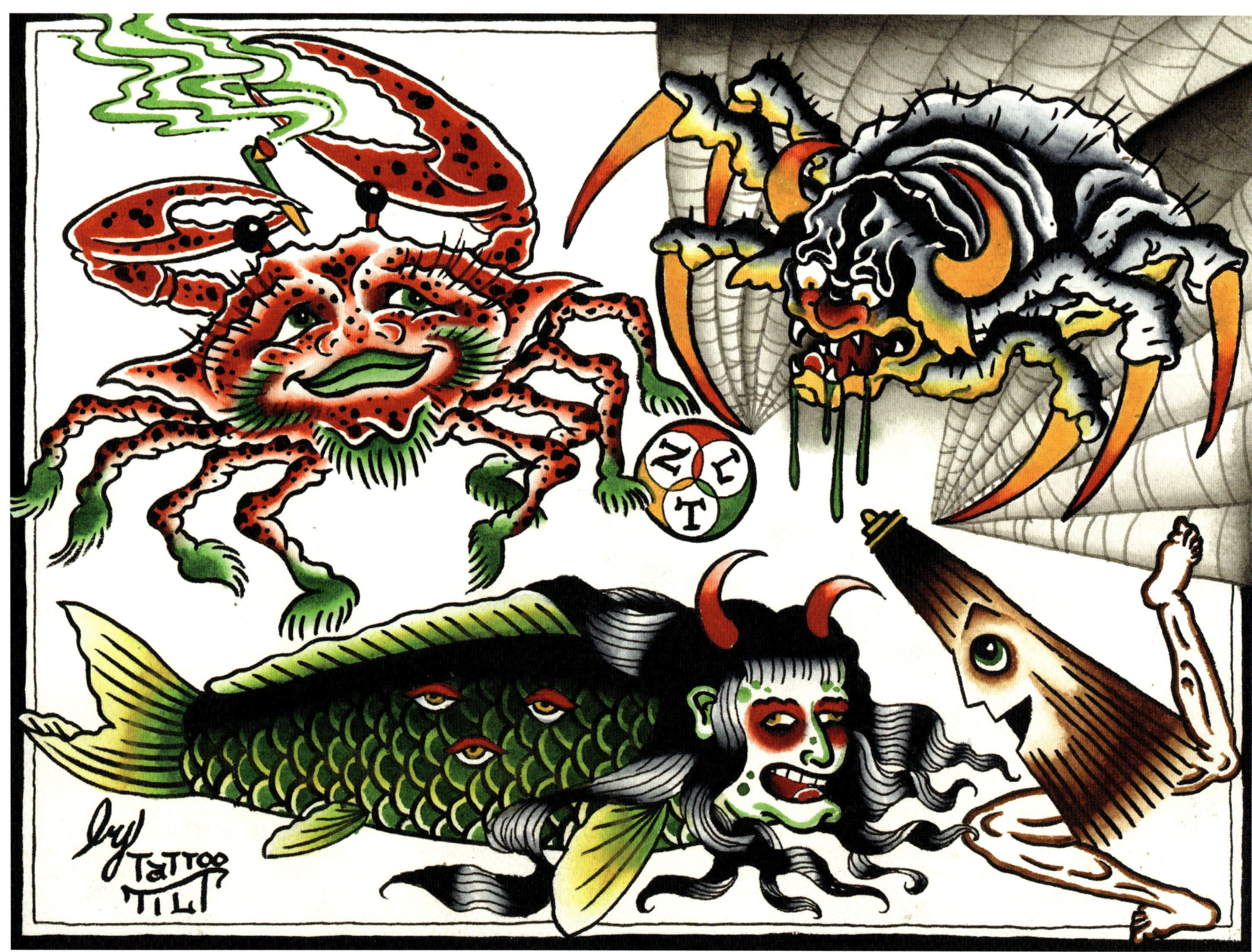
TaTToo
TILI

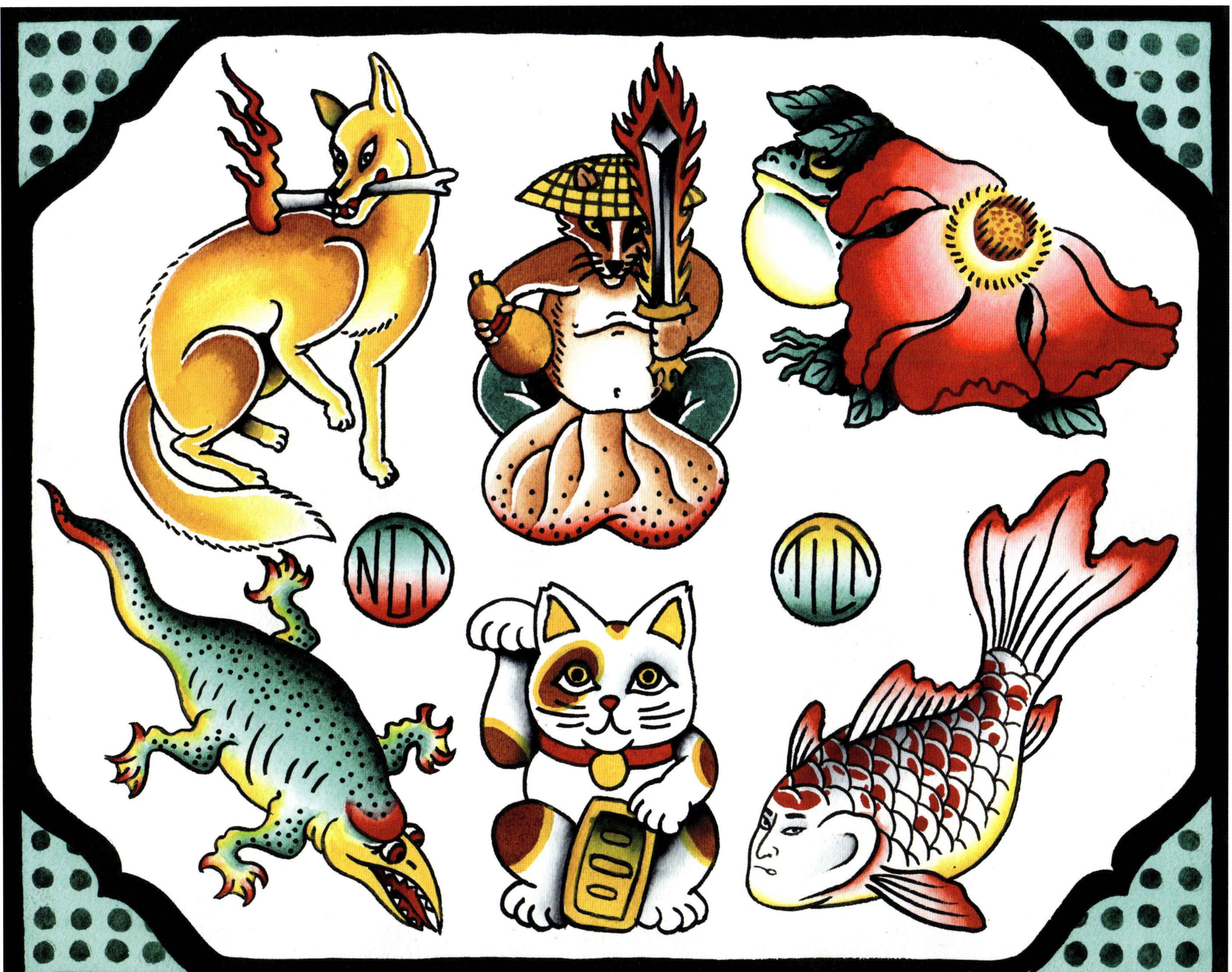
TILT

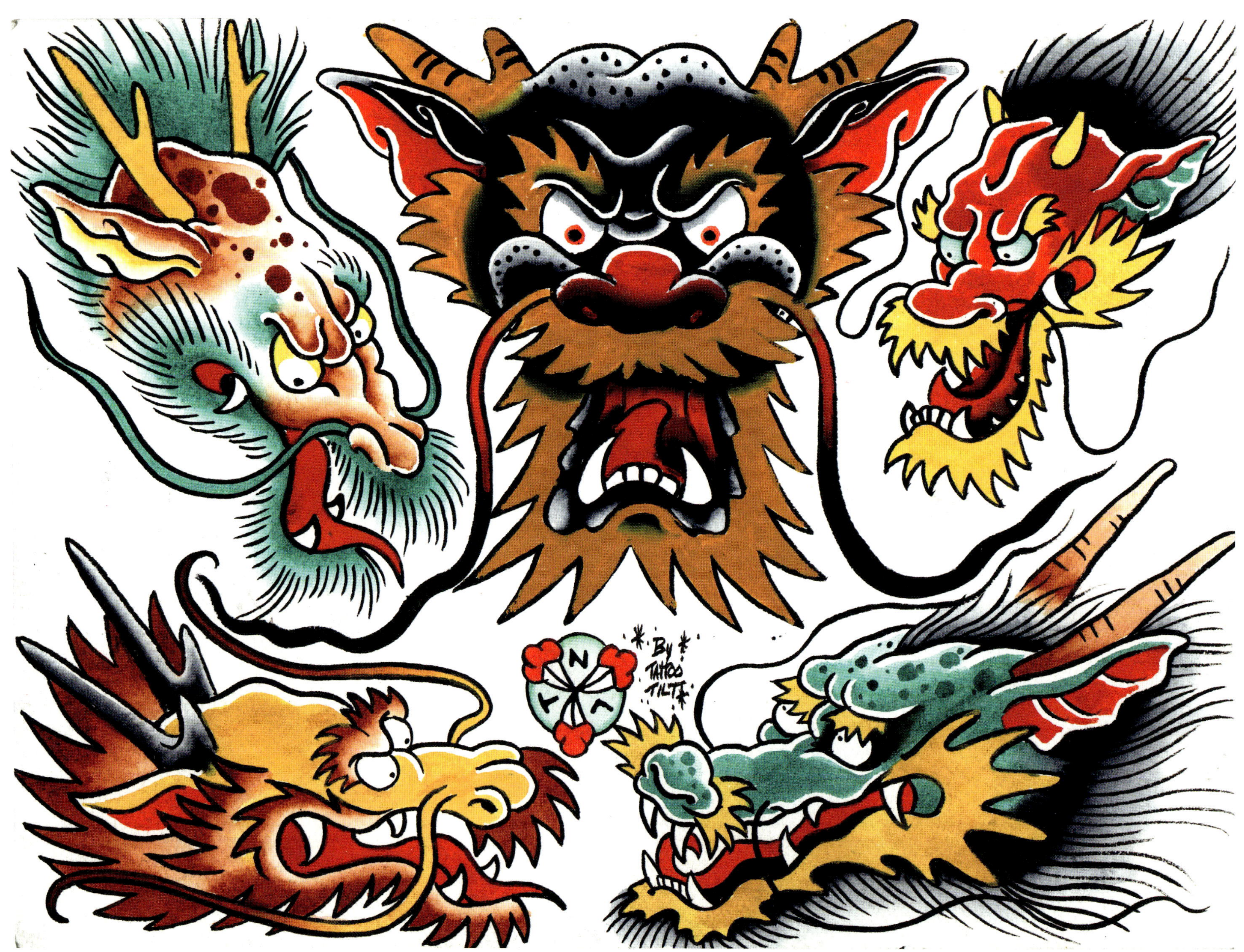
By
TATTOO
TILT

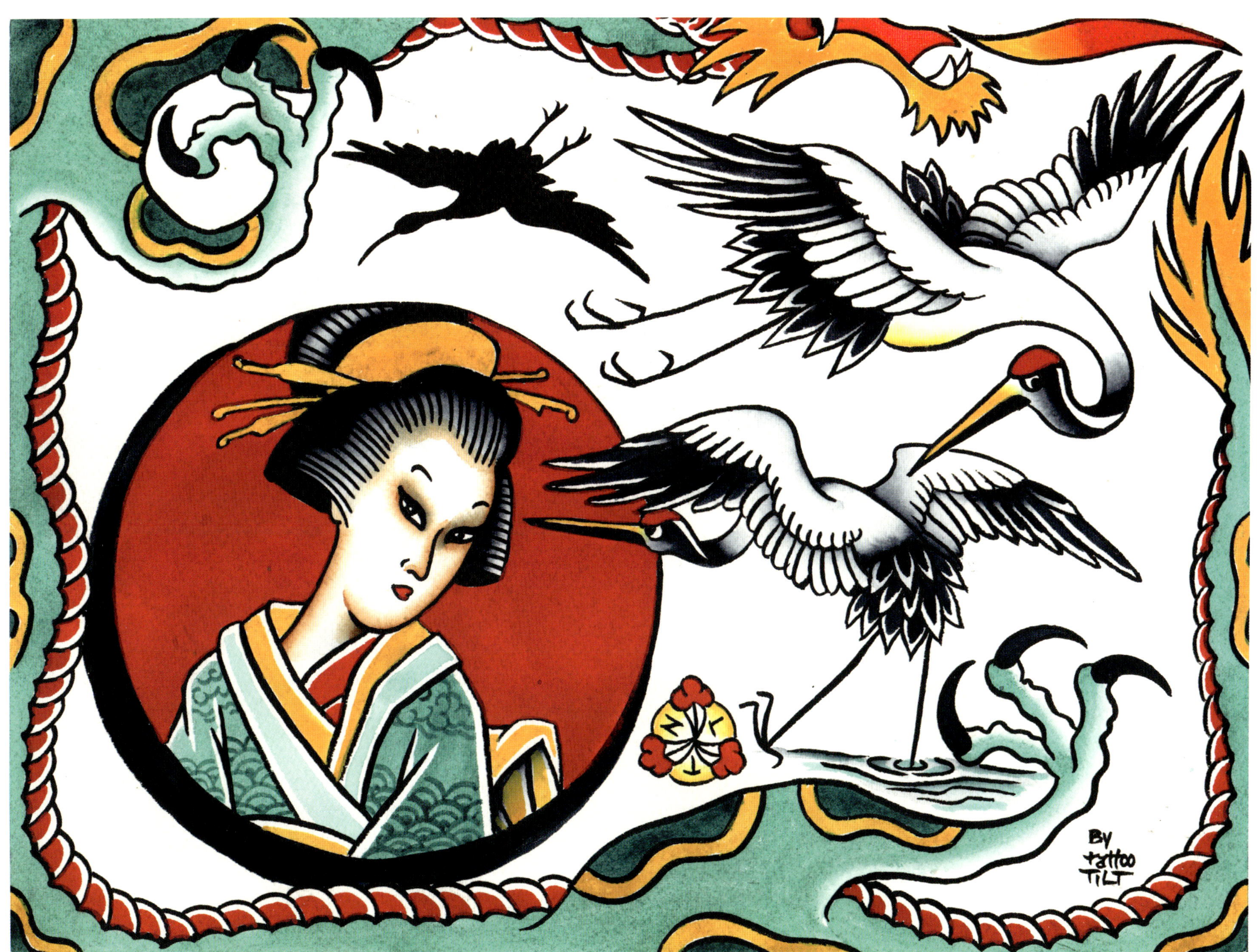
By
tattoo
TiLT

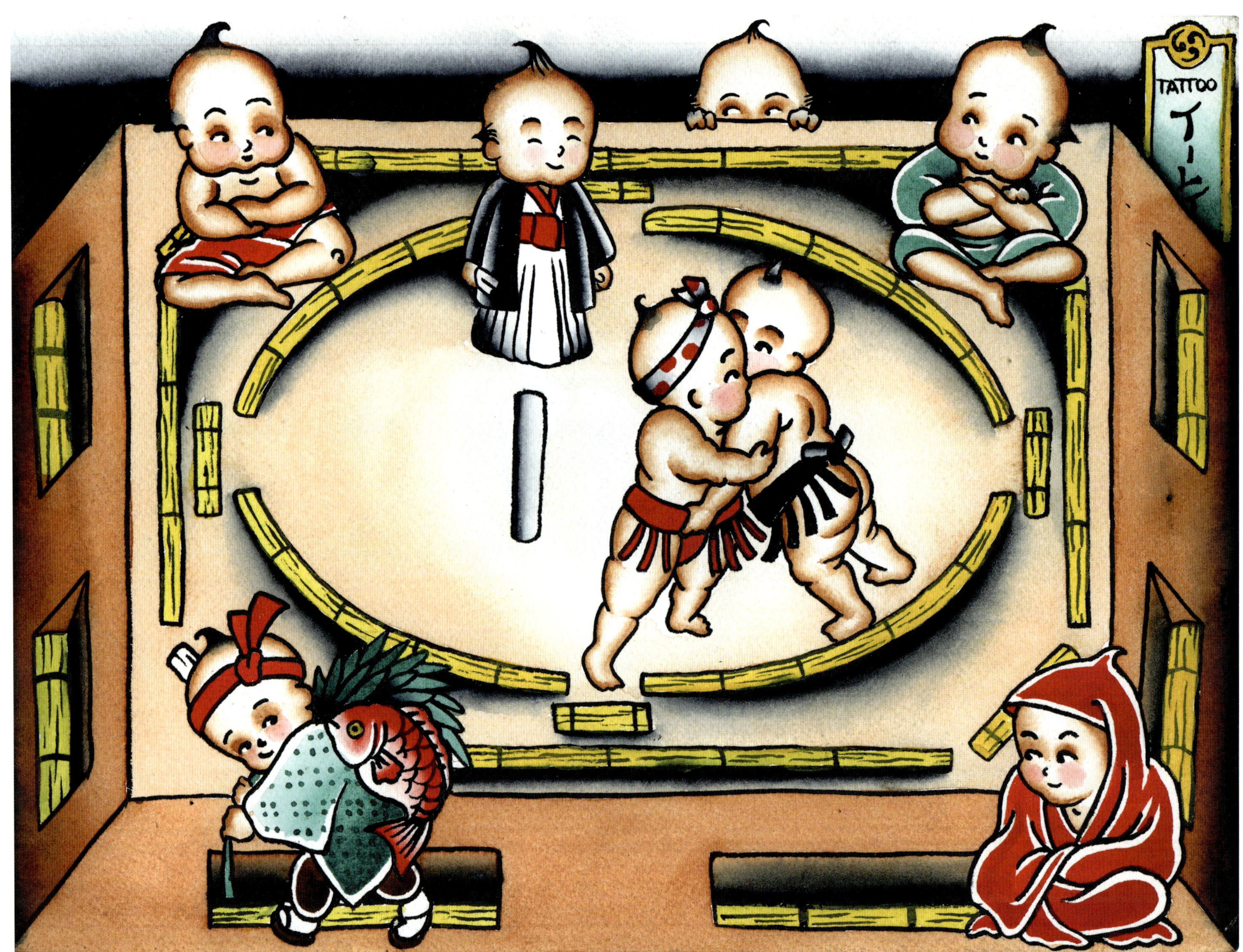
TATTOO
イーヒ

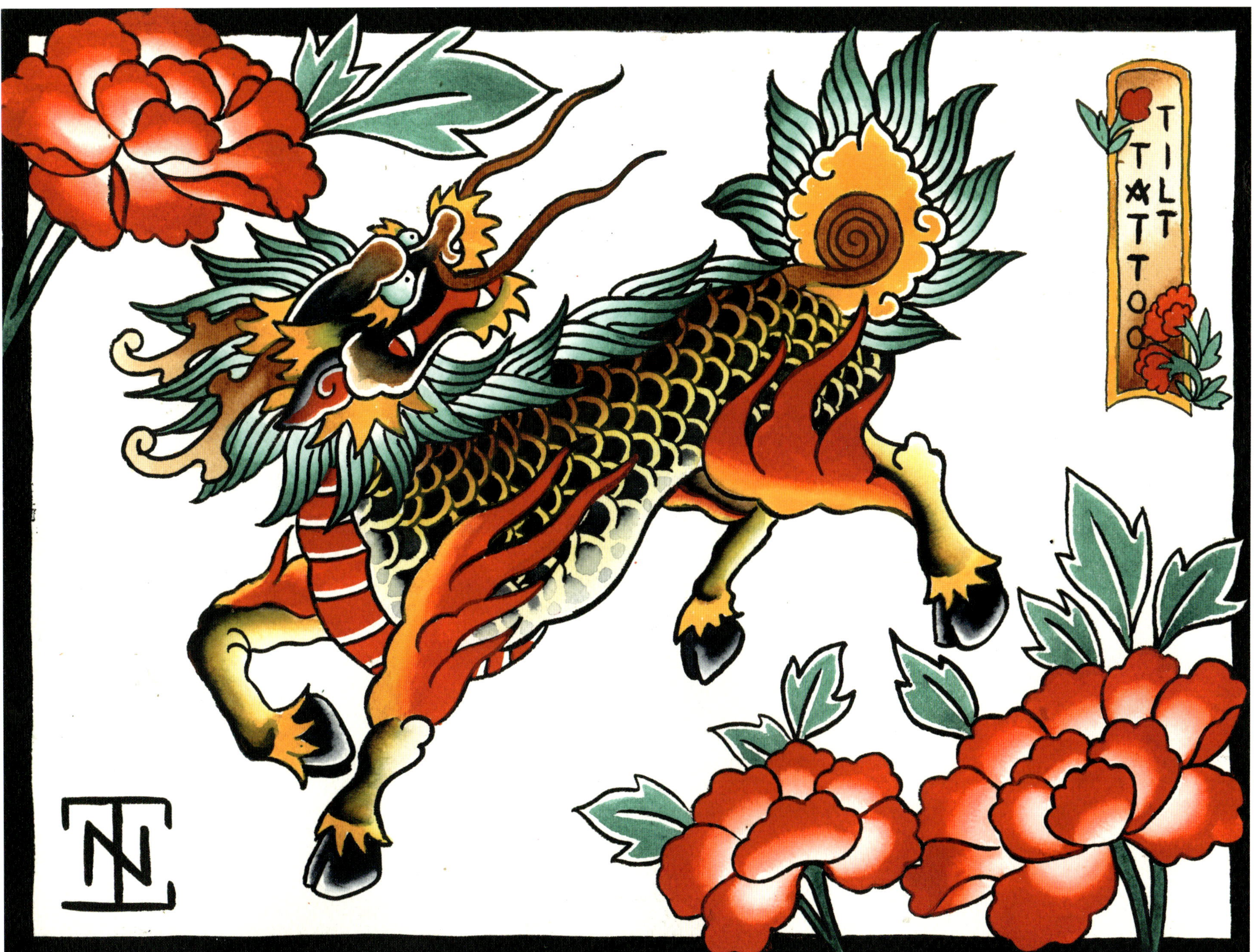
TILT
TATTOO

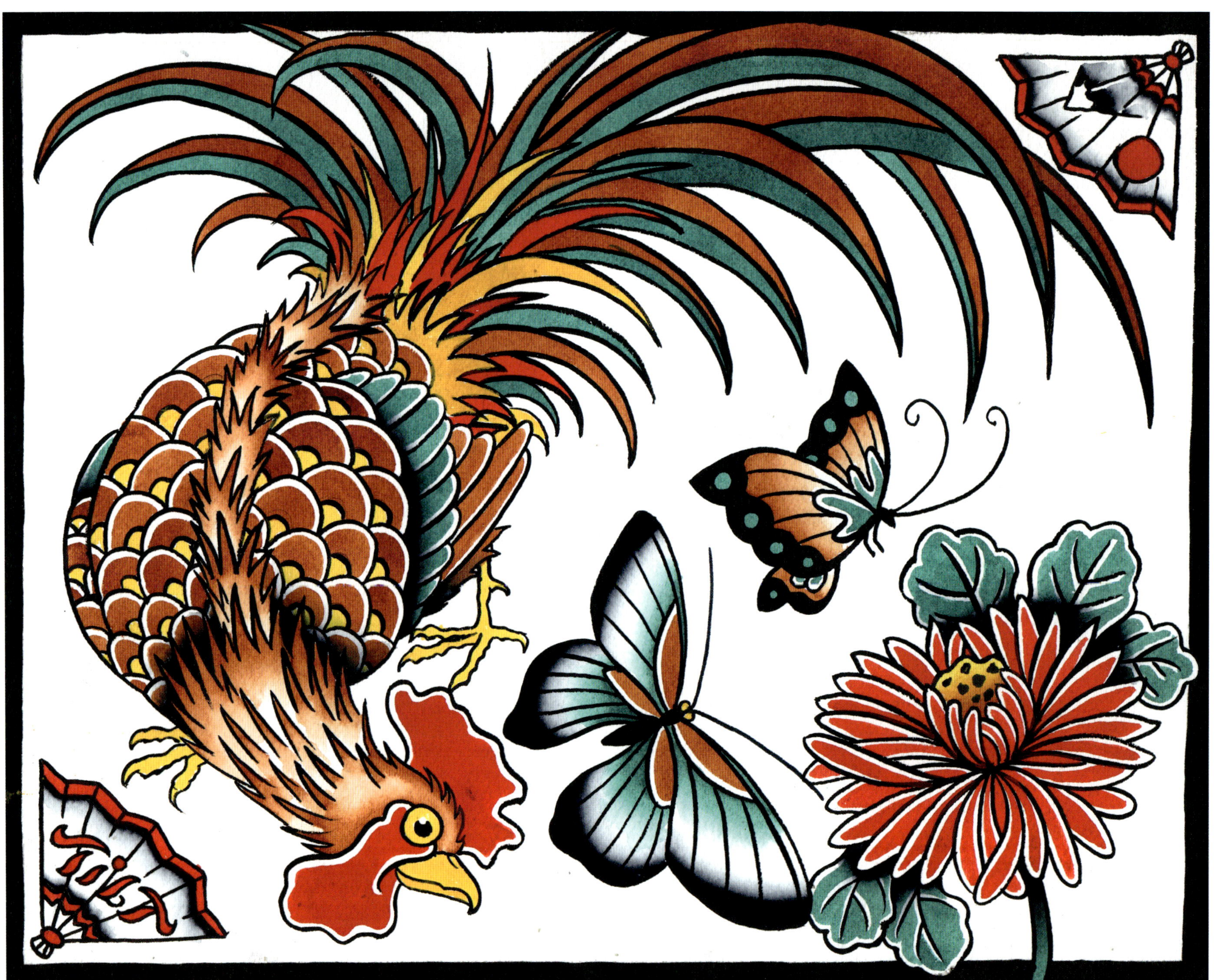

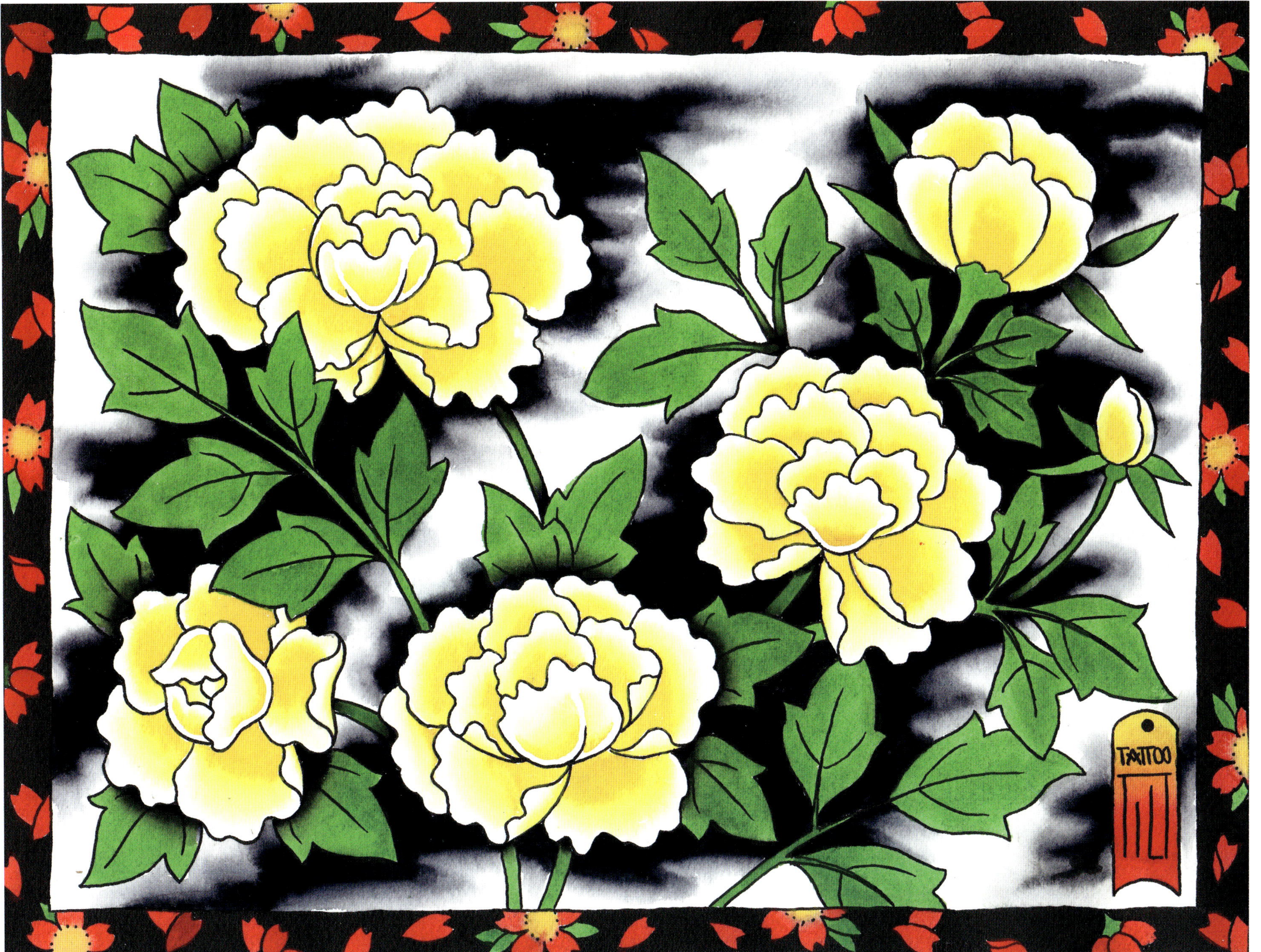
TATTOO

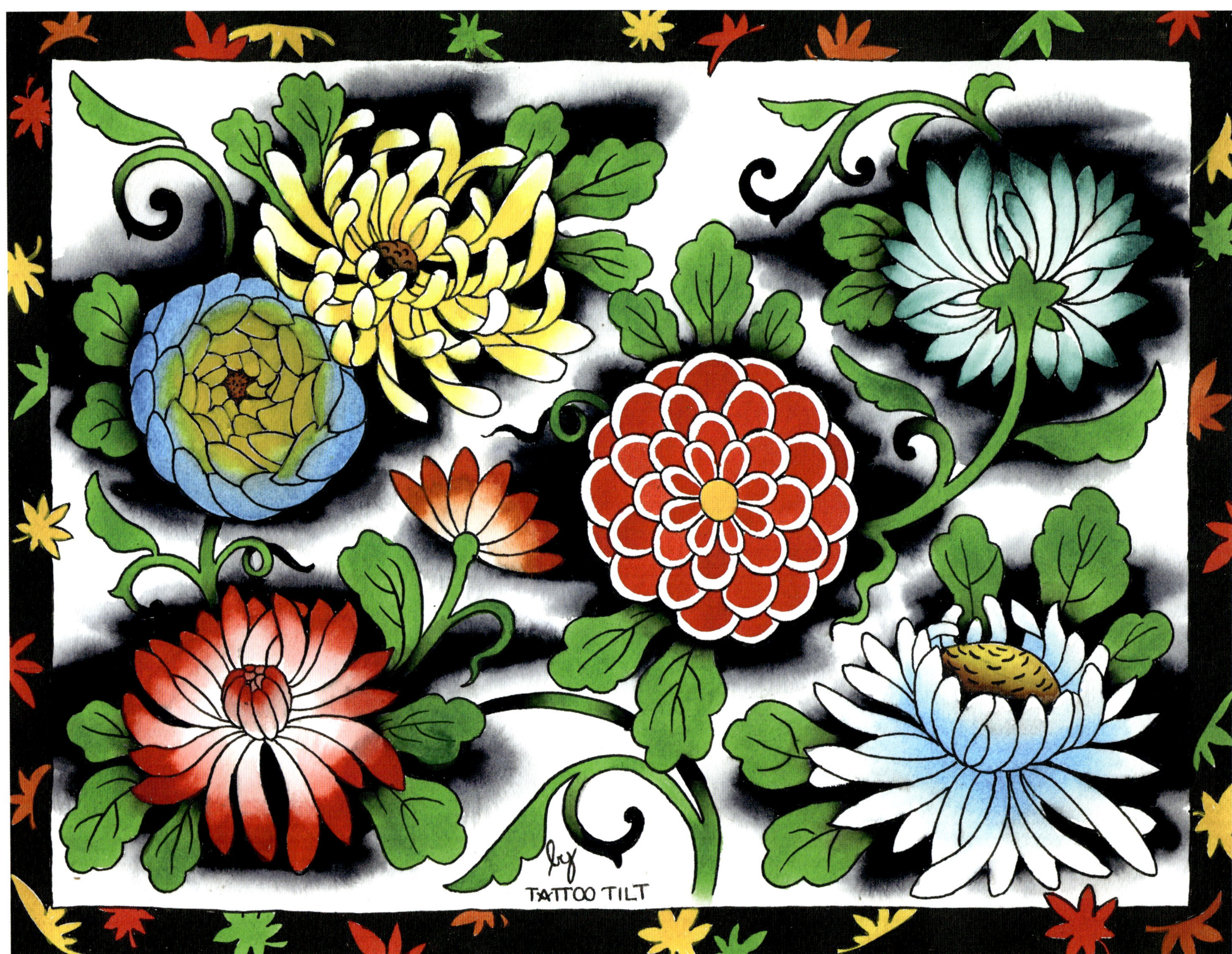
by
TATTOO TILT

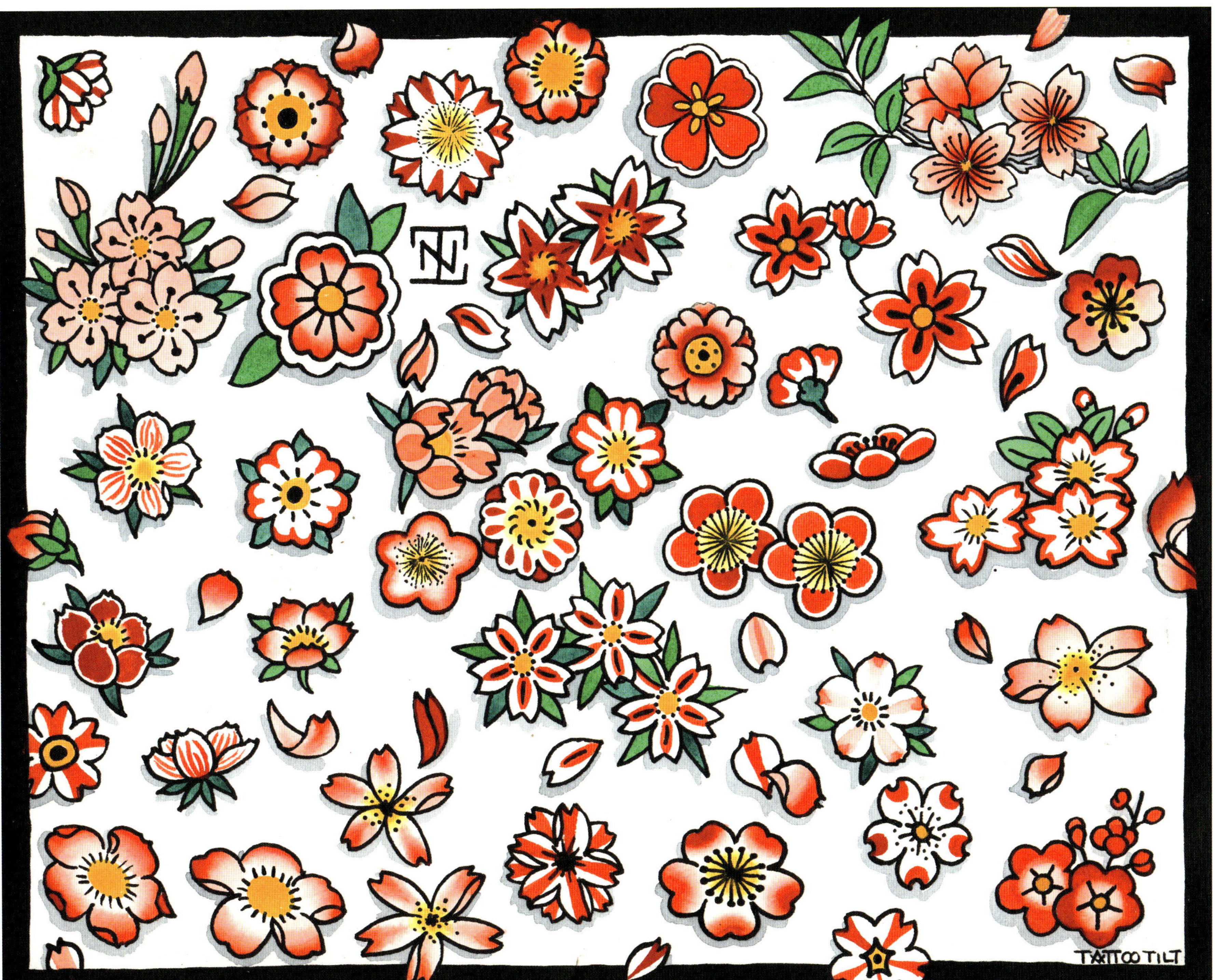
TATTOO TILT

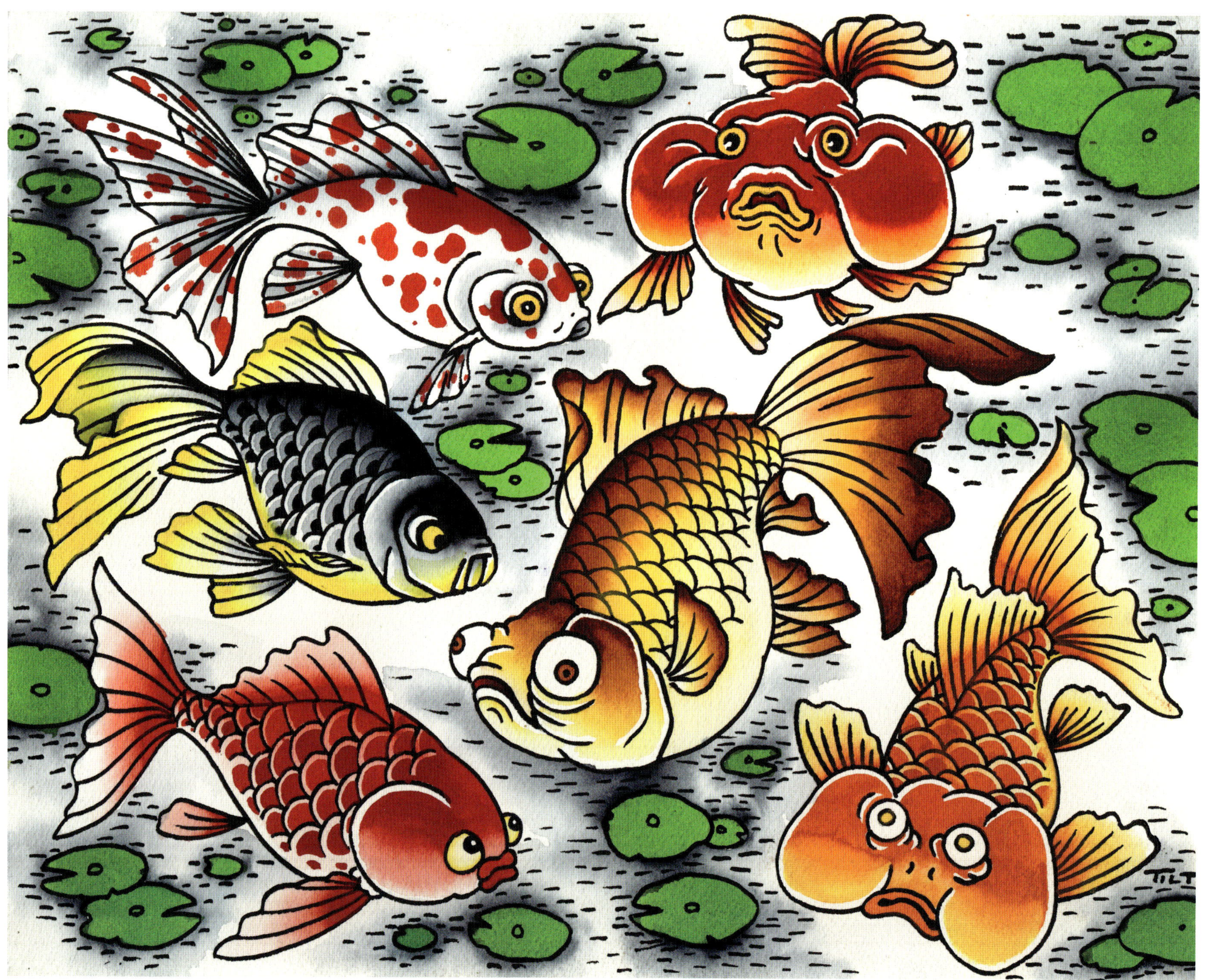
TILT

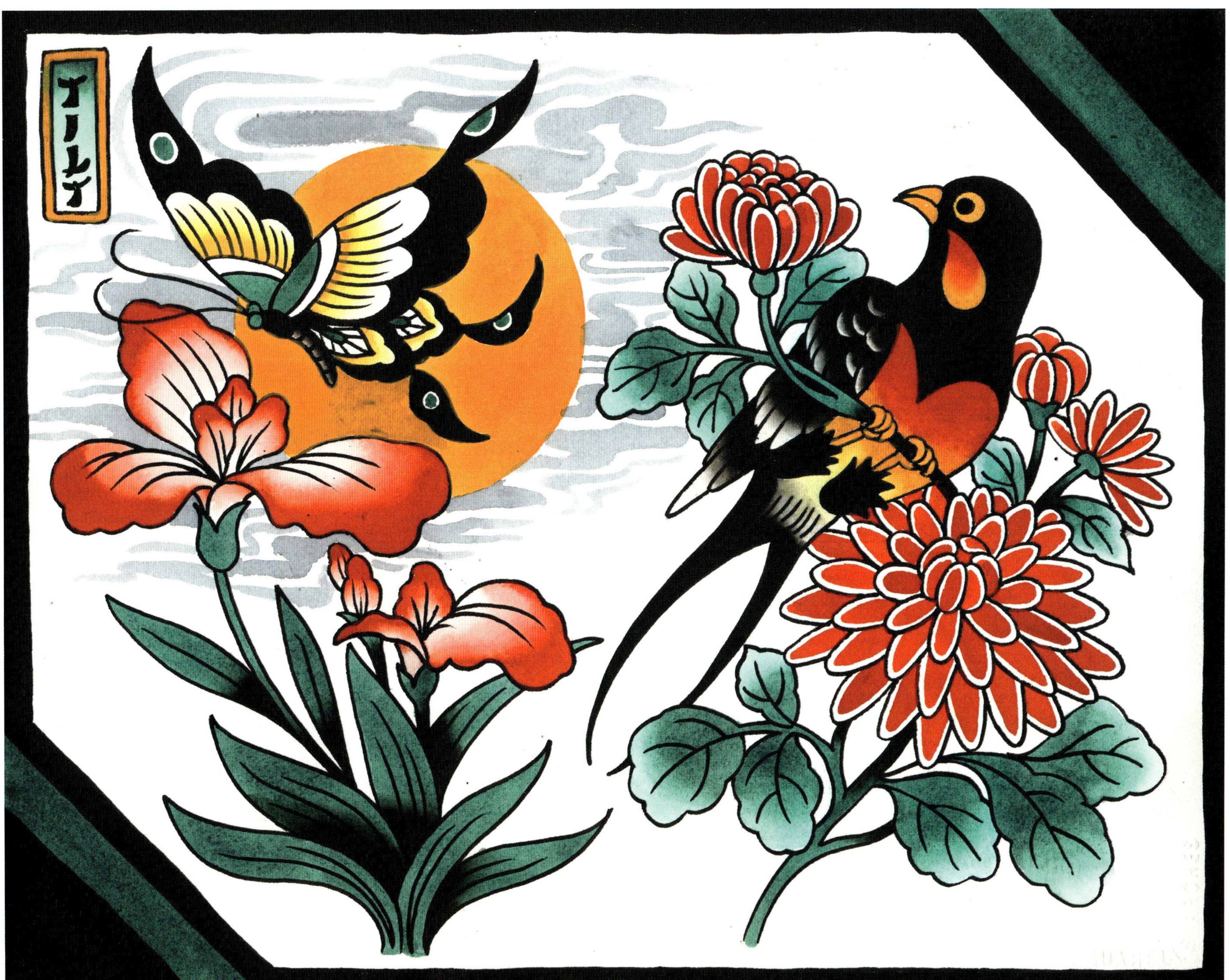

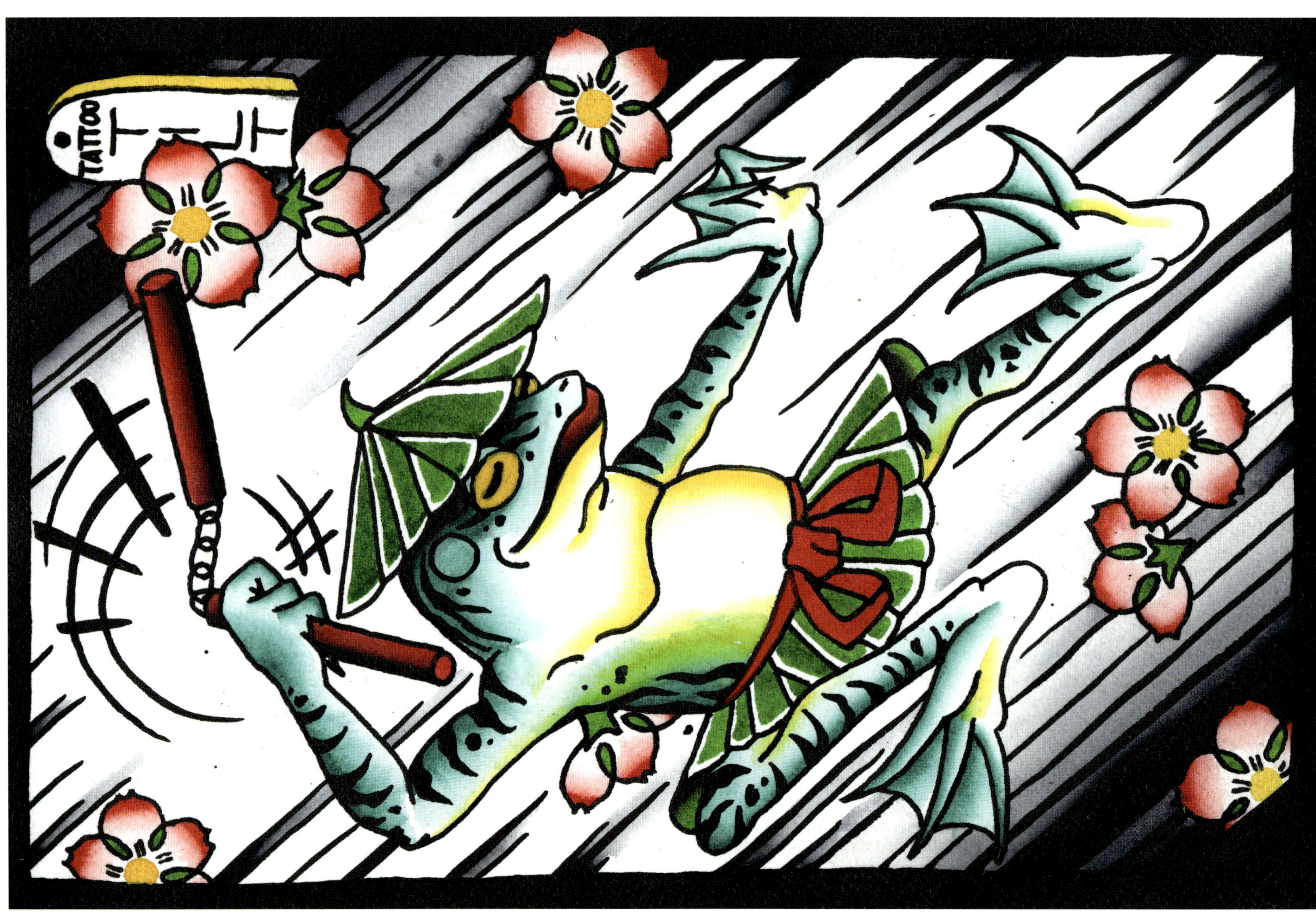
TATTOO
TLT

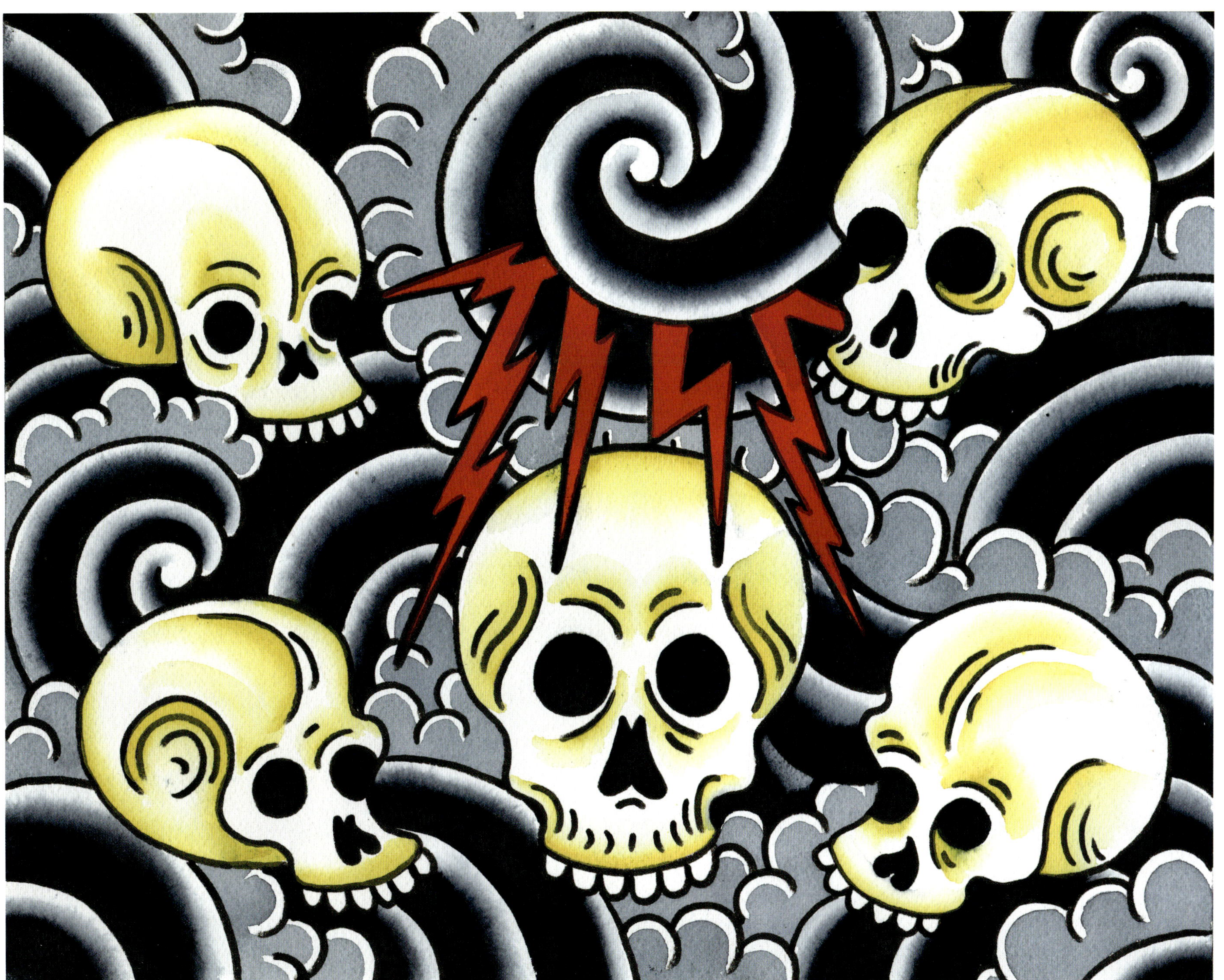

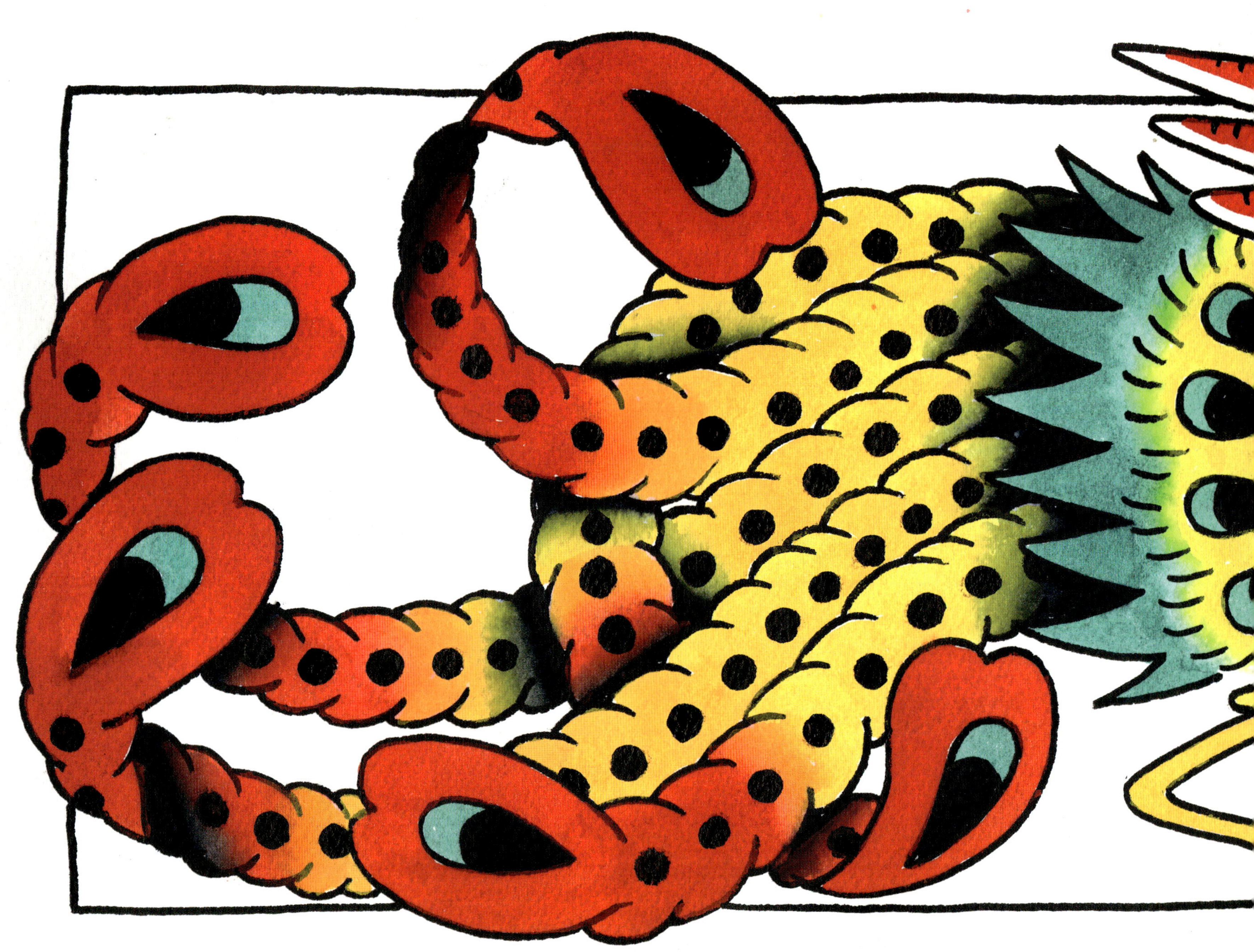

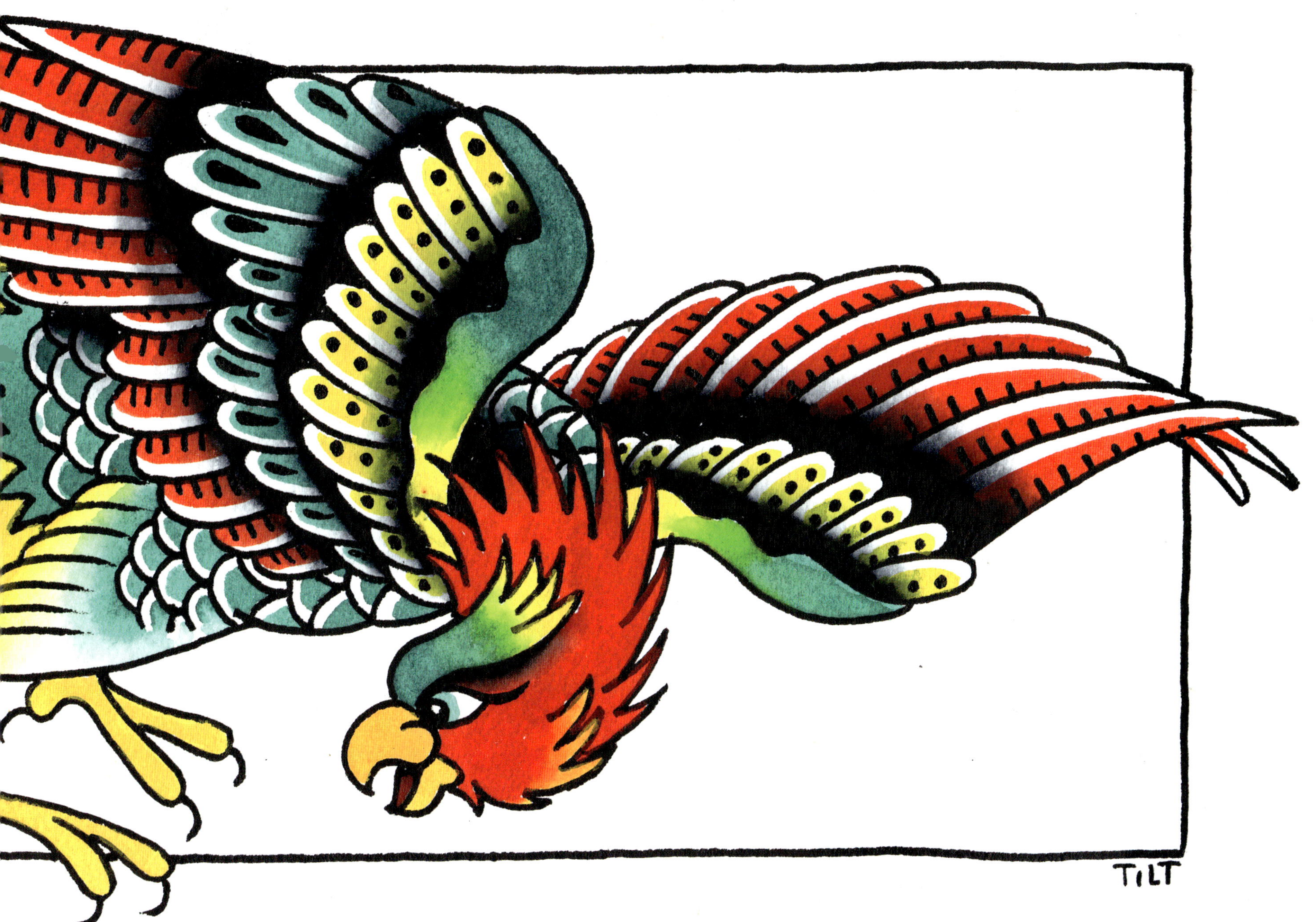
TILT

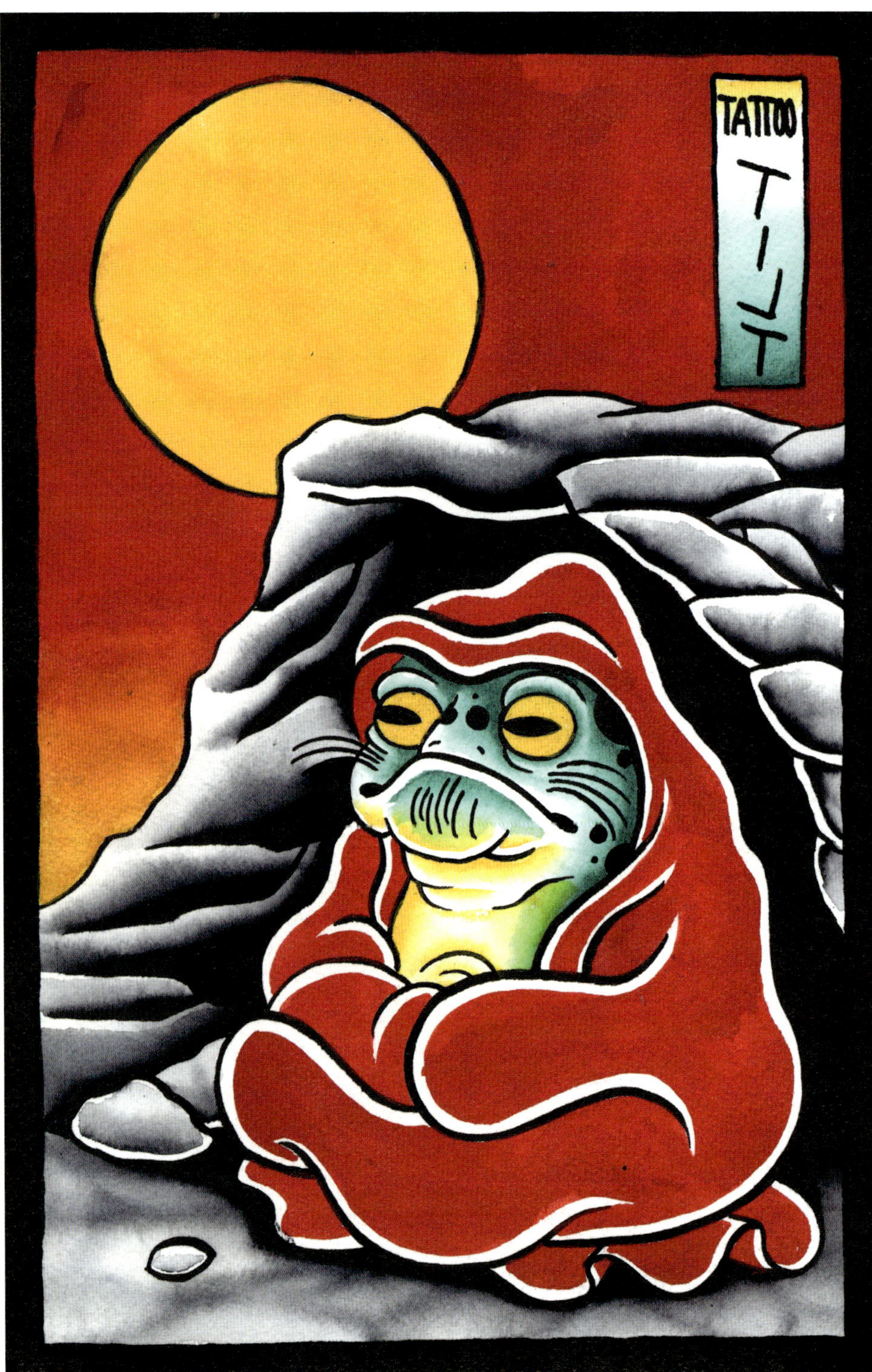

ABOUT THE AUTHORS

Jeromey "Tilt" McCulloch is a professional tattooer in Champaign, Illinois, where he has owned and operated NewLife Tattoos for fourteen years. Tilt has a deep respect and passion for the Japanese style of tattooing. He is committed to studying and carrying on the tradition of tattooing.

Justin Sellers, a.k.a. Lowercase j, started tattooing and painting flash in Florida in 2005 with his brother TimmyTatts. He later moved back to State College, Pennsylvania. He works at Tattoo Mark's at 127 East Beaver Avenue, still alongside his brother. He collects antique tattoo memorabilia and also builds tattoo machines. He is proud to be a part of keeping up the old-time tattoo religion.